WOMEN IN GERMAN YEARBOOK 4

Feminist Studies and German Culture

WOMEN IN GERMAN YEARBOOK 4

Feminist Studies and German Culture

Edited by

Marianne Burkhard
Jeanette Clausen

UNIVERSITY
PRESS OF
AMERICA

Lanham • New York • London

Copyright © 1988 by

University Press of America,® Inc.

4720 Boston Way
Lanham, MD 20706

3 Henrietta Street
London WC2E 8LU England

Printed in the United States of America

British Cataloging in Publication Information Available

"Totale Feminisierung", "Die Kätzin, die Rättin,
und die Feminismaus", "Carl Maria, die Männe", and
"Sind Herren herrlich und Damen dämlich?" ©by Luise F. Pusch

"E.T.A. Hoffman's "Der Sandmann": An Early Example of
Ecriture Féminine?" ©1988 by Ricarda Schmidt

"Novellistic Representation of *die Berufstätige* during the
Weimar Republic" ©1988 by Renny Harrigan

"Gespräch mit Herrad Schenk" ©1988 by Susan Wendt-Hildebrandt

Co-published by arrangement with the Coalition of Women in German

ISBN: 0-8191-6704-5 (pbk. alk. paper)
ISBN: 0-8191-6703-7 (alk. paper)
LCN: 85–642607

All University Press of America books are produced on acid-free
paper which exceeds the minimum standards set by the National
Historical Publication and Records Commission.

ACKNOWLEDGEMENTS

The individuals listed below served as consultants to the editors for this volume. We gratefully acknowledge their assistance.

Leslie Adelson, The Ohio State University
Angelika Bammer, Emory University
Jeannine Blackwell, University of Kentucky
Helen Cafferty, Bowdoin College
Susan L. Cocalis, University of Massachusetts, Amherst
Ruth Dawson, University of Hawaii
Thomas C. Fox, Washington University
Miriam Frank, New York City
Elke Frederiksen, University of Maryland
Sandra Frieden, University of Houston
Gertraud Gutzmann, Smith College
Renny Harrigan, University of Wisconsin-Milwaukee
Ritta Jo Horsley, University of Massachusetts, Boston
Anna Kuhn, University of California, Davis
Sara Lennox, University of Massachusetts, Amherst
Richard McCormick, New York University
Linda S. Pickle, Westminster College
Joan Reutershan, New York University
Marc Silbermann, University of Texas-San Antonio
Edith J. Waldstein, Massachusetts Institute of
   Technology
Martha K. Wallach, University of Wisconsin-Green Bay
Sydna Stern Weiss, Hamilton College

Special thanks to Victoria M. Kingsbury for manuscript preparation.

Publication of this volume was supported in part by a grant from the Indiana University President's Council on the Humanities.

TABLE OF CONTENTS

PREFACE

Each <u>Women in German Yearbook</u> has expanded the
boundaries of our field a little more, and the present
volume is no exception. Several of the papers collected
here make new connections between feminist <u>Germanistik</u>
and other fields, while others continue the process of
rediscovery and reinterpretation that is essential to a
feminist re-vision of criticism and the canon.

Feminist linguistics, an area too little studied by
Germanists, especially in the U.S., is represented here
by contributions from Luise F. Pusch, its leading
practitioner in the FRG. Pusch was our invited guest at
the 1985 Women in German conference. Her work
articulates, in both content and form, a radical vision
encompassing far more than its immediate object, sexist
usages in the German language. We are also pleased to
present two papers that explore the potential of
<u>écriture féminine</u> for German literary and film criti-
cism, Ricarda Schmidt's critique of Hélène Cixous's
"Sandmann" interpretation, and Renate Fischetti's adap-
tation of Luce Irigaray's work for a feminist reading of
"Ticket of No Return." In a different vein of film
criticism, Jan Mouton grounds her analysis of mother
figures in German women's film in American psychoanalytic research.

Analysis of sexual stereotypes--one of the first
critical strategies developed by feminist literary
scholars almost two decades ago--is the basis for
Charlotte Armster's rereading of <u>Katharina Blum</u>. The
category of criticism dubbed "spadework" by Annis Pratt
in the early 1970s is also well represented here. Renny
Harrigan and Lynda King have uncovered neglected
writings from the twenties and thirties that provide a
fresh look at literary reflections of societal change
(Harrigan) and a portrait of one author, Hermynia zur
Mühlen, writing to try to effect societal change. Helga
Madland has studied 18th-century journals to discover
parallels between the manipulation of women by the media
then and now. Linda Worley's analysis of Louise von
Francois's "odd woman" fiction and Sigrid Brauner's

ix

"Hexenjagd in Gelehrtenköpfen" both expand on studies published in volume 3. The two contributions that conclude the present collection aim to introduce Yearbook readers to very recent literature. Susan Wendt-Hildebrandt has contributed an interview with West German feminist Herrad Schenk. Not unlike Luise Pusch, who has published autobiographical prose in addition to her scholarly books and papers, Schenk resists categorization, alternating between research and teaching in her academic field, sociology, and creative writing. Dorothy Rosenberg has prepared a bibliography of GDR women writers whose works are of interest for feminist scholars.

Volume 4 marks a turning point for the Women in German Yearbook: at the October 1986 Women in German conference, we voted to make the Yearbook part of membership in WIG, rather than a publication to be purchased separately, as in the past. This decision represents a commitment to our members as well as to the profession as a whole on behalf of feminist research in the field of German studies.

In closing, I wish to thank Marianne Burkhard, who is retiring as Yearbook editor after co-delivering four volumes. We are fortunate to have had her experience and expertise, for without them the journal simply would not be what it is. On a personal level, as a neophyte co-editor this past year, I have learned much from Marianne's good-humored unflappability when confronted with the mix-ups and delays that are probably inevitable in a venture involving so much unpaid work by so many people. Thanks, Marianne! You've earned a respite. Marianne and I invite you to join us in welcoming Helen Cafferty of Bowdoin College, the new coeditor beginning with volume 5.

Jeanette Clausen
Indiana University-Purdue
University at Fort Wayne

with

Marianne Burkhard
University of Illinois

January 1987

x

Totale Feminisierung:
Überlegungen zum umfassenden Feminimum

Luise F. Pusch

> Es werden zur Zeit Untersu-
> chungen über . . . den gesamten
> symbolischen Apparat unserer
> Männerkultur veröffentlicht,
> über die Bedeutung von Meta-
> phern und speziell sexuellen
> Metaphern. Was aber noch immer
> nicht erkannt ist, ist die Be-
> deutung der einen, alles durch-
> dringenden Metapher, die in
> unserer Sprache verankert ist:
> Ich meine die Metapher des
> Genus selbst. (Alma Sabatini)[1]

1. Einleitung: Grammatik und Mathematik: Die Metapher des Genus

Alma Sabatini ist Italienerin - sie weiß, wovon sie
spricht. Denn in der italienischen Sprache ist die
Metapher des Genus womöglich noch "durchdringender" als
im Deutschen. Wie alle romanischen Sprachen besitzt das
Italienische nur zwei Genera: Maskulinum und Femininum,
während wir im Deutschen immerhin noch das Neutrum
haben. Dieses Neutrum gibt uns z.B. die Möglichkeit, das
Kind, das eine Frau erwartet, realitätsgerecht, ge-
schlechtsneutral eben, zu bezeichnen. Unsere Sprache
macht "es" nicht schon vor der Geburt zu einem kleinen
Mann, wie es die romanischen Sprachen tun. Allerdings -
das Neutrum hat bei uns auch seine Tücken: Ist das Kind
geboren, heißt es "der Junge" oder "das Mädchen". Das
männliche Kind wird also sprachlich als männlich eingeordnet, das weibliche Kind hingegen als sächlich.

Diese Art Einordnung in die richtige oder falsche
"Geschlechts-Schublade" mit Hilfe des richtigen oder
falschen Genus nennt Sabatini "die Metapher des Genus".
Männer werden immer richtig eingeordnet, Frauen fast

1

nie, denn in unserer Sprache gilt die Regel: 99 Sängerinnen und 1 Sänger sind zusammen 100 Sänger (merke aber: 99 Birnen und 1 Apfel sind zusammen nicht 100 Äpfel, höchstens 100 Früchte!) Futsch sind die 99 Frauen, nicht mehr auffindbar, verschwunden in der Männer-Schublade. Die Metapher bewirkt, daß in unseren Köpfen nur Manns-Bilder auftauchen, wenn von "Arbeitern", "Studenten", "Ärzten", "Dichtern" oder "Rentnern" die Rede ist, auch wenn jene "Ärzte" oder "Rentner" in Wirklichkeit überwiegend Ärztinnen bzw. Rentnerinnen waren. Eine Bekannte erzählte mir neulich von dem neuen Lehrling in ihrem Geschäft. Obwohl ich seit Jahren gegen den perfiden Einfluß der Metapher in meinem eigenen Kopf andenke, hab ich mir natürlich ganz automatisch einen Jüngling vorgestellt. "Der" Lehrling war aber - eine junge Frau! Undenkbar ist es in unserer Kultur auch, daß ein Buch etwa über "Die Anatomie des Menschen" auf dem Umschlag einfach eine Frau darstellt. Eine Frau kann in unserem Denken nicht "den Menschen" symbolisieren - dieses Privileg bleibt dem Mann vorbehalten, nicht zuletzt dank einer nur scheinbar harmlosen Grammatikregel, die aus beliebig vielen Frauen Männer macht, sowie ein einziger Mann hinzukommt. Auf die Spitze getrieben: Die gesamte Erdbevölkerung könnte aus Milliarden von Frauen und einem Mann bestehen - diese Regel würde die Frauen noch immer als "Erdbewohner" statt "Erdbewohnerinnen" zählen, und spätere Generationen hätten einige Mühe, sich unter diesen "Erdbewohnern" überhaupt Frauen vorzustellen.

Ist es denn so schlimm, wenn wir alle uns - auf den Leim geführt durch die Metapher des Genus - unter einem Menschen eigentlich nur einen Mann vorstellen können? Diese häufig gestellte Frage zeugt von ungeheurer Naivität oder davon, wie gut die Metapher des Genus bereits gewirkt hat ("Frauen sind unwichtig, zählen ja nicht") und in fast jeder sprachlichen Äußerung weiterwirkt: Stellen wir uns zum Vergleich nur einmal vor, es habe eine CDU-Veranstaltung stattgefunden, bei der auch ein SPD-Mitglied zugegen war. Am nächsten Tag berichtet die Presse von einer SPD-Veranstaltung. Die CDU würde aufjaulen. Ganz anders die 99 Sängerinnen, von denen oben die Rede war. Wir Frauen sind es gewohnt, der "Gegenpartei" zugezählt und somit ausgelöscht zu werden; die Metapher des Genus hat ganze Arbeit geleistet.

So jedenfalls sah es bis vor kurzem aus. Inzwischen aber, etwa seit Beginn der Neuen Frauenbewegung, wehren sich immer mehr Frauen gegen die männliche Vorherrschaft in der Sprache. Im folgenden möchte ich

(1) die Geschichte dieses Protests skizzieren,
(2) weitere unschöne Aspekte der Metapher des Genus diskutieren,
(3) davor warnen, eine Strategie, die für das Englische (eine Sprache <u>ohne</u> Genus!) entwickelt wurde, sozusagen blindlings auf Genus-Sprachen zu übertragen,
(4) eine Reihe von Argumenten für die "totale Feminisierung" anstelle der bisher als Lösung propagierten "partiellen Feminisierung" vortragen.

2. Unschön und schwerfällig - Die "englische Lösung" der partiellen Feminisierung, angewandt auf die europäischen Genus-Sprachen

   Der Protest gegen den Sexismus in der Sprache begann in den USA, und vor etwa acht Jahren setzte die Diskussion über die Feminisierung und somit Therapierung der patriarchalischen Sprachen auch in Europa ein. Als Vorbild dienten dabei die Methoden, die von den US-amerikanischen Feministinnen für die Therapierung der englischen Männersprache (Manglish) entwickelt worden waren. Nur: Es gibt einen gravierenden Unterschied zwischen dem Englischen und den meisten anderen europäischen Sprachen: Das Englische besitzt kein grammatisches Genus, was dessen Therapierung zu einer relativ simplen Sache macht: Wenn von "a doctor, a student" o.ä. im allgemeinen die Rede ist, wird anschließend mit "he or she" oder "s/he" fortgefahren, und damit hat sich die Sache. Die Mehrzahl der europäischen Sprachen hingegen ist geprägt vom grammatischen Genus und der Herrschaft des maskulinen über das feminine Genus:

   [Französisch, Spanisch, Italienisch, Rumänisch, Portugiesisch, Russisch, Polnisch, Tschechisch, Serbokroatisch, Deutsch, Griechisch und - mit Einschränkungen - die skand. Sprachen Norwegisch, Schwedisch und Dänisch sowie das Niederländische] stimmen in folgenden Regularitäten überein: Frauen haben nicht dieselben Chancen des Gemeintseins wie Männer. Maskulina können sich generell nicht nur auf männliche Referenten beziehen, sondern auch auf gemischtgeschlechtliche Gruppen. Diese zweite Funktion wird als sog. generische oder geschlechtsabstrahierende Funktion bezeichnet. Feminina haben dagegen eine ausschließlich geschlechtsspezifizierende Funktion.

3

Danach kann eine Personengruppe, die aus 49 Studentinnen und einem Studenten besteht, im Deutschen wie in allen anderen der genannten Sprachen nicht als "fünfzig Studentinnen" bezeichnet werden, es muß vielmehr heißen "fünfzig Studenten".

Die Konsequenz des Gebrauchs generischer Maskulina ist die Unsichtbarkeit von Frauen und ihren Leistungen in den betreffenden Sprachen.

Die zweite Regularität betrifft die Bedeutungs-Asymmetrie maskuliner und femininer Ausdrücke. Dabei kommt dem Femininum generell ein niedrigerer Rang zu als dem Maskulinum; vg. engl. master/mistress, dt. Gouverneur/Gouvernante; ital. maestro "Lehrer, großer Meister"/maestra "Lehrerin"; filosofo "Philosoph"/filosofessa "pedantische, eingebildete Frau"; dän. professor "Professor"/professorinde "Frau des Professors". Diese Asymmetrie hat Auswirkungen auf den Status abgeleiteter Feminina im allgemeinen; die Feminina werden als zweitrangig empfunden - auch von vielen Frauen.

Daraus ergibt sich eine dritte Regularität: die Bezeichnung von Frauen mit einem Maskulinum wird als Aufwertung interpretiert, während die Bezeichnung von Männern mit einem Femininum als Degradierung empfunden wird. Dies hat Konsequenzen für die Entwicklung des Wortschatzes patriarchalischer Sprachen. Die Neubildung maskuliner Ausdrücke von vorhandenen Feminina wird generell vermieden; vgl. die folgenden Beispiele: ital. la levatrice "Hebamme" - das zugehörige Maskulinum müßte il levatore lauten; stattdessen - um negative Assoziationen zu vermeiden - wird ein neues Maskulinum mit anderem Stamm gebildet: l'ostetrico; ähnlich dän. sygeplejerske "Krankenschwester" --> *sygeplejer --> sygeplejerassistent; span. azafata "Stewardess" --> *azafato --> comisario de abordo; dt. Kindergärtnerin --> *Kindergärtner --> Erzieher (nach Hellinger 1985: 3f).

4

Besonders die letzten Beispiele zeigen deutlich, daß die Regularitäten patriarchalischer Sprachen weniger linguistisch als vielmehr machtpolitisch, genauer gesagt: frauenfeindlich, motiviert sind: Maskulina funktionieren genau wie Oberbegriffe und die entsprechenden Feminina wie deren Unterbegriffe: Ein Gartenhaus (Unterbegriff) ist ein Haus (Oberbegriff) - aber die Umkehrung (ein Haus ist ein Gartenhaus) "gilt nicht". Genauso verhält es sich mit Sätzen wie "Eine Studentin ist ein Student" im Gegensatz zu "Ein Student ist eine Studentin". Ein Femininum (ja nicht einmal dessen maskuline Rückbildung, vgl. das nicht akzeptierte *Kindergärtner) darf unter keinen Umständen zum Oberbegriff avancieren, auch wenn das die einfachste und nächstliegende Lösung wäre.

Die mittels der Genera Maskulinum und Femininum in die meisten europäischen Sprachen zutiefst verankerte Metapher männlicher Macht und weiblicher Ohnmacht erschwert deren Therapie ungeheuer - zumindest die Therapie nach dem englischen Vorbild, welche männliche Interessen ungeschoren läßt. Nehmen wir zur Verdeutlichung einen Ausspruch von W.H. Auden:

> However pitiful a handful his readers, a poet at least knows this much about them: they have a personal relation to his work (W.H. Auden, 1967).

Heute hätte Auden wahrscheinlich geschrieben:

> However pitiful a handful his or her readers, a poet at least knows this much about them: they have a personal relation to his or her work.

Die Übersetzung in eine Genus-Sprache wie das Deutsche sieht wie folgt aus:

> Mögen auch ihre oder seine Leserinnen und Leser nur eine traurige Handvoll sein: eine Dichterin oder ein Dichter weiß jedenfalls dies über sie: Sie haben eine persönliche Beziehung zu ihrem oder seinem Werk.

Wie wir sehen, ist die Therapierung einer Sprache wie Englisch, die kein grammatisches Genus besitzt, relativ einfach, während die Feminisierung von Genus-Sprachen es keineswegs ist. Die Resultate der Therapie werden gewöhnlich als "unschön" und "schwerfällig" beurteilt. Es ist aber nicht unsere Schuld, daß für Frauen in den patriarchalen Sprachen kein Platz ist. Das geben Männer, Lexikographen, die es wissen müssen, bisweilen sogar selber zu:

> . . . bis in neue zeit [beherrscht] der mann sprache und literatur fast allein (Alfred Götze, Grimmsches Wörterbuch Bd. 28, Sp. 336).

Es ist nicht unsere Schuld, daß sprachliche Gleichbehandlung von Frauen und Männern (das aus dem engl. Sprachraum übernommene Ziel) für die Genus-Sprachen kaum praktikabel ist. Sie belastet nicht nur Männer, sondern Frauen genau so, bedeutet sie doch eine Verdoppelung fast aller Personenbezeichnungen. Frauen nehmen aber derzeit die Belastung noch auf sich - und werden für ihre aufopferungsvolle Arbeit auch noch gescholten (ein klassisches Beispiel für die männliche Strategie des "blaming the victim" - 'dem Opfer die Schuld geben').

Sofern Männer sich mit der Unsichtbarkeit der Frau in der Sprache überhaupt befassen und uns dabei nicht einfach für überspannt erklären, plädieren sie gewöhnlich für die "Strategie", es alles beim alten zu belassen:

> Übrigens wenden wir uns ebenso an Leserinnen und Psychoanalytikerinnen wie an die männlichen Vertreter dieser Genera, und wir schreiben für Patienten und für Patientinnen. Die generische Verwendung des Maskulinums, mit der wir die Gattung Leser und das Genus Psychoanalytiker ansprechen, ist die bequemste Lösung (m.H.) eines schwierigen Problems. Die Verwendung des generischen Femininums würde zumal dann verwirrend wirken, wenn wir der Gerechtigkeit wegen von einem Kapitel zum anderen wechselten. So belassen wir es beim gebräuchlichen generischen Maskulinum . . . (Thomä & Kächele 1985: XXI).[2]

Aber "die bequemste Lösung" ist bequem nur für Männer und wird deshalb auch nicht funktionieren, weil Frauen weiterhin darauf bestehen werden, auch in Genus-Sprachen sprachlich sichtbar zu sein, wie "unbequem" auch immer das für Männer sein mag. Für Sprachen mit einem Genus Neutrum wie Deutsch oder Griechisch gibt es die Möglichkeit, dieses Genus zu aktivieren und die

femininen Endungen abzuschaffen (vgl. Pusch 1980) - eine
Lösung, die unter dem Namen "der verrückte Pusch-Vorschlag" bekannt wurde. Nach diesem Vorschlag sähen
deutsche Texte etwa so aus:

> Barbara ist eine gute Student; ihre Pro-
> fessor ist sehr zufrieden mit ihr. Früher
> war sie übrigens Sekretär bei einer Archi-
> tekt. Im Moment suchen wir noch ein
> zweites Gutachter für ihre Dissertation,
> am besten ein Dozent, das was von Hydro-
> geologie versteht.

Es gibt aber natürlich noch eine dritte, sehr
einfache und effektive Strategie: die totale Feminisierung, d.h. die Ersetzung des generischen Maskulinums
durch ein generisches Femininum. Sehen wir uns einmal
an, wie W.H. Auden die totale Feminisierung bekommt:

> However pitiful a handful her readers, a
> poet at least knows this much about them:
> they have a personal relation to her work.

> Mögen auch ihre Leserinnen nur eine trau-
> rige Handvoll sein: eine Dichterin weiß
> jedenfalls dies über sie: Sie haben eine
> persönliche Beziehung zu ihrem Werk.

3. Argumente für den Gebrauch des generischen Femininums, d.h. für die totale Feminisierung

3.0. In den vergangenen Jahren habe ich in West-
deutschland, der Schweiz und Österreich etwa 500 Vorträge zum Thema "Sprache, Geschlecht und Macht" gehalten, üblicherweise vor Auditorien von 50 bis zu 600
Personen. Das zentrale Anliegen in den jeweils sich
anschließenden Diskussionen war **immer** die Frage: Was
sollen wir nun praktisch tun? - eine Frage, die sich so
für Englischsprachige überhaupt nicht stellt, weil ihre
Lösung der partiellen Feminisierung ja so leicht durch-
führbar ist und sich deshalb auch schon längst weitgehend durchgesetzt hat. Es ist an der Zeit, daß die
europäische Frauenbewegung sich diesbezüglich von ihrem
Anglozentrismus emanzipiert.

In den Diskussionen bestand und besteht Einigkeit
über folgende Punkte:

1. Der Gebrauch des generischen Maskulinums wird entschieden abgelehnt.

2. Die konsequente partielle Feminisierung (das sogenannte Splitting) wird als so umständlich empfunden, daß die Mehrheit ihr langfristig kaum Chancen einräumt. Trotzdem wird derzeit viel Energie darauf verwendet, sie zu praktizieren und zu propagieren, weil andere/bessere Lösungen bisher nicht gefunden worden sind. Die obersten Behörden der Bundesländer Hessen und Bremen haben 1985 sogar in Runderlassen die Abschaffung der maskulinen Oberbegriffe angeordnet - ein immerhin erstaunlicher Erfolg zäher feministischer Sprachpolitik. Allerdings untergräbt es die "Kampfmoral" erheblich, daß Frauen dem stereotyp und hämisch vorgebrachten Einwand der Männer, diese Lösung führe zu "unerträglichen Schwerfälligkeiten", insgeheim zustimmen.

3. Gewünscht wird eigentlich eine Sprache, die sowohl echt geschlechtsabstrahierende als auch geschlechtsspezifizierende Ausdrucksmöglichkeiten besitzt, und zwar in der Form, daß erstens keines der beiden Geschlechter sprachlich benachteiligt wird und zweitens alle die Sprache als "bequem" und "nicht schwerfällig" empfinden. Wie jedoch unsere überkommenen, durch und durch patriarchalischen Genus-Sprachen in einen solchen Zustand zu überführen sind, zumal von Frauen, die ja nicht an der Macht sind, bleibt einstweilen unklar.

Angesichts des sprachpolitisch bisher Erreichten (hohe Sensibilisierung, Beurteilung der partiellen Feminisierung als nicht optimal, sondern bestenfalls als "kleineres Übel") ist es offenbar Zeit für eine nüchterne Strategie-Diskussion, die ich hiermit einleiten möchte. Ich bin der Ansicht, daß sich die totale Feminisierung als natürliche (Übergangs)Lösung - so etwa für die nächsten zwei-, dreitausend Jährchen - anbietet. Von einer "radikalen Minderheit" (ich schließe mich ein) wird sie bereits seit langem konsequent praktiziert und propagiert. Von Männern wird sie - natürlich - vehement abgelehnt, von den meisten Frauen ebenso. Häufigstes Argument der Frauen gegen diese Strategie ist: Wenn wir den Spieß umkehren, gewinnen wir nichts. Wir ziehen nur denselben Vorwurf auf uns, den wir immer den Männern gemacht haben. Wir machen uns lächerlich, wenn wir etwa die 97% Professoren und 3% Professorinnen an unseren

Universitäten entschlossen, aber wirklichkeitsfremd als Professorinnen bezeichnen. Niemand wird im Ernst diese Strategie unterstützen, mittragen. Einige von der "Neuen-Weiblichkeits"-Fraktion meinen auch, das Femininum sei "echt zu schade", um damit "Schwanzträger" zu bezeichnen.

Nun die Argumente der "kleinen radikalen Minderheit":

Wenn wir
a) das generische Maskulinum ablehnen
b) der partiellen Feminisierung für Genus-Sprachen langfristig keine Chancen einräumen
c) zu machtlos sind, um die letztlich angestrebte optimale Lösung (entweder Abschaffung des Genus-Systems, was allerdings tiefgreifende Folgen für die Syntax der betreffenden Sprachen hätte, oder so etwas wie den "verrückten Pusch-Vorschlag") hier und heute, auf direktem Wege, durchzusetzen

– dann bleibt uns eigentlich nur die dialektisch motivierte, indirekte/paradoxe Strategie, über das Ziel hinauszuschießen, um es zu treffen. Was wir zur Zeit versuchen, ist gleichsam der Sprung von der These zur Synthese unter Umgehung der Antithese (ob aus Angst vor männlichen Sanktionen oder angeborenem weiblich-demokratischem Empfinden, will ich nicht entscheiden). Ich meine also, wir müssen so konsequent und radikal sein, daß wir mit unserer Sprachpolitik nicht nur – wie bisher – den Männern auf die Nerven gehen, sondern ihren Nerv treffen. Der Nerv, auf dem Männer erwiesenermaßen sprachlich zu treffen sind, und nicht nur sprachlich, sondern gesamtkulturell, ist: Feminisierung. Die männliche Angst vor dem Verlust der männlichen Identität (durch Feminisierung) ist das Zentrum der grotesken Gesamtveranstaltung, die sich Patriarchat nennt. Feminisierung ist für den Mann sozusagen die ultimative Bedrohung, das schlechthin Unerträgliche. Um dem zu entgehen bzw. nicht länger ausgesetzt zu sein, wird er möglicherweise zur Kooperation bei der Entwicklung einer für beide Geschlechter gerechten und bequemen Sprache bereit sein.

Soweit das Hauptargument. Es betrifft ein Faktum, das Männer nicht zugeben können, da die Geheimhaltung dieser Tatsache – sogar vor sich selbst (Verdrängung) – ihre Welt zusammenhält und bedingt. Ich werde deshalb nunmehr ein paar äußerlichere Argumente zusammentragen, die für den Gebrauch des generischen Femininums sprechen, denn schließlich müssen wir, um das Fernziel zu erreichen, auch das Zwischenziel argumentativ absichern und ernstnehmen.

Die Argumente für das Zwischenziel "totale Feminisierung" zerfallen in zwei Gruppen, eine halb ironisch-spielerisch vorzutragende und eine sehr ernstgemeinte.

3.1 Ironisch-spielerische Argumente für die totale Feminisierung:

a) Das Arbitraritäts-Argument: Männer pflegen ja zu betonen, daß wir "sowieso nur an Symptomen herumkurieren", daß unsere Bemühungen um eine gerechte Sprache am Kern der Sache vorbeigehen, daß Sprachveränderung nichts bewirkt. Nehmen wir sie also beim Wort. Wenn Sprachveränderung nichts bewirkt, dann wird es ihnen sicher egal sein, wenn sie feminisiert werden.

b) Das strukturelle Argument: Es leuchtet - rein strukturell betrachtet - nicht ein, daß das längere Femininum im kürzeren Maskulinum "enthalten" sein soll. Wo, bitteschön, ist in dem Wort Lehrer das Wort Lehrerinnen enthalten? Die umgekehrte Behauptung ergibt offensichtlich viel eher einen Sinn: Das Maskulinum Lehrer (Singular und Plural) ist in den Feminina Lehrerin und Lehrerinnen hör- und sichtbar enthalten, ähnlich wie man in woman und poet in poetess und nicht umgekehrt.

c) Das biologische Argument: So sieht es ein deutscher Humanbiologe: "Das weibliche Bild stellt . . . den unmittelbar im Erbgut festgelegten Bauplan des Menschen dar. Der Mann dagegen ist eine Spezialform, die irgendwann in der langen tierischen Stammesgeschichte als Abweichung des weiblichen Bauplans entstanden ist. . . . Die Natur hat . . . eigens für die Fortpflanzung die Sonderform des männlichen Geschlechts [geschaffen]. Dies charakterisiert das Wesen des Mannes. Er ist nur ein Ableger der Frau, eine menschliche Sonderform für die Fortpflanzung. . . . Der Mann ist das sekundäre Geschlecht, aus der 'Rippe' der Frau gemacht - genau umgekehrt, als [sic] es die Bibel meint!" (Knußmann 1982: 22 und 29f).

10

b&c) Das strukturell-biologische Argument: Wir er-
    lauben uns, daran zu erinnern, daß jeder Mann vor
    der Geburt tatsächlich "in der weiblichen Form
    enthalten war". Behauptungen zum Beweis des
    Gegenteils gehören in den Bereich des Mythos.

d) Das statistische Argument: Frauen sind mehr als
   die Hälfte der Weltbevölkerung. Allgemeine Aus-
   sagen wie "Amerikanerinnen sind freundlich",
   "Engländerinnen sind reserviert", "Die Nächste
   bitte", "Die Kundin ist Königin", "Jeder das
   Ihre", "Die Inhaberin dieses Passes ist
   Deutsche", haben deshalb einen statistisch höher-
   en Wahrheitsgehalt als wenn das generische Maskulinum benutzt würde. Zugegebenermaßen gibt es
   (noch) zahllose Berufe, in denen das männliche
   Geschlecht statistisch weit überwiegt, aber erstens soll dieser Zustand ja bald überwunden sein
   und zweitens werden ja die angeblich geschlechts-
   neutralen Maskulina auch hemmungslos für überwiegend und sogar für rein weibliche Gruppen
   eingesetzt (vgl. etwa "Die Menstruation ist bei
   jedem ein bißchen anders"). Und für wirklich
   männliche Gruppen bleibt uns ja immer noch das
   Maskulinum. Es wird geschlechtsspezifizierend benutzt, genau wie bisher das Femininum. So werden
   wir also nicht statt die Päpste plötzlich die
   Päpstinnen sagen.

e) Das Aufwertungsargument: Der Einwand, das Femininum könnte "zu schade" sein, um damit Männer zu
   bezeichnen, ist ernstzunehmen, weisen doch sogar
   Männer immer wieder darauf hin, das weibliche sei
   das bessere, weil (z.B.) friedlichere Geschlecht.
   Aber seien wir doch ein bißchen großzügig und
   betrachten wir den Gebrauch des Femininums für
   Männer als eine (hoffentlich) sich selbst er-
   füllende Prophezeiung, auf daß dereinst auch das
   männlich Geschlecht echt weiblich-friedfertig
   sein möge. Wie wir wissen, ist es höchste Zeit!

3.2 Ernsthafte Argumente für den Gebrauch des generi-
    schen Femininums

a) Das international Argument: Feminismus ist international, da das Patriarchat international ist.
   Partielle Feminisierung ist (relativ) bequem nur
   für die Sprachen ohne grammatisches Genus. Totale

Feminisierung ist für alle Sprachen bequem und einfach.

b) Das historische Argument: Die Geschichte lehrt, daß unterdrückte Gruppen ihre Energien darauf konzentrieren sollten, <u>ihre</u> Situation zu verbessern. Gleichzeitige Berücksichtigung der Interessen des Unterdrückers ist taktisch absurd.

c) Das Autarkie-Argument: Der Einwand, daß Männer diese Lösung "nicht mittragen" werden, ist nicht stichhaltig, da sie ja auch die partielle Feminisierung nicht oder kaum (d.h. nur widerwillig) mitmachen. Jedenfalls gilt dies für die Genus-Sprachen, wenn es auch für das Englische anders sein mag.

d) Das Gerechtigkeits-Argument: Phyllis Chesler[3] sagt: "Die Gleichbehandlung Ungleicher ist ungerecht", und ich stimme ihr zu. Stellen wir uns einen verfetten Menschen und einen unterernährten vor. Es wäre nicht nur ungerecht, sondern für die verfettete Person auch ungesund, ihr ebensoviel Nahrung zu geben wie die unterernährte Person benötigt.

Auf die Sprache übertragen, bedeutet das: Wenn es unser Ziel ist, die Position von Frauen und dadurch die Frauen selbst zu stärken – warum sollten wir nicht ein wenig bei Männern in die Lehre gehen? Offenbar waren ja ihre Strategien zur Stärkung des eigenen Selbstbewußtseins sehr erfolgreich. Eine ihrer Maßnahmen war das "generische Maskulinum". Diese Selbstvergrößerungsdroge funktioniert offenbar hervorragend. Warum sollten wir uns nur eine halb so starke Nahrung gönnen?

Es besteht kein Zweifel daran, daß die Frau sprachlich (natürlich auch in jeder anderen Hinsicht) extrem benachteiligt ist. Was ihr zusteht und was sie braucht, ist nicht Gleich-, sondern Besserbehandlung, kompensatorische Gerechtigkeit, eine gezielte und umfassende "affirmative action". Der Mann hingegen braucht dringend eine "Abmagerungskur" zur Therapie seines immer gefährlicher werdenden Größenwahns. Außerdem braucht er Einfühlungstraining. Es wird ihm guttun, es im eigenen Gemüt zu erleben, wie es sich **anfühlt**, <u>mitgemeint</u> zu sein, sprachlich dem anderen Geschlecht zugezählt zu werden, diesen ständigen Identitätsverlust hinzunehmen. Wir werden ihm immer wieder mütterlich und geduldig versichern, er sei natürlich mitgemeint, eingeschlossen - aber solche Mitteilungen werden höchstens intellektuell verarbeitet, das Gefühl reagiert anders (als Frauen haben wir da unsere Erfahrungen machen können). Und dieses Gefühl muß der Mann erlebt haben, um die Notwendigkeit einer grundlegenden Sprachreform zu begreifen.

Die bisherigen sprachtherapeutischen Maßnahmen (Splitting-Empfehlungen, Runderlasse zur Abschaffung des generischen Maskulinums) hatten nur einen geringen Effekt, der etwa mit dem des neuen Namensrechts vergleichbar ist: Seit 1976 kann in der BRD auch der Name der Frau als Familienname gewählt werden. Wenn beide Geschlechter "Gleiche" wären, hätten in den letzten 10 Jahren genau 50% der Männer bei Eheschließung ihren Namen ändern ("feminisiert werden") müssen. Es waren aber nur 2%. Für das Namensrecht hätte es also zur Herstellung des Gleichgewichts eines kompensatorischen Gesetzes bedurft: "Ab sofort wird der Name der Frau zum Ehenamen". Die normative Kraft des Faktischen hätte dann im Laufe der Zeit den Ausgleich bewirkt. Aber: Die Gesetzgeber waren Männer - und sie werden sich nicht selbst "entpatrifizieren", genau so wenig wie das Nazi-Regime sich selbst entnazifiziert hat.

4. Schlußbemerkung

Ich bin überzeugt, daß die Strategie, die ich skizziert habe, die einzig erfolgversprechende zur Herstellung sprachlicher Gleichberechtigung ist. Genauso überzeugt bin ich davon, daß sich nur wenige meiner Meinung anschließen und noch weniger diese Strategie-Überlegungen in die Praxis umsetzen werden. Die praktischen Auswirkungen des neuen Namensrechts sind zu ernüchternd, als daß ich mich Illusionen hingeben könnte. Trotzdem werde ich diese Ideen zu verbreiten suchen, denn immerhin ist die Sache einen Versuch wert, weil sie Spaß macht, erkenntnisfördernd ist und das weibliche Selbstbewußtsein kräftigt: Frauen, die konsequent das generische Femininum verwenden, empfinden dies als sehr lustvoll - auch weil die Reaktionen der Männer auf diese Strategie so komisch und entlarvend sind.

Anmerkungen

Alle Übersetzungen aus dem Englischen sind von mir, LFP.

[1] Sabatini 1985: 64.

[2] Diesen Fund verdanke ich Jennifer Hartog, die Thomä empfohlen hatte, es doch mal mit dem generischen Femininum zu versuchen, woraufhin er mit seiner "bequemsten Lösung" aufwartete.

[3] Chesler 1985: 435.

Literatur

Auden, Wystan Hugh. 1967. "A short defense of poetry". Address given at a round-table conference on "Tradition and innovation in contemporary literature" at the International PEN Conference in Budapest, Oktober 1967. Abgedruckt in und zitiert nach The New York Review of Books, vol. 33, no. 1, 30. Januar 1986, p. 15.

Chesler, Phyllis. 1985. Mothers on trial: The battle for children and custody. New York: McGraw-Hill.

Hellinger, Marlis. Hrsg. 1985. Sprachwandel und feministische Sprachpolitik: Internationale Perspektiven. Wiesbaden: Westdeutscher Verlag.

Knußmann, Rainer. 1982. Der Mann: Ein Fehlgriff der Natur. Hamburg: Gruner & Jahr (STERN-Buch).

Pusch, Luise F. 1980. "Das Deutsche als Männersprache – Diagnose und Therapievorschläge", Linguistische Berichte 69 (1980), S. 59-74. Nachdruck in: Das Deutsche als Männersprache. Aufsätze und Glossen zur feministischen Linguistik. Frankfurt/M.: Suhrkamp (edition suhrkamp 1217), S. 46-68.

Sabatini, Alma. 1985. "Occupational titles in Italian: Changing the sexist usage", in Hellinger, ed., 1985, 64-75.

Thomä, Helmut & Horst Kächele. 1985. Lehrbuch der psychoanalytischen Therapie. Band 1: Grundlagen. Berlin, Heidelberg, New York, Tokyo: Springer Verlag.

Die Kätzin, die Rättin und die Feminismaus

Luise F. Pusch

Jetzt ist er raus, der fünfte Band von Grass' Tier-
leben: Die Rättin (nach Katz und Maus, Hundejahre, Aus
dem Tagebuch einer Schnecke und Der Butt). Ich habe nur
den ersten (und kürzesten) Band der monumentalen Pen-
talogie gelesen. Es ging darin weder um Katzen und Mäuse
noch um Kätzinnen und Mäusinnen, sondern um einen
Adamsapfel - ein Thema, das uns Frauen von jeher kaum zu
fesseln vermag.

Apropos Adam. Da gab es doch diese falsche Schlange,
oder war es vielleicht ein Schlangerich? Wir werden das
Geschlecht des Tieres wohl nie erfahren, und doch
glauben alle steif und fest, es sei weiblich gewesen.
Schließlich heißt es die Schlange, und außerdem hat sie
den Menschen ins Verderben gelockt!

Vor Jahren brachte mir ein Professor der Germanistik
einen Zeitungsausschnitt mit. "Kätzin entlaufen" stand
da zu lesen. Was ich denn davon hielte, so als feministische Linguistin, fragte er listig. Und vor einer Woche
erzählte mir eine Buchhändlerin von dem neuen Grass, den
sie sogar schon gelesen hatte (Buchhändlerinnen müssen
von Berufs wegen alles mögliche lesen). Sie fand, der
Titel "Die Rättin" müßte mir doch auf Anhieb zusagen und
war verblüfft, als ich das verneinte.

Die Wortschöpfung "Rättin" verstößt gegen die Regeln
der deutschen Grammatik, und das hat der Günterich wohl
schlau einkalkuliert. Heldin seines Werks ist eine weibliche Ratte, ein Rattenweibchen. Aber "Die weibliche
Ratte" oder "Das Rattenweibchen" - das klingt für einen
Buchtitel natürlich wenig verkaufsfördernd.

Thomas Mann hat vornehm darauf verzichtet, seine Erzählung Herr und Rüde zu nennen. Er vertraute - mit
Recht - darauf, daß mann sich bei "der Hund" sowieso nur
ein männliches Tier denkt. Der weiße Wal, der weiße Hai
- wer käme wohl auf die Idee, von einem "Walerich" oder

15

einem "Haiermann" zu sprechen, damit sich auch niemand irrigerweise ein Weibchen vorstellt?

Und genau das ist das Problem. Die Tiere – sie sind nun mal unsere Vettern, niemals unsere Basen oder Cousinen. Ein Mensch ist männlich, es sei denn, das Gegenteil ist erwiesen. Für Tiere gilt in unserer Herrenkultur dasselbe. Und dagegen stemmt sich der Günter. Er will nicht, daß wir uns unter seiner Ratte einen tierischen Vetter vorstellen. Seine Ratte ist eine Rättin, weil sie eine echte Ausnahme ist. Kein langweiliges Männchen, wie sonst alle Tiere, sondern, höre & staune: ein Weib!

Danke, Günter! Du hast uns nachhaltig daran erinnert, daß sogar eine feminine Bezeichnung nichts gegen eure Vorstellung vermag, daß auch alle Tiere männlich sind. Mit Ausnahme der Schlange natürlich.

Carl Maria, die Männe

Luise F. Pusch

Der Mann hinkt mit seiner Emanzipation der Frau hoffnungslos hinterher. Alle sind sich einig, daß etwas geschehen muß, um diese Schmach zu lindern. Aber was? Aus aktuellem Anlaß sei hier an zwei ermutigende historische Beispiele erinnert, die überraschende Lösungs-Perspektiven eröffnen.

Die Gedenkbriefmarke zum 200. Geburtstag von Carl Maria von Weber zeigt ein feingeschnittenes, sehr "weibliches" Gesicht, umrahmt von zarten Löckchen und einem weichen Halstuch. Carl Maria gehört zu den ganz seltenen Ausnahme-Komponisten, die sich von einer Frau ein Libretto schreiben ließen. Den Mißerfolg der Oper (Euryanthe, Textbuch: Helmina von Chézy) führen die Musikhistoriker natürlich auf ebendiese "bedauerliche Fehlentscheidung" zurück. Über eine Begegnung mit Beethoven berichtet Weber: "Wir brachten den Mittag mit einander zu, sehr fröhlich und vergnügt. Dieser rauhe, zurückstoßende Mensch machte mir ordentlich die Cour, bediente mich bei Tische mit einer Sorgfalt wie seine Dame". Und in den Briefen an seine Frau Karoline, die er "liebe Weibe" nennt, bezeichnet er sich selbst als "Männe". Nun werden viele Männer von ihren Frauen "Männe" genannt, aber "die Männe" - das ginge den meisten denn doch zu weit. Carl Maria aber findet offenbar nichts dabei: "Meine Lebensordnung, liebe Weibe, ist freilich fast jeden Tag anders; in der Regel aber folgende. Um 8 Uhr, zuweilen wohl auch 1/2 9, steht die Männe auf, trinkt ihren langweiligen Tee und geht dann zu Smart". Oder: "Nun habe ich alle meine Leiden recht von Herzen geklagt, im Vertrauen auf Deine Vernunft, daß Du daraus nicht neuen Stoff zu Angst und Sorgen saugst, sondern höchstens die arme Männe bedauerst, die wirklich zum Leiden geboren ist".

Carl Maria starb 1826. Genau hundert Jahre später starb Rainer Maria, auch so eine "arme, zum Leiden geborene Männe", weich, zartbesaitet, sensitiv - kurz: vom Männlichkeitswahn ziemlich weit entfernt.

17

Mag sein, daß die beiden bekanntesten Maria-Männer unserer Geistesgeschichte nur zufällig auffallend "weiblich" geraten sind, aber vielleicht handelt es sich auch um eine Auswirkung des Gesetzes "nomen est Omen". Unser (von Männern festgelegtes) Namensrecht schreibt strikte Geschlechtertrennung vor, nicht ohne Grund. Einzige Ausnahme ist eben "Maria" als Zweitname für Knaben. Ich schlage vor, diese Ausnahme zur Regel zu machen und auf sämtlich weiblichen Vornamen auszudehnen - Männer hießen dann also etwa Helmut Agathe Kohl, Johannes Paula II. bez. Rau, Ronald Nancy Reagan, Michail Natascha Gorbatschow, François Madeleine Mitterand, etc. Wie die obigen Fälle zeigen, besteht eine gewisse Hoffnung, daß damit die Emanzipation der Männer endlich ein Stück vorankäme.

Sind Herren herrlich und Damen dämlich?

Luise F. Pusch

Als Vortragsreisende in Sachen "Frauen, Männer und Sprache" verfolgt mich diese Frage nun schon seit sieben Jahren. Gestellt wird sie meist von verunsicherten Frauen aus dem Publikum, denen ihr jeweiliger Freund, Gatte, Vater, Bruder oder sogar Sohn den Uralt-Kalauer mal wieder um die Ohren gehauen hat. Mich selbst hat mann ebenfalls seit meiner Kindheit mit diesem anscheinend unausrottbaren Schwachsinn einzuschüchtern versucht.

Also: Wenn dir das nächste Mal einer unserer herrlich galanten Herren mit den "dämlichen Damen" kommt, musterst du ihn kühl und wählst gelassen zwischen folgenden drei Möglichkeiten des Konterns:

1) Entweder du schüttelst befremdet das Haupt ob seiner linguistischen Unbedarftheit und empfiehlst ihm, sich anhand des nächstbesten etymologischen Wörterbuchs (Grimm, Kluge, Duden o.ä.) gefälligst selbst fortzubilden,

2) oder du stimmst eifrig zu: Natürlich, Herren seien herrlich, Damen dämlich, Winzer winzig und ihr Wein zum Weinen. Erzbischöfe seien aus Erz, unser Schicksal schick, die Amazone eine erotische Zone und die Lüneberger Heide heidnisch. Die Wale gehörten in die Walhalle, die Elefanten nach Rüsselsheim und der Ur-Opa in den Urwald. Mozart sei dir zu zart, Gulasch zu lasch, und vom starken Geschlecht würde dir schlecht. Immer feste druff - was dir halt an Kalauerinnen so einfällt.

3) oder (falls du grad in nachsichtiger Stimme bist) du klärst ihn selber auf: Das Wort "herrlich" kommt von "hehr", vgl. "hoch und hehr". Das Wort "Herr" geht zurück auf "heriro", eine Steigerungsform dieses "hehr". Die Herren finden sich also nicht nur herrlich, sondern sozusagen "super-herrlich". Anscheinend haben sie's nötig.

19

"Dame" hingegen geht zurück auf das lateinische "domina" - 'vornehme, hochgestellte Frau'.

"Dämlich" schließlich wird abgeleitet vom süddeutschen "Damian", vgl. "du Depp, damischer!" oder vom niederdeutschen "Dämel", "Dämlack" (Dummkopf). "Damian", "Dämel" und "Dämlack" sind Maskulina; weibliche Varianten gibt es nicht.

E.T.A. Hoffman's "Der Sandmann":
An Early Example of Écriture Féminine?
A Critique of Trends in Feminist Literary Criticism

Ricarda Schmidt

Since the introduction of the term écriture féminine by French post-structuralist theoreticians there have been many attempts to find literary precursors and examples of it—in literature written by men. Taking Hélène Cixous's interpretation of "Der Sandmann" in Prénoms de personne (Paris: Editions du Seuil, 1974) as an example, I want to examine how convincing the establishing of a male ancestral line for "feminine writing" is.

I will first describe those characteristics of Hoffmann's "Der Sandmann" which Cixous portrays as revolutionary precursors of writing directed against logocentrism and phallocentrism. Then I will analyze the narrative context of romantic art and philosophy, and, situating the tale in the historical context of romantic art and philosophy, I will formulate a critique of Cixous's interpretation which is directed at her use of the terms desire, dissolution of identity, decentralized narrative, and disorientation of the metaphorical, the qualities she identifies as anti-phallogocentric aspects of Hoffman's tale.

I. Cixous's Analysis of "Der Sandmann"

Cixous puts literature and desire on the same level. For her, literature expresses desire and, at the same time, produces desire. She distinguishes a predominant libidinal economy, the Realm of the Proper—character-ized by possession, appropriation, consumption, death—from the one she is interested in, the Realm of the Gift: an economy of life without limits, of whole life, of generosity and giving without a thought of return. In Prénoms de personne Cixous analyzes how the latter has been expressed and sought in literature by men (Hoff-mann, Kleist, Poe, Joyce) since the 19th century. In her later writing Cixous terms the two libidinal economies

21

masculine and feminine without meaning to imply any biological determination.[1] The fact that in Prénoms de personne Cixous looks for a feminine libidinal economy in literature by men is evidence of her intention to use these concepts as cultural constructs, not as biological essences.[2]

Cixous defines the aim common to all the texts she analyzes in her book as the wish to transcend a limit, a limit that she identifies as death in all its forms. According to Cixous these texts are also dizzy summits from which one can perceive other things, the other. Cixous sees liberation from confining social and affective ways of life prefigured in fiction:

> C'est personne, toujours plus d'un, qui est le "héros" divers de toutes les oeuvres dont il est ici fait récit: un sujet capable d'être tous ceux qu'il sera, désireux d'infini, risqué loin d'un moi central, et insubordonnable. Partout où il passe, les structures éclatent, l'économie sociale ou affective change de forme, des possibilités inconnues de désir et de vie surgissent, l'échange perd son privilège, et le don l'emporte (6).

This means that what Derrida described as typical of western thought (identity, unity, dominance, presence, etc.) and what Irigaray specified as phallogocentric discourse, Cixous sees already questioned and combatted in male literature of the previous century--although she concedes that the authors in question lived too early to arrive at what they desired (cf. 8).

Cixous is convinced that literature has been working for a long time on the subversion nowadays attributed to avant-garde literature: fighting both on the front of subjectivity, by breaking up logocentrism and the unity of the subject, and on the front of intersubjectivity, by criticizing phallocentrism and writing of a desire that is no longer determined by castration, death, calculation, preservation, and dominance. According to Cixous the same struggle took place in different forms in pre-Marxist, pre-Freudian, pre-structuralist times:

> Bien avant Bataille, Hoffmann, Kleist faisaient le procès virulent de l'idéalisme hégélien, et de la "dialectique" enfermante de la Reconnaissance. Chanteurs

de la dépense, poètes de la contestation,
ébranleurs du narcissisme conservateur,
briseurs des jougs et des liens, ils ar-
rachent le sujet à l'asservissement, fen-
dent le propre, disloquent la marionnette,
coupent les fils, troublent les miroirs.
Déjà Hoffmann libère le difficile enivre-
ment de savoir que je est plusieurs (10).

Cixous elaborates these theses in her detailed
analysis of E.T.A. Hoffmann's "Der Sandmann" by relating
features of the textual structure to a libidinal economy. The beginning of the tale, with the three letters
written by characters in the story and the subsequent
appeal by the narrator to the intense emotional experiences of his "beloved reader," is intepreted by Cixous
as a device by which Hoffmann draws the reader into the
magnetic circle of the tale, where nobody is or can be
indifferent, where the reader may not adopt the role of
spectator. "Le désir réclame sans cesse d'autres éner-
gies; et toi lecteur tu n'y couperas pas. Si tu lis,
avance, cherche à prendre, et sache que tu es toi aussi
désigné à saisie [sic]" (39).

The reader, Cixous maintains, is drawn into a whirl-
pool of desire in which categories like inside and
outside are dissolved. She emphasizes that Hoffmann's
text does not offer a continuous model of identification. Rather, digressions, ruptures, flashbacks, and
decentralization of the action produce fleeting possibilities of identification in which intensity, not
durability, counts most. Cixous sets this kind of textual structure parallel to the structure of seduction:

> Digression et séduction opèrent conjointe-
> ment; c'est le même geste, textuel ici,
> sexuel ici, geste d'éloignement calculé.
> Ce qui compte en effet, c'est d'entretenir
> à vif le plaisir. Et c'est ce calcul,
> cette distance, même réduite, qui assure
> au récit son défaut de réalité (41).

When Cixous talks of an absence of reality and the
abolition of the reality principle in Hoffmann's tale,
she is referring to the reality of the dominant
libidinal economy, which is here replaced by something
new: "Ce n'est past que notre seuil d'incrédulité soit
abaissé. C'est que notre relation au vraisemblable et
notre relation à l'identité et à l'identification auront
été - délicieusement - modifiées" (41).

23

Cixous interprets Nathanael as the embodiment of the new kind of desire: Nathanael is interested in the indefinable, in what is alien to identity (Olimpia, Coppelius, Coppola). The well-known (the image of Clara) does not hold him. He wants giddiness, the abyss, ecstasy (cf. 45). Cixous describes his desire as one that spends itself and thus escapes the dominant libidinal economy of conservation: ". . . rien ne le retient en un moi, pour lequel il n'a jamais un regard. Il ne se retourne pas sur lui-même, il se jette, regard amoureux du vide que son désir constitue en oeil-absolu" (42 f.).

This characterization already contains the main idea of Cixous's interpretation, for she defines the theme of "Der Sandmann" as the desire of the eye, the subject's relation to the complex order of seeing (cf. 49). For Cixous, Nathanael's overflowing desire is expressed in his way of seeing, which shapes the digressive, yet intense, narration. Nathanael is capable of being an anti-Nathanael (cf. 96): that is, more than one, not identical with himself, containing the other. Nathanael's wish to see is interpreted by Cixous as the desire to enlarge life and to open up the subject. Knowledge for him is to see himself seeing (cf. 98). Nathanael ends in madness because of the frightening insight that Olimpia is himself, an insight he cannot accept without being alienated from himself (cf. 81).

Apart from Nathanael's overflowing desire and the dissolution of his identity--which correspond to the achronological, decentered, digressive, intense mode of narration in Hoffman's tale--Cixous also perceives a clash with logocentrism in Hoffmann's use of metaphors with regard to femininity. Here Cixous speaks of a "glissement" (47) of the difference between animate and inanimate. Clara, whom Nathanael calls a lifeless automaton, is " - nous le verrons - et Nathanaël ne s'y trompe pas, réductrice, figeante, refroidissante, par opposition à l'effet de ferveur que la vue d'Olympia produit" (71). In Clara, who corresponds to conventional images of femininity, Hoffmann has created a "false" portrait. Cixous takes Clara as a parody of Goethe's good fiancées (cf. 48). There is rather too much of the automaton in the woman and, on the other hand, rather too much of the woman in the automaton. This heterogeneity is disturbing and threatening to the social order. Olimpia, who is given the value of a woman, causes a disorientation of the metaphorical for which Cixous cites Olimpia's second appearance as an example. From his room Nathanael sees her in the window of the house opposite as a "schöne Bildsäule" (beautiful statue). Cixous concludes that she (the woman) looks like a metaphor (cf. 65). Olimpia's charm is based on this ambiguity, which is not articulated as such. According to Cixous, Olimpia functions on two levels, that of appearance and also that of representation, thus cancelling out the difference between the two terms which ensures the functioning of the Law of the Proper.

Cixous comes to the conclusion that Hoffmann, in his tale "Der Sandmann," has shaken the singularity of the model, the principle of identity, the dominant libidinal economy, and the reality principle--that is, the pillars of phallogocentrism.

II. Nathanael's Desire within the Narrative Concept of "Der Sandmann"[3]

Cixous says of her interpretation of "Der Sandmann" that it is a reading from within; she dissociates herself from the alternative, "external" and rational, interpretation (cf. 72). The category "within" manifests itself in Cixous's endeavor to comprehend Nathanael's inner life, to follow his desire. Although she states at the beginning that the reader identifies briefly with any passing character, rather than with any one single person, it is nevertheless only Nathanael with whose desire Cixous identifies. She tries to see through Nathanael's eyes alone the world which is unfolded in the story, and thus Hoffmann's narrative concept is shifted to the edge of her field of vision. By adopting a perspective from within Nathanael, Cixous alters Hoffmann's tale in favor of her analytic interest much as she has accused Freud of doing in his famous interpretation of "Der Sandmann" (cf. 21-23).[4] For the characteristic trait of Hoffmann's tale is precisely the shifting between closeness and distance, between a perspective from within and one from without. When critics take the figure of the young enthusiastic artist, which crops up so often in Hoffmann's writing, for the prototype of the artist with ideals in a stupid, narrowly bourgeois world, or even for Hoffmann's own image, then they equate--with regard to "Der Sandmann"-- the level of the characters with the level of the abstract author. The difference between hero, narrator, and abstract author is of vital importance in Hoffmann's writing. The abstract author has the ironic distance which his heroes so often lack. Irony can be found on three levels in Hoffmann: in the colloquial sense of the word that what is said is the opposite of what is meant; in the sense that two incompatible spheres of life are contrasted; and in the romantic-philosophical meaning of the word. Ingrid Strohschneider-Kohrs elucidates Schlegel's romantic concept of irony, which she argues is formative in Hoffmann's writing, as

> eine bestimmte Möglichkeit und Methode künstlerischen Schaffens, indem der Künstler durch freies Verhalten zu sich selbst sich zu Besonnenheit bestimmt und die künstlerische Erfindung und Begeisterung mit Bewußtsein modifiziert. Eine solche Art künstlerischer Haltung und Schaffensweise kann sich am objektivierten Werk in formalen Prinzipien ausprägen, die wie der "Buffo" oder die "Parekbase" eine bewußte Durchbrechung der nur gegenständlichen oder erlebnisbedingten Darstellung zu erkennen geben.[5]

Examples of "breaking through" the level of narration are the direct address to the reader and the discussion of possible ways to begin the story. Here the persona of the narrator reflects on the mode of narration. These reflections are themselves in turn transformed into fictional form by a narrator who imagines the experiences and feelings of a fictional reader, whom he playfully projects into the role of the author. This multiplication of roles and the combination of literary production, reception, and criticism in a complex and amusing puzzle are a hint that on the level of the abstract author more than merely immediate identification of the reader is intended. Here the abstract author also makes the reader into an accessory, appealing to his capacity for enthusiasm as well as for ironic distance, to his emotion and reason. For in all his Fantasie- und Nachtstücke, with their elements of romantic yearning, Hoffmann nonetheless has a tendency towards enlightenment.

In "Der Sandmann" this tendency towards enlightenment manifests itself in comments by the narrator and in the figure of Clara. Clara, the one who sees clearly, gives an explanation in her letter of the sinister power by which Nathanael feels threatened: to have an effect on us the dark power must assume the form of "unser eignes Spiegelbild" (340), our own reflection. Referring to her brother Lothar's comment she writes: "Es ist das

Phantom unseres eigenen Ichs, dessen innige Verwandtschaft und dessen tiefe Einwirkung auf unser Gemüt uns in die Hölle wirft, oder in den Himmel verzückt" (341). Cixous concedes a certain analytic sharpness to the pre-Freudian naivete of Clara's explanation, but basically she conceives of her as mechanical and strangely comical. Clara, however, in fact functions less as a comic figure than as an on-the-whole trustworthy interpreter. The narrator agrees with her point of view several times. Furthermore, he describes her as possessing a profound heart and clear, keen understanding (cf. 345), capable of recognizing half-baked ideas as such and of dealing with them ironically. My reading of Clara's function as that of conveying to the reader a comprehensible interpretation of Nathanael's fantastic emotional life is moreover confirmed by the fact that she says almost the same about the "strange power" as the figure Ludwig in "Die Automate."[6] In this tale, which was written shortly before "Der Sandmann," Ludwig's role is also that of bringing clarification. He can even be seen as Hoffmann's mouthpiece since he articulates Hoffmann's theory of music in "Der Dichter und der Komponist"[7]--a tale which is closely connected to "Die Automate" with regard to its time of origin as well as to its dialogic structure and its constellation of characters.

In "Der Sandmann" the presentation is more complex and more mediated than in the two earlier dialogic tales. Clara is not simply the author's mouthpiece. From her perspective we do not see the whole truth. She embodies one pole of Hoffmann's world, the pole of level-headedness (Besonnenheit). Thus, while not to be dismissed as comical, she is yet limited, for there is nothing of the spark of genius in her. She does not undergo any development, any conflict. She does not become but is, and that, moreover, in a narrow bourgeois world. Thus she is one of the countless unevolving female figures in male literature. Hoffmann's female characters are statically fixed either in heaven, or with the philistines, or in bourgeois reason. Within the spectrum of Hoffmann's female characters--good, angelic, 16-year-old Julies, Aurelies, Antonies, career-minded, calculating Veronikas, Candidas, Ännchens, evil schemers like Benzon--clever Clara with her "lebenskräftige Fantasie des heitern unbefangenen, kindischen Kindes" (345) is probably the most positively and fully drawn female figure, without, however, offering the reader the possibility of simple identification with her. The narrator unfolds Clara's character by presenting several people's views of her, and he also gives expression to his own attitude towards her. Clara, with her gift of irony and wit, is even complex enough to be treated ambivalently by the narrator: his sympathy, which was so apparent at the beginning of the tale and expressed itself in his taking her side against Nathanael, seems to be withdrawn from her in the last paragraph. In the narrator's depiction of Clara's settling down in a cozy bourgeois life there is a note of distance which Cixous rightly emphasizes (cf. 48 f.). However, it is not simply unreliability that manifests itself in the narrator's ambivalence, but the author's intention to relativize opposing positions and to effect a distance from the level of the acting characters.

The narrator's ambivalent attitude towards Nathanael is a constant structural characteristic of the whole tale.[8] The hero's exalted feelings and actions are a fascinating thing which the narrator depicts from within by merging his perspective with that of Nathanael, but which he also follows with sober, ironic, critical eyes. For example, even before breakfast Nathanael reads to his fiancée from, as the narrator ironically puts it, all kinds of mystical books ("aus allerlei mystischen Büchern"; 346 f.), as well as poetry which he wrote while under the spell of Coppola, the evil power. Clara, who formerly listened to his stories "mit dem innigsten Vergnügen" (347), now reacts to his new gloomy, incomprehensible, formless tales as unerringly as in the narrator's previous descriptions of her reactions to the "Nebler und Schwebler" (345), who have little success with her. Her rejection, which is justified by the narrator ("Nathanaels Dichtungen waren in der Tat sehr langweilig"; 347), puts Nathanael on the same level as those airy-fairy poets, the "Nebler und Schwebler." Nathanael's reaction to Clara's negative opinion of his "ganzen mystischen Lehre von Teufeln und grausen Mächten" (346) is described by the narrator with humorous insight into Nathanael's contradictory feelings and behavior: "Der dachte kalten, unempfänglichen Gemütern erschliessen sich nicht solche tiefe Geheimnisse, ohne sich deutlich bewußt zu sein, daß er Clara eben zu solchen untergeordneten Naturen zähle, weshalb er nicht abließ mit Versuchen, sie in jene Geheimnisse einzuweihen" (346). By means of this ironic description, which echoes the airy-fairy poets' accusation that Clara is "kalt, gefühllos, prosaisch" (345), the reader is assigned the role of critical spectator, whose elimination Cixous has claimed to be the aim of Hoffmann's way of telling the story (cf. Cixous, 40).

The narrator exposes Nathanael as being in love with his allegedly extraordinary fate. Nathanael seems to feel singled out by the threatening force in the shape of Coppelius/Coppola, worthy of special attention. He therefore tries hard to keep alive the image of the evil power hanging over him:

> Die Gestalt des häßlichen Coppelius war, wie Nathanael selbst es sich gestehen mußte, in seiner Fantasie erbleicht und es kostete ihm oft Mühe, ihn in seinen Dichtungen, wo er als grauser Schicksalspopanz auftrat, recht lebendig zu kolorieren. Es kam ihm endlich ein, jene düstre Ahnung, daß Copelius sein Liebesglück stören werde, zum Gegenstand eines Gedichts zu machen (347).

Thus it is less the intention of the abstract author to remove the law of reality than to explore the relationship between inner and outer world and to depict the discrepancy between reality and Nathanael's view of reality.[9] Nathanael is so completely dominated by his fantasy world that he can no longer distinguish between fantasy and reality.[10] The inner world of Nathanael's desire becomes rampant, yet Hoffmann does not represent this as the "overflowing" and bursting open of the enslavement of the subject, as Cixous suggests, but as an egocentic deformation. Nathanael's relationship to seeing is possessive: he wants to see = know = define = dominate others. Furthermore he wants to determine the way others see him. Nathanael's angry reaction to Clara's letter, his desire that Clara should not learn "sichten und sondern" (342), as well as his endless attempts to instruct Clara and to wring enthusiasm for his poems out of her, all show that he is very intensely concerned with his ego. Far from desiring in an overflowing, self-forgetful way and being interested in what is alien to identity, he cannot bear contradiction, criticism, or any image of himself but the one he himself has constructed. Thus Nathanael calls Clara "Du lebloses, verdammtes Automat!" (348) because she does not feel inflamed by his poem. The automaton-doll Olimpia, on the other hand, he thinks capable of a high knowledge of the spiritual world and the eternal Beyond (cf. 357), for she does not contradict him. The narrator's disparaging judgment of Nathanael's literary mass production and his irony towards Nathanael's belief in having found an understanding of his poetic genius in

Olimpia are unmistakable. They are deliberately used by the abstract author to direct the reader's reactions:

> Aus dem tiefsten Grunde des Schreibpults holte Nathanael alles hervor, was er jemals geschrieben. Gedichte, Fantasien, Visionen, Romane, Erzählungen, das wurde täglich vermehrt mit allerlei ins Blaue fliegenden Sonetten, Stanzen, Kanzonen, und das alles las er der Olimpia stundenlang hintereinander vor, ohne zu ermüden. . . . Er erbebte vor innerm Entzükken, wenn er bedachte, welch wunderbarer Zusammenklang sich in seinem und Olimpias Gemüt täglich mehr offenbare; denn es schien ihm, als habe Olimpia über seine Werke, über seine Dichtergabe überhaupt recht tief aus seinem Innern gesprochen, ja als habe die Stimme aus seinem Innern selbst herausgetönt. Das mußte denn wohl auch sein; denn mehr Worte als vorhin erwähnt, sprach Olimpia niemals (357 f.).

Far from lifting the limitations of social exchange in favor of multiplicity and the gift, as Cixous describes the progressive part of the story, Nathanael wants something quite specific in return: his mirror image, larger than life-size. That is to say, his desire has traditionally masculine characteristics, just as Luce Irigaray has described them in Speculum. Society's shocked reaction to Nathanael's infatuation with a doll--caricatured in the portrayal of enamored men asking their fiancées for grotesque signs of real life and feeling--establishes moreover a close connection between the dreamer Nathanael and philistine society. For the abstract narrator's message is that Nathanael's fate is latent reality for many men since they, too, treat women like dolls.

The narrative concept aims at combining the tragic and the comic. Understanding and sympathy, as well as laughter mixed with consternation and horror, are awakened in the reader. The horror originates from, among other things, the fact that Hoffmann presents the intermingling of Eros and Thanatos in Nathanael's infatuation. For Nathanael's desire does not drive out death in order to enlarge life, as Cixous writes. Rather, his desire is directed at the dead. Elsewhere Hoffmann writes about the lifelike, dead automaton-doll:

"Mir sind", sagte Ludwig, "alle solche
Figuren, die dem Menschen nicht sowohl
nachgebildet sind, als das Menschliche
nachäffen, diese wahren Standbilder eines
lebendigen Todes oder eines toten Lebens,
im höchsten Grade zuwider. Schon in früher
Jugend lief ich weinend davon, als man
mich in ein Wachsfigurenkabinett führte,
und noch heute kann ich kein solches
Kabinett betreten, ohne von einem unheim-
lichen grauenhaften Gefühl ergriffen zu
werden. Mit Macbeths Worten möchte ich
rufen: 'Was starrst du mich an mit Augen
ohne Sehkraft?'. . .
    Schon die Verbindung des Menschen mit
toten das Menschliche in Bildung und Bewegung nachäffenden Figuren zu gleichem
Tun und Treiben hat für mich etwas
Drückendes, Unheimliches, ja Entsetz-
liches. Ich kann mir es denken, daß es
möglich sein müßte, Figuren vermöge eines
im Innern verborgenen Getriebes gar künst-
lich und behende tanzen zu lassen, auch
müßten diese mit Menschen gemeinschaftlich
einen Tanz aufführen und sich in allerlei
Touren wenden und drehen, so daß der
lebendige Tänzer die tote hölzerne Tänzer-
in faßte und sich mit ihr schwankte,
würdest du den Anblick ohne inneres Grauen
eine Minute lang ertragen?"[11]

In "Der Sandmann" Hoffmann unfolds such a scene in
detail. He describes a masculine desire with the utmost
intensity and at the same time criticizes it without,
however, putting anything new in its place. It seems unintentionally comical to me that Cixous interprets such
a classical masculine desire as, of all things, the precursor of an anti-phallogocentric desire. The comical
effect comes about because Cixous--misjudging the irony
of the presentation--equates the level of the characters
with that of the abstract author, as can be seen for example in her characterization of writing: "Écrire, c'est
donc regarder le réel avec les yeux 'communicants' de
Nathanaël" (99). But the intention of the text is not
identical with Nathanael's point of view, for Nathanael
is not depicted as the ideal, the model of the poet.
Cixous's failure to recognize Hoffmann's irony also
becomes apparent in her misinterpretation of Hoffmann's
"Der vollkommene Maschinist," a tale from the Kreisleriana collection.[12] She summarizes Kreisler's ironic

31

speech as if it had been meant literally, as if Kreisler/Hoffmann had really spoken in favor of a theater in which the theatrical machinery becomes visible as such and thus shatters the spectator's illusion. Cixous makes Hoffmann into a precursor of modern theatre à la Artaud when she interprets Kreisler's description of the allegedly perfect machinist as follows:

> Il faut que le théâtre se donne en spectacle: qu'il fasse valoir sa vérité et qu'il détruise la prétendue vérité du décor. Que la perfection du travail soit de se manifester comme tel. Il faut théatraliser le théâtre, empêcher le faux mystère, convier le spectateur à découvrir et contrôler les ficelles de la mise en scène: lui donner le plaisir <u>double</u> de la représentation, celui qui surgit de cette appartenance à deux lieux à la fois, qui maintient la valeur de jeu, et donc à la fois expulse le sérieux, l'appropriation, l'aliénation, interdit toute forme de possession, mais ouvre de réel au théâtral une scène intermédiaire et particulièrement délectable où s'effectue la transition d'un terme à l'autre . . . (110).

Yet Kreisler's speech means the opposite of what is said from beginning to end. In this case, Hoffmann does identify with the hero throughout. He makes use of the persona of Kreisler to give vent to some of his own exasperations and frustrations as a theatrical director, but in a humorous, indirect way. By overstating his praise he ridicules coarse, unimaginative machinists who do not succeed in producing a perfect illusion. For in Hoffmann's eyes, that is the desirable aim of theater since only the spectators' complete translation from everyday life could carry them into the higher realm of poetry.[13] Although Cixous completely misunderstands the meaning of this text she cannot entirely ignore the humor and parody in the manner of presentation. She compares the narrative technique to a Möbius strip on which one finds oneself suddenly—without being able to say when—transported onto the other side, the side of parody. After having up to this point given a literal rendering of Kreisler's ironic text, Cixous now claims that it is impossible to determine the author's position and to clearly separate seriousness, humor, and parody (cf. 111).

32

It strikes me as remarkable that in her interpretation of this continuously ironic text which is narrated from one and the same perspective, Cixous emphasizes a multiplicity and ambiguity of aspects. In the complex Sandmann tale with its changing narrative points of view, on the other hand, Cixous sees the meaning of the text solely from Nathanael's perspective. In both cases she misses the intention of the text, which is conveyed ironically, in order to emphasize elements which she assimilates to her own anti-phallogocentric theory. Hoffmann was conscious of the danger that irony can be misunderstood and he reduced this possibility by projecting it, through one of the Serapion brothers, onto the opposite sex: "'Willst du', rief Lothar, 'überall den Maßstab darnach, was den Weibern gefällt, anlegen, so mußt du alle Ironie, aus der sich der tiefste ergötzlichste Humor erzeugt, ganz verbannen; denn dafür haben sie, wenigstens in der Regel ganz und gar keinen Sinn.'"[14]

Sarah Kofman writes of Freud's literary interpretations that they are "un fantasme de maîtrise et de réappropriation des prédécesseurs,"[15] which repeats a typical gesture of western philosophy. Does not Cixous, too, come close to this phantasm? Does not she, too, transform literature into the childhood of her own theory?

III. Dissolution of Identity

Her anti-logocentric theory also shapes Cixous's claim that Nathanael bursts the limits of the identity of the subject, that he contains the other. It seems to me that the claim made here of a dissolution of identity illustrates the use of a fashionable term that is widely applied to everything lacking a unified identity. I think it is a misinterpretation to see in Hoffmann's presentation of the identity problem a liberating dissolution of identity, the ecstasy of knowing that "je est plusieurs" (10). Hoffmann's theme is rather the pain of being torn by opposite poles within the subject if the subject does not succeed in unifying them harmoniously, or madness if one of the poles is eliminated.

Hoffmann depicts the diversity of the subject in terms of the dissociations, repressions, projections of men whose actions are compulsive, who are haunted, threatened, and dominated by their drives because they do not recognize them. It is to be noted that women

never have such a diverse "I" in Hoffmann's writing.[16]
Hoffmann often portrays women ironically in their weaknesses or he transfigures them into angelic beings. Some
are robbed of their identity by an evil magnetist, but
none is as split, haunted, and driven by their other "I"
as are Medardus, Nathanael, Kreisler, and the goldsmith
in "Das Fräulein von Scuderi." Moreover, the dis-
integration of the "I" in Hoffmann's male figures remains largely within the romantic dualism between ideal
and reality, fantasy and sober reasoning, mind and
sensuality. In this context the splitting of identity in
Hoffmann's writing has a teleological tendency towards
wholeness and integration of the parts. Influenced by
the popular romantic philosopher G.H. Schubert,[17] who
conceived of historical development as a linear, upward
movement after an original unity has fallen apart, Hoffmann shared the romantic longing for a higher world--a
spiritualized, ideal, transcendental state--of which, so
he believed, art was able to impart an idea. In this
sense the most romantic of all the arts for Hoffmann was
music, which has only infinity as its subject and opens
the gate to the spiritual realm of immensity, vastness,
and infinite longing.[18] In this conception of art the
typical contemporary dualism manifests itself between a
higher spiritual world, the ideal, and art on the one
hand, and the lower material world, the reality of the
philistines, on the other. However, Hoffmann does not
situate the artist within the ecstatic realm of infinite
longing, but bases his greatness on his ability to
mediate between the finite and the infinite. He demands
enthusiasm of him and, at the same time, distance,
rationality. The latter Hoffmann expresses with the term
Besonnenheit, which is repeatedly mentioned as a characteristic of genius in his essay on Beethoven. The level-
headed composer "trennt sein Ich von dem innern Reich
der Töne und gebietet darüber als unumschränkter
Herr."[19]

Hoffmann's ideal artist is thus distinguished by an
integration of opposing aspects, by the attainment of a
definite identity in which opposites are harmoniously
balanced. Nathanael, who writes with Besonnenheit only
once after his encounter with Coppola, when he puts his
vision of the destruction of his and Clara's love into
verse, does not achieve this balance because he cannot
distinguish his self from outside reality. Without attaining this gentle happiness and the poetic talent of
the hermit Serapion, Nathanael, too, is shaped by the
failure to recognize the Duplizität of being which
Lothar diagnosed in Serapion:

34

Armer Serapion, worin bestand dein Wahn-
sinn anders, als daß irgendein feindlicher
Stern dir die Erkenntnis der Duplizität
geraubt hatte, von der eigentlich allein
unser irdisches Sein bedingt ist. Es gibt
eine innere Welt, und die geistige Kraft,
sie in voller Klarheit, in dem vol-
lendetsten Glanze des regesten Lebens zu
schauen, aber es ist unser irdisches Erb-
teil, daß eben die Außenwelt in der wir
eingeschachtet, als der Hebel wirkt, der
jene Kraft in Bewegung setzt. Die innern
Erscheinungen gehen auf in dem Kreise, den
die äußeren um uns bilden und den der
Geist nur zu überfliegen vermag in dunklen
geheimnisvollen Ahnungen, die sich nie zum
deutlichen Bilde gestalten.[20]

Nathanael's madness is complementary to Serapion's:
Serapion lives happily in his own mad world while denying the existence of outside reality. Nathanael is
haunted by the projections of his inner world onto an
external force. Hoffmann is fascinating in his portrayal
of the split identity, in which he describes processes
which were not psychoanalytically analyzed until much
later. Furthermore, his ability to relativize both poles
of the split identity, the split world, to insist on the
transcendental and on the common sense of the real
world, and thus to adopt a position comprising elements
of romanticism as well as of enlightenment, is unique.
Yet at the same time, the identity problem in Hoffmann's
work is tied to his time (that is, to logocentrism) with
regard to its dualistic principle and its teleological
tendency. Hoffmann is never concerned with an ecstatic
celebration of the dissolution of identity, but aims at
the establishment of an ideal identity on a higher
level--a tendency which also becomes apparent in having
Nathanael commit suicide in madness since he does not
succeed in attaining that higher unity. This tendency
only applies to men however. For Hoffmann is also a
child of his time in his misogyny which imprisons women
in the realm of being and denies them any conflict of
identity. Given his many one-dimensional, static female
characters one could see Hoffmann more as a typical representative of phallogocentrism than as a precursor of
anti-phallogocentric thinking, although he does describe
the Nachtseiten (dark sides) of the male character.

IV. Decentralized Narrative

While Cixous praises Hoffmann's digressive narrative she herself brings him into line by describing him one-sidedly as a writer of ecstasy, of generous prodigality, and of unlimited desire. But it is necessary to ask, first, whether Hoffmann's narrative reality is as digressive and decentralized as Cixous claims, and, second, whether digression necessarily coincides with anti-phallogocentrism.

In "Der Sandmann," only the narrator's intervention after the three letters really is a digression. After the narrator has offered his reflections on story-writing, and given necessary background information and a portrait of Clara, the story continues quite chronologically. More interesting material for examples of decentralized narrative can be found in Hoffmann's Lebens-Ansichten des Katers Murr and Prinzessin Brambilla.

Cixous interprets the digressive narrative as a technique which seduces and captivates the reader, and keeps the enjoyment of the text alive by well-calculated diversions and evasions. It seems to me that behind this assessment of Cixous's is the idea that digression = seduction follows the pleasure principle and does not subordinate spontaneous emotion to rational control in order to achieve linearity and unity. Seduction is thus opposed to logocentrism, and seems untainted by phallogocentrism. Yet on the sexual level, it has always been the prerogative of the phallocrats to give in to seduction, to flutter from blossom to blossom. On the textual level, digression, the breaking free from linear unity, is already an element of the literary tradition to which Hoffmann had ready recourse. In this respect, Hoffmann is influenced above all by Shakespeare and Sterne.

In his essay on Beethoven, Hoffmann writes:

> Ästhetische Meßkünstler haben oft im Shakespeare über gänzlichen Mangel innerer Einheit und inneren Zusammenhanges geklagt, indem dem tieferen Blick ein schöner Baum, Blätter, Blüten und Früchte aus einem Keim treibend, erwächst; so entfaltet sich auch nur durch ein sehr tiefes Eingehen in Beethovens Instrumental-Musik die hohe Besonnenheit, welche vom wahren

Genie unzertrennlich ist und von dem
Studium der Kunst genährt wird.[21]

This description characterizes Hoffmann's own writing
praxis too, especially if we think of Kater Murr. With
the metaphor of the tree and the seed Hoffmann returns
to Herder's famous topos from the Sturm und Drang
period. In the reading of Shakespeare in this period,
the argument that the apparently disparate parts in his
plays nevertheless form a natural inner unity became a
standard assertion with which the representatives of
Sturm und Drang signalled their opposition to the rules
of French classical drama. This opposition was embedded
in the context of a philosophy justifying new social
positions: nature, as opposed to artificiality, becomes
the ideological term which is used to fight restrictive
authority.

On the level of aesthetics, this conception of nature raises writing practices, previously excluded from
the aesthetic canon in Germany, to the status of avant-
garde models. The strategy of argumentation for this re-
evaluation shows, however, that decentralized aesthetic
forms can be absorbed by a logocentric tradition. For
the positive value of "unity" in a work of art is not
disputed by the representatives of Sturm und Drang; only
the definition of "unity" is altered so that disparate
aesthetic elements can be attributed a unity defined by
analogy with nature, with the organically grown.

In Hoffmann's time, Shakespeare had become known to
a wide public through the translations of Schlegel and
Tieck, and Hoffmann, an ardent theater-goer, was very
familiar with Shakespeare, as is shown by the great
number of quotations from and allusions to him in
Hoffmann's work. Moreover, Shakespeare's technique of
contrasting and interlocking scenes, of breaking up
linear courses of action, of mirroring plots, of comic
reflection on the action, influenced Hoffmann's own
technique of writing. The fact that the inner unity of
an apparently disparate text, as expressed by Hoffmann
in the metaphor of the tree, was not only his ideal but
can actually be found in the text, is demonstrated by
Ingrid Strohschneider-Kohrs in her hermeneutical interpretation of Prinzessin Brambilla.[22]

I think, therefore, that a style which is characterized by digression and decentralization does not
lie as far outside of the phallogocentric cultural
tradition as Cixous claims. The masterpiece of

digressive narration, Laurence Sterne's <u>The Life and Opinions of Tristram Shandy</u> (1759-67; rpt Harmondsworth: Penguin, 1977) was a stimulating model for Hoffmann. Sterne devotes an amusing chapter in Volume I of <u>Tristram Shandy</u> to a reflection on digression:

> Digressions, incontestably, are the sunshine;--they are the life, the soul of reading;--take them out of this book for instance,--you might as well take the book along with them;--one cold eternal winter would reign in every page of it; restore them to the writer;--he steps forth like a bridegroom,--bids All hail; brings in variety, and forbids the appetite to fail.
> All the dexterity is in the good cookery and management of them, so as to be not only for the advantage of the reader, but also of the author, whose distress, in this matter, is truly pitiable: For, if he begins a digression,--from that moment, I observe, his whole work stands stock still;--and if he goes on with his main work,--then there is an end of his digression (95).

As is well known, Sterne shifts the relation between progression and digression so far that it takes almost four volumes before he has described the day of his hero's birth. He finally has the novel end four years before Tristram's birth. Continuous progression is abandoned to such an extent in this novel that Hoffmann's tales and novels seem quite linear by comparison. Furthermore, Sterne emphasizes the unconscious part of the writing process which escapes rational control: "But this is neither here nor there--why do I mention it?-- Ask my pen,--it governs me,--I govern not it" (403). This remark could easily be interpreted as an indication of anti-phallogocentric writing in Sterne. In the narrator's description of his way of writing, Sterne, like Cixous, mixes the sexual and textual levels. The metaphors of the bridegroom and of unfailing appetite, however, seem to indicate not so much a break with the phallogocentric order, but rather an evocation of the desire for inexhaustible male potency which exists within that order.

The ruling symbolic order, the masculine libidinal economy, is not as homogenous and uncontradictory as

theories of an _écriture féminine_ describe it. It is capable of integrating diverse strategies of writing. The
ambivalence between being tied to its time and being
distanced from it characterizes all literature; the element does not exclude a text from the canon of tradition. On the contrary, it is precisely the break with
some aspects of tradition which assures a text's place
within it. In order to judge the status of an innovative
text in relation to phallogocentrism, I suggest one
would have to analyze the narrative concept more closely
than Cixous does, to locate it more precisely within
literary history, and to examine it with regard to its
strategies of signifying femininity and masculinity.

V. Disorientation of the Metaphorical

Cixous herself examines the signification of femininity in "Der Sandmann" in relation to metaphor. She
claims the Law/the Proper would break down if the metaphor transported its meaning from one term (representation) to the other (appearance) so that one would
not know which of them stands for the other.
". . . qu'une femme soit une poupée, voilà qui ne menace
personne si l'on reste dans la métaphore, car la
métaphore subordonne un de ces deux termes à l'autre.
Mais supposons que la femme _soit_ une poupée, que la
métaphore n'ait été qu'un écran à l'intolérable" (53).
According to Cixous, the social foundations of the
subject would dissolve if the metaphor did not guarantee
the distancing and valorization of one term (which is
assumed to be the proper one) against the other (cf.
Cixous, 53-55, 65 f., 69-73, 104-106).

However, it seems to me that it is not so much a
shaking of the pillars of phallogocentrism as an old
comic device when the metaphor glides towards reality,
when the metaphor is in play together with its concrete
source, and the distance between representation and
appearance is abolished. A scene from _A Midsummer-
Night's Dream_ may serve as an example for such comedy,
where the humor is derived from the fact that the
metaphorical is at the same time the concretely real. In
Act III, Scene I, Bottom the weaver really has an ass's
head, but knows nothing of his curious transformation.
He then uses the term "ass" metaphorically, relating it
to himself, but only in order to reject the relation:

> _Snout_. O Bottom, thou art chang'd! What do
> I see on thee?

Bot. What do you see? You see an asshead
of your own, do you?

Exit Snout

Re-enter Quince

Quin. Bless thee, Bottom, bless thee! Thou
art translated.   Exit
Bot. I see their knavery: this is to make
an ass of me; to fright me if they could.
But I will not stir from this place, do
what they can; I will walk up and down
here, and I will sing, so that they shall
hear I am not afraid (William Shakespeare,
A Midsummer-Night's Dream in The Complete
Works, ed. Peter Alexander London and
Glasgow: Collins, 1978 , III/I, p. 208).

The audience can see, however, that in both the literal
and the metaphorical sense, or to use Cixous's terms, on
the levels of appearance and reality, he is an ass.
Hoffmann employs the same comic device of a metaphorical
expression which, as is clear to the reader but not to
the fictional characters, is also literally true. To
Nathanael, Olimpia appears as beautiful as a statue, her
voice like crystal. On this level of the characters,
Olimpia really turns out to be a statue, a doll. On the
level of the abstract author lies the critical message:
if Olimpia, the divine woman, is finally unmasked as a
doll, then that implies that the doll is the ideal of
femininity in this society. By playing with the con-
stituents of the metaphor Hoffmann achieves comic-eerie
and socially critical effects, but the foundations of
the subject are surely not being dissolved by this
traditional literary device.

Neither is the singularity of the model--which,
according to Cixous, is one of the pillars of phallogo-
centrism--really shaken by this play with metaphor.
Cixous argues that a copy which cannot be distinguished
from the model threatens the dominant economy of subjectivity, because it destroys the notion of the singularity of the model and thus the concepts of identity
and property (cf. 104 f.). With regard to works of art
in general, the "age of technical reproducibility" (cf.
Benjamin) has shown that reproduction can well be
integrated into the dominant economy. As for Hoffmann's
tale, it does not shake the singularity of the model, as
claimed by Cixous, but aims at precisely the opposite.

40

By having Nathanael call the real woman (Clara, the original) a doll, while the copy (the doll Olimpia) becomes the model of femininity raised to Olympian levels for Nathanael—and, as the author's sardonic remark shows, also for philistine society—the abstract author articulates his critique of a society which suppresses individuality, singularity, originality, in favor of perfectionism and polish. "Der Sandmann" argues for the very economy of subjectivity which, according to Cixous's interpretation, the tale dissolves.

From this examination of Cixous's interpretation of "Der Sandmann" I would draw the conclusion that the use of the term écriture féminine, or anti-phallogocentric writing, for this text--and probably also for others by male authors—is misleading in several ways. This approach isolates certain elements of the text without examining them in the context of the narrative concept or of literary history. Thus the text's structure and content are distorted in order to appropriate it to a new theory. Furthermore, in her method of interpretation Cixous disregards the fact that, in spite of interesting innovations the text does contain, there are a number of masculine prerogatives on various textual levels which reflect the phallogocentrism prevalent in the writer's time. Feminist research should not neglect the historical perspective, and should be wary of the search for past models for a contemporary theory.

Notes

1 Cf. Hélène Cixous, "Le Sexe ou la tête?" Les Cahiers du GRIF, 13 (1976), 5-15 and the collection of Cixous's writing that appeared in German translation as Weiblichkeit in der Schrift, Berlin: Merve, 1980.

2 In spite of this intention, Cixous sometimes falls back into dualist thinking, attributing value to one position by denouncing the other and making femininity into mystic essentialism. Toril Moi criticizes this in Sexual/Textual Politics (London and New York: Methuen, 1985): "Fundamentally contradictory, Cixous's theory of writing and femininity shifts back and forth from a Derridean emphasis on textuality and difference to a full-blown account of writing as a voice, presence and origin" (119). "Within her poetic mythology, writing is posited as an absolute activity of which all women qua women automatically partake. . . . In her eagerness to appropriate imagination and the pleasure principle for

41

women, Cixous seems in danger of playing directly into the hands of the very patriarchal ideology she denounces. It is, after all, patriarchy, not feminism, that insists on labelling women as emotional, intuitive and imaginative, while jealously converting reason and rationality into an exclusively male preserve" (123).

[3] E.T.A. Hoffmann, "Der Sandmann," in Fantasie- und Nachtstücke, ed. Walter Müller-Seidel and Wolfgang Kron (München: Winkler, 1976), pp. 331-63.

[4] Cf. Sigmund Freud, "Das Unheimliche," in E.T.A. Hoffmanns Leben und Werk in Daten und Bildern, ed. Gabrielle Wittkop-Ménardeau (Frankfurt/M.: Insel, 1968), pp. 7-18.

[5] Ingrid Strohschneider-Kohrs, Die romantische Ironie in Theorie und Gestaltung, Hermanea, Germanistische Forschungen, Neue Folge 6, 2. durchgesehene und erweiterte Auflage (1960; Tübingen: Niemeyer, 1977), p. 38.

[6] Cf. E.T.A. Hoffmann, "Die Automate," in Die Serapions-Brüder, ed. Walter Müller-Seidel and Wulf Segebrecht (München: Winkler, 1976), pp. 328-55. Like "Der Sandmann," this tale also deals with an automaton-doll. A telling difference, however, lies in the fact that in "Die Automate" it is the clever speeches in many different languages of a male doll which cause astonishment and admiration. The attraction of the female doll in "Der Sandmann," on the other hand, consists of her muteness which Nathanael can fill out with his own speeches. Like Clara in "Der Sandmann," the figure Ludwig in this tale interprets the strange power as projection: "Es ist die psychische Macht, die die Saiten in unserm Innern, welche sonst nur durcheinander rauschten, anschlägt, daß sie vibrieren und ertönen, und wir den reinen Akkord deutlich vernehmen; so sind wir aber es selbst, die wir uns die Antworten erteilen, indem wir die innere Stimme durch ein fremdes geistiges Prinzip geweckt außer uns verständlicher vernehmen und verworrene Ahndungen, in Form und Weise des Gedankens festgebannt, nun zu deutlichen Sprüchen werden; so wie uns oft im Traum eine fremde Stimme über Dinge belehrt, die wir gar nicht wußten, oder über die wir wenigstens im Zweifel waren, unerachtet die Stimme, welche uns fremdes Wissen zuzuführen scheint, doch nur aus unserm eignen Innern kommt und sich in verständlichen Worten ausspricht" (343; cf. also 354).

42

[7] Cf. E.T.A. Hoffmann, "Der Dichter und der Komponist," in Die Serapions-Brüder, pp. 76-99.

[8] Cf. Wolfgang Kayser, Das Groteske: Seine Gestaltung in Malerei und Dichtung (Hamburg: Gerhard Stalling, 1957), p. 80 and footnote 24 on p. 214. Kayser perceives the narrator's irony and distance towards Nathanael as a stylistic rupture within a new narrative perspective he analyzes in Hoffmann, one which occasionally merges the narrator's perspective with that of the characters. In making this assertion, however, he overlooks the fact that the shifting between closeness and distance runs through the whole tale. Cf. also James McGlathery, Mysticism and Sexuality: E.T.A. Hoffmann, Part One: Hoffmann and His Sources, Europäische Hochschulschriften, Vol. 450 (New York, Berne, Frankfurt/M.: Peter Lang, 1981); Part Two: Interpretations of the Tales, Europäische Hochschulschriften, Vol. 819 (New York, Berne, Frankfurt/M.: Peter Lang, 1985). McGlathery assumes a position which is diametrically opposed to Kayser's. By situating Hoffmann solely within the tradition of comic sexual humor, he attributes only distance and irony to him. The element of romantic yearning, of the tragic within the comic, is flattened out of McGlathery's interpretation.

[9] There is also a tendency among literary critics not writing within a post-structuralist framework to interpret Hoffmann's work as exploding the law of reality. Cf. e.g., Wolfgang Preisendanz, "Eines matt geschliffnen Spiegels dunkler Widerschein. E.T.A. Hoffmanns Erzählkunst," in E.T.A. Hoffmann, Wege der Forschung, Vol. CDLXXXVI, ed. Helmut Prang (Darmstadt: Wissenschaftliche Buchgesellschaft, 1976), pp. 270-91.

[10] Cf. Peter von Matt, Die Augen der Automaten. E.T.A. Hoffmanns Imaginationslehre als Prinzip seiner Erzählkunst (Tübingen: Niemeyer, 1971). Von Matt writes of the projection of Hoffmann's heroes: "Sie begegnen alle dem konkretisierten Lichtentwurf ihres eigenen kreativen Seelengrunds, aber da sie ihn nicht als solchen erkennen und ihnen auch die Gabe eines milden Wahnsinns fehlt, können ihnen diese Erscheinungen ebensosehr zu tödlichem Grauen wie zu überirdischer Beseligung gereichen. Je nachdem, meinen sie auf Dämonen oder gute Geister zu stoßen, bedroht oder beschenkt zu werden, aber de facto erleben sie niemals Jenseitiges, weder den Teufel noch den Lieben Gott, sondern nur sich selbst und ihre phantastisch ausgefächerte Innenseite" (23). He calls this "autistische Daseinserfahrung" (74).

[11] E.T.A. Hoffmann, "Die Automate," pp. 330 and 346. Cf. also Sarah Kofman, Quatre romans analytiques (Paris: éditions galilée, 1974), pp. 135-81. In her psychoanalytic interpretation of "Der Sandmann," Kofman emphasizes the aspect of death. She interprets the magic, alchemical scene in which Nathanael watches his father and Coppelius as the "real" return to an imaginary scene, the primitive, primary scene. In this primary scene Nathanael had such strong incestuous drives, Kofman conjectures, that as a consequence he renounced woman and identified with a father whom he imagined as passive. He replaced genital enjoyment, which he never experienced, by narcissistic enjoyment: eyes for genitals. The replacement of the function of sexual reproduction by the eye causes Nathanael to draw a kind of perverse satisfaction from the creation of doubles. Imitation of life takes the place of life for him. Kofman identifies "double" with "diable" (devil) and with the death instinct. Thus she comes to conclusions about this tale which are quite the opposite of Cixous's.

[12] Cf. E.T.A. Hoffmann, "Der vollkommene Maschinist," in Fantasie- und Nachtstücke, pp. 58-66.

[13] Cf. also the discussion of the function of decoration in Hoffmann's "Seltsame Leiden eines Theater-Direktors," in Fantasie- und Nachtstücke, pp. 674-82. The aim of the painter of theater sets should be "jene höhere Illusion hervorzubringen, die mit dem Moment der Handlung sich selbst in der Brust des Zuschauers erzeugt" (676). The overall aim must be "die vollkommene Einheit des Spiels" in which there is nothing "Fremdartiges" (682).

[14] E.T.A. Hoffmann, "Der Artushof," in Die Serapions-Brüder, p. 169.

[15] Kofman, p. 18.

[16] Cf. Susanne Asche, Die Liebe, der Tod und das Ich im Spiegel der Kunst. Die Funktion des Weiblichen in Schriften der Frühromantik und im erzählerischen Werk E.T.A. Hoffmanns, Hochschulschriften Literaturwissenschaft, Vol. 69 (Königstein: Hain, 1985). Asche claims that Hoffmann does not engage in a power discourse on femininity; femininity does not have to embody the other but remains an undefined vacancy in Hoffmann's writing. However, if femininity is not denounced as narrowly bourgeois, it is a vacancy onto which Hoffmann's heroes project their dreams and their ego. In this and in the

non-development of his female characters Hoffmann certainly is a representative of a masculine discourse.

[17] Cf. G.H. Schubert, Ansichten von der Nachtseite der Naturwissenschaft (1808; rpt. Darmstadt: Wissenschaftliche Buchgesellschaft, 1967). Cf. also the analysis of teleological tendencies in Hoffmann's writing in Karl Ochsner, E.T.A. Hoffmann als Dichter des Unbewußten, Wege zur Dichtung, Vol. XXIII (Frauenfeld/Leipzig: Huber, 1936).

[18] Cf. Hoffmann's essay on Beethoven which first appeared as a review and was later made a part of the "Kreisleriana" under the title "Beethovens Instrumental-Musik," in Fantasie- und Nachtstücke, pp. 41-49; esp. pp. 41 and 43. The same idea of art in which the hope for a higher, better world expresses itself, Hoffmann portrays elegiacally in "Ombra Adorata" and in ironic reversal in "Gedanken über den hohen Wert von Musik," where he has supposed unfortunate enthusiasts and madmen voice his own views. Cf. Fantasie- und Nachstücke, pp. 33-41, especially pp. 34 and 39.

[19] E.T.A. Hoffmann, "Beethovens Instrumental-Musik," p. 44. Cf. also the final words of the "Rahmenfigur" Ottmar in Die Serapions-Brüder, p. 995; Ottmar believes that an "erregter Seelenzustand zwar einen glücklichen genialen Gedanken, nie aber ein in sich gehaltenes geründetes Werk erzeugen kann, das eben die größte Besonnenheit erfordert."

[20] E.T.A. Hoffmann, Die Serapions-Brüder, p. 54.

[21] E.T.A. Hoffmann, "Beethovens Instrumental-Musik," p. 44.

[22] Cf. Strohschneider-Kohrs, Die romantische Ironie in Theorie und Gestaltung, pp. 362-424.

I would like to thank Chris Lyons for helping me with the translation of this paper which was originally written in German. Thanks also to Jeanette Clausen for many helpful comments.

A German version of this paper appears in Annegret Pelz et al. (eds.), Frauen-Literatur-Politik. Dokumentation der Tagung vom Mai 1986 (Berlin: Argument, 1987.)

Écriture Féminine in the New German Cinema: Ulrike Ottinger's Portrait of a Woman Drinker

Renate Fischetti

The question of whether or not there is a specifically feminine aesthetic remains an open question and
the subject of much debate among feminists in the U.S.
and in Europe. In film criticism, this debate was
stirred up in the early and mid-seventies by Claire
Johnston and Laura Mulvey, two British film critics, and
has continued in the leading journals ever since.[1]
Beginning in the early eighties, the first books appeared on the subject, among them Annette Kuhn's Women's
Pictures: Feminism and Cinema, and E. Ann Kaplan's Women
and Film: Both Sides of the Camera. Both authors analyze
films by women using the tools of psychoanalytic neo-
structuralism and displaying varying degrees of ortho-
doxy.[2] Re-Vision: Essays in Feminist Film Criticism
offers a collection of analyses by prominent feminist
critics, while Alice Doesn't: Feminism, Semiotics, Cinema by Teresa de Lauretis situates feminist criticism
among the avant-garde of film theory. The best summary
of the questions raised by feminist criticism is found
in the article "Aesthetic and Feminist Theory: Rethinking Women's Cinema," also by Teresa de Lauretis, in
the winter 1985 issue of New German Critique. Lauretis
admits that posing the question of what constitutes a
feminine aesthetic implies remaining trapped "in the
master's house."[3] In other words, using the tools of
patriarchal discourse, which for so long has subjected
women to non-presence, feminist theorists would endorse
that very system, and "legitimate the hidden agendas of
a culture we badly need to change" (158). Lauretis
highlights the very point in question: should feminist
critics spend their efforts deconstructing patriarchal
discourse, to unmask the mechanisms of power sustaining
an ideology long recognized by feminists as alien to the
needs of women? Or should there be an attempt to reread
the texts by women, of which there have appeared a
considerable number, to discover whether they differ
from texts by men, or, more precisely, to ask what sets
feminist texts off from non-feminist texts, and whether

47

there is such a thing as a feminine discourse. Finally, how can the feminist critic offer such a reading without falling into the traps of the dominant discourse?

These very questions have been asked by the French feminist theorists, most notably by Julia Kristeva, Hélène Cixous, and Luce Irigaray, all of the post-structural school, with varying backgrounds. French feminists began to articulate a "feminine discourse" as early as the late sixties, reading the texts of dominant discourse against the grain and discovering instances of écriture féminine, or feminine writing, throughout the history of civilization, in cases where dominant discourse was subverted or rendered meaningless.[4] Of particular interest is the approach of Luce Irigaray, a linguist and philosopher as well as a practicing psychoanalyst, who seems to offer the most revealing insights into the psycho-sexual position of women, their non-language, and the options for finding a discourse of their own, which she prefers to call "feminine discourse" or "feminine syntax." In Speculum of the Other Woman, Irigaray undertakes a deconstruction of Freud's theory of female sexuality as well as a rereading of classical philosophy, finding, in most instances, a total lack of representation of women, who have been defined as outside of the dominant discourse. Her collection of essays This Sex Which Is Not One offers further views on the position of women in the dominant discourse, which Irigaray sees psychoanalytically, i.e., established through Freud's theory on infant sexuality, and through Lacan's rereading of Freud in linguistic terms. Both Freud and Lacan had defined sexuality through the phallus. In Freudian and Lacanian psychoanalysis, the phallic principle is responsible for the articulation of desire, and ultimately for all symbolic representation. This leads Irigaray to see the laws of phallic discourse as ultimately "hom(m)osexual" (This Sex, 129), meaning there is only one sexuality which it admits, one identity on which it is built. Women, who lack the phallus, are the other, and are excluded from the processes which involve the establishment of symbolic systems. Therefore Irigaray, in her deconstruction of Freud, Lacan, and dominant Western philosophy, sees woman defined as a non-person, as possessing no sexuality, no desire, no articulation, no language, all of these concepts being part of a discourse which is determined by the phallic principle alone. Using a favorite metaphor of Lacan's, Irigaray speaks of the logic of the dominant discourse as follows:

As for the priority of symmetry, it correlates with that of a flat mirror--which may be used for the self-reflection of the masculine subject in language, for its constitution as subject of discourse.

In this symmetry of the flat mirror, woman can only emerge "as the inverted other of the masculine subject (his alter ego), or as the place of emergence and veiling of the cause of his (phallic) desire, or again as lack. . . ." In other words, this system of representation does not allow women to see themselves or speak for themselves as subjects. Feminine discourse will not be possible until women recognize that "this flat mirror cannot be privileged and symmetry cannot function as it does in the logic and discourse of a masculine subject" (129). To put it differently, woman, if she is to truly articulate her desire, will need more than the flat mirror. As we shall see in our analysis of Ottinger's Ticket of No Return, that mirror needs to be shattered.

Since Irigaray's work provides the stimulus for re-reading texts of all sorts, for repositioning women with regard to these texts, her thoughts shall serve as the framework for our reading of Ottinger's film. It is hoped that an analysis of this text as an example of écriture féminine, as an attempt at feminist discourse, will encourage similar readings of texts by other women.

Ticket of No Return, or in literal translation of the German title Portrait of a Woman Drinker, is the fourth film by Ulrike Ottinger, and her second full-length feature. Shot in 1979 in Berlin, it opened at the 1979 Hof Festival, ran the following year during the "Semaine de la Critique" at Cannes, and later that year at Berlin and Edinburgh. As with her previous films, Ottinger wrote the script, did camera, and directed. The plot is easily summarized: "A woman of great beauty," as the voice-over informs us toward the beginning of the film,[5] leaves some mythical Southern place, "La Rotonda," buys a ticket of no return to Berlin Tegel, and, having decided to forget or leave her past by concentrating on one thing, "her thing," which is to drink, engages on a drinking tour of Berlin, "a sightseeing tour" suited to "her particular needs." The film is built around the various drinking episodes, contains several dream sequences, and violates many of the rules of narrative film, most notably by representing the

49

protagonist as silent, without speech.[6] Compared to
Ottinger's earlier films, however, Ticket is relatively
accessible, less chaotic through its insistence on the
one character and the portrayal of her "passion," a term
Ottinger uses to describe the Drinker's addiction.
Critical reaction to the film was mixed. Reviewed
favorably by most,[7] it failed to get the approval of the
feminist critics in Frauen und Film.[8] The reasons for
their rejection had to do with the film's apparent
aestheticism, its glossy surface. What was missed was
emotional involvement, the portrayal of women in be-
lievable situations, social criticism, in other words, a
case study. Instead, the film offered a woman character
of grotesque appearance and behavior with whom it was
impossible to identify, and whose actions were utterly
stupid. The strongest objections raised were against her
appearance, which seemed to reduce her to the status of
object, or seemed to convey the feeling that much of the
film played on images which were being exploited by
sexist ads. Significantly, one critic also mentions the
Drinker's silence as something objectionable and sees it
as a manifestation of nonsensical artifice:

> die tödliche passion der dame, die da
> mickrig auf pfennigabsätzen, in quarantäne
> gekleidet (weil saufen eine seuche) die
> straßen auf und ab tickert, dauernd
> irgendwo einkehrt und sich vollaufen läßt,
> ohne sinn und verstand, sprachlos, al-
> koholeinnahme als solche, ein spektaku-
> läres unternehmen, ganz und gar gewollt
> präsentiert, stümperhaft vorgeführt, eine
> tödliche passion, der man weder das töd-
> liche abnimmt, noch die passion glaubt
> (Reschke, 29).

The fetishistic character of the Drinker's appearance is
also the focus of Miriam Hansen's paper, "Visual
Pleasure, Fetishism and the Problem of Feminine Discourse: Ulrike Ottinger's Ticket of No Return," which
appeared in the winter 1984 issue of New German Critique.
Quoting Laura Mulvey's thoughts on woman as fetish in
conventional cinema, a function determined by man's
desire to be a voyeur as well as by his fear of
castration, Hansen reads the film as a parody:

> The emancipation of visual pleasure
> through a parodistic display of its
> fetishistic guises is not least a function

of the overall organization of the film's narrative (105).

In her analysis of the narrative structure, Hansen concludes that voyeurism is not possible as a response to the film since it is its major theme, parodied as "the stereotypical social response to the appearance of the Drinker," and a distancing device.[9] Instead, visual pleasure is "re-connected to its source, female narcissism," which Hansen reads historically as an "inversion of the aesthetic impulse" women experienced but were unable to express other than by overly concerning themselves with their own image (102). Evoking the work of Oscar Wilde whose Dorian Gray was to be the title hero of Ottinger's next film (Dorian Gray im Spiegel der Boulevardpresse), Hansen concludes by reading Ottinger's affinity for turn-of-the-century art as a reflection of her aestheticism, as a "stylistic equivalent of the cult of narcissism" (107), a tradition historically reserved for male discourse, but "reappropriated" by Ottinger for the purpose of parody through ultimately feminist discourse (108). Hansen is right in pointing to the references which seem to link the film with European aestheticism of the late 19th century. At the same time, her reading is somewhat reductive, neglecting the more powerful psychological statements of the film.

Ticket of No Return undoubtedly does have narcissism as a central theme. Not only is there a reference to it in the introduction, where the narrator speaks of the Drinker's "narcissistic-pessimistic cult of loneliness,"[10] there are the many instances of mirroring and seeking a double image, mostly in the encounters with the bag woman, and there is the blatant loneliness of the Drinker, her social isolation, most clearly inscribed in her lack of speech. There are also instances of parody, most obvious in the treatment of the three women representing social virtues: "gesunder Menschenverstand," "soziale Frage," and "exakte Statistik," ridiculing sociologists in their claim to solve the world's problems. These allegorical characters cross the path of the Drinker throughout the film. They are voyeurs to her exploits, which they readily and amply comment on in silly platitudes. They are dressed grotesquely in "Pepita," black and white checkered suits and cloaks, with matching hats:

While the film is often humorous, there are also many serious moments, as toward the end, when Ottinger herself appears in the frame, sitting on a park bench, bottle in hand, reading passages from a book by Peter Rosei:

> soweit mir Trinker bekannt sind, wollen sie nicht trinken, sondern sterben. Wundersamer Plan, ein Vergnügen so zu steigern, daß es über Qualen in den Tod führt. . . .

As she reads this, a transvestite is tossed out of a taxi and crawls to the bench, only to be left there to himself, the book in hand, from which he in turn recites. Serious also are the final sequences in the underground passages of the Zoo Station as the Drinker, having reached a stage of delirium, is seen staggering through corridors, and down and up staircases. The unusual sightseeing tour comes to a bizarre ending, as both the Drinker and the bag woman, who has come to her rescue, are run over by a crowd on a busy stairway of the train station. These elements of pathos make the film more than a parody; it appears that Ottinger meant more than an exercise in aestheticism. To do the film justice, it may be necessary to attempt a different reading.

Costumes, Make-Up, Accessories

Costumes are a major signifier in this film, as in all of Ottinger's films, with the exception of her latest, a documentary on China. Tabea Blumenschein, who plays the Drinker, designed them under Ottinger's guidance in striking colors and shapes. Blumenschein wears these costumes with dignity, letting us know that she is aware of her masquerade. The way she exhibits them is reminiscent of the way the living sculptures in Laokoon und Söhne and Die Betörung der blauen Matrosen wore their drapes and costumes. This is especially true in the opening and closing sequences, and in the sequence on the Straße des 17. Juni, in all of which she is shot from extremely low angle. The Drinker also reminds the spectator of Madame X, the cultist pirate who rules over the women seeking adventure with her:

Her dress is exaggerated, theatrical. The colors are red, black, yellow, burgundy, pale blue, black, and silver, indicating, one may suggest cautiously, a preference for colder colors toward the end. The materials are soft in the beginning and progress to harsher textures, her final dress being of an aluminum-like metallic substance:

The shapes are flowing in the beginning--she wears wide overcoats in the opening sequence and at Café Möhring--but soon there is a preference for tight-fitting, sleeveless evening robes, with gloves or glove- and wing-like attachments to the arms:

At one point she is nude, her upper torso revealed, as she and the bag woman celebrate a bubble bath with champagne. Her make-up is at all times exaggerated, mask-like. Mostly she wears her hair back and up, and often adorns it with fancy hats or bows. She wears exaggerated jewelry, like the tin coils that dangle from her ears during the casino episode, or the strap she has tied around her neck during the "Kneipentour" with the bag woman. She is always in high heels, which are in center frame during much of the opening sequence, and which again dominate the very last shot. The heels' clicking often dominates the sound track, a monotonous and threatening noise. Among her accessories are lipstick, pills, an address booklet, and a switchblade. These are shown in a very brief close-up toward the end of the film, after she has dropped her bag on a lone walk with the bag lady toward the Siegessäule. Her friend is eager to assemble the items, but a photographer, who has witnessed the event, grabs the remainder. He sits down on the curb, spreads the Drinker's belongings out, and proceeds to photograph them. Among them is the switchblade.

Several times, the Drinker assumes the appearance of a man. Twice this occurs in dream sequences, the first time in a taxi on the way to the casino, the second time in the longer dream sequence framed in a park across from Charlottenburg Castle. During the first change of sex roles, she is a young man with black mustache, hair combed back, wearing a black leather jacket. The young man drinks from a small leather liquor bottle which is passed between him and the driver, an action continued from the previous shot, where the Drinker had done the same. His eye-level medium shots are intercut with reverse shots of what is outside, followed by a crashing noise and a fast cut to the young man being thrown back. Then there is a cut to a long shot of the bag woman and her cart, knocked over, presumably as the taxi was avoiding her. The bag woman hurls curses at the taxi as it disappears into the frame. The reverse shot has the Drinker converted back into her female role, with the three social virtues appearing in a taxi along to her right.

The second time a sex change takes place, the young man is framed in a high angle shot as he climbs a set of stately stairs. Again sporting a black mustache, he now wears a black business suit, a black hat, and carries a black folder under his right arm. Following, there is a cut to a close shot of his fragmented mirror image, providing multiple reflections of him:

The sequence ends with a medium shot, as he presents the three social virtues, who are seated along a table, with a catalog, obviously in the function of salesman.

Finally, there is a third image of the Drinker as young man in a glossy unframed color photograph which we initially see pinned onto the wall to the right above her bed. This photograph shows a frontal view of her head and upper torso, again with her hair combed back, though here it is light brown in color; and again there is the mustache. She is dressed in a yellow jacket over a dark shirt. During the latter part of the film, this photograph has disappeared.

A psychoanalytic reading of the Drinker's costumes, make-up, and accessories suggests, above all, ambivalence toward her sexual identity. The surface femininity is misleading; there is more to her than the initial images suggest. She is wearing a mask, her bizarre fashions are part of the masquerade. Unconsciously, she sees herself differently. Her feminine image is complemented by its opposite, a masculine identity, which stays in hiding most of the time and is called forth in dreams. The photo and the switchblade are traces of this hidden identity that surface into her waking states. She is undoubtedly narcissistic, for she is unable to form any relationships except those which reflect her own self. But her narcissism is determined by a search for identity, by the need to reconcile both masculine and feminine traits of her personality. Returning to the theoretical framework of Luce Irigaray, we may read the Drinker as a subversive woman, one who negates the clear definition ascribed her by masculine discourse. In her aggressive behavior, by dwelling on masculine traits, and in her secret desire to see herself as a young man, this woman questions the sexual identity given her by man. She remains silent, but her gestures speak clearly. From the beginning, she is a woman of action, not a passive object of desire. She has chosen to destroy herself, out of her own free will. She is in control, there is no man in her life for whom she might serve as reflection. She is a phallic woman, visually symbolized in her possession of the knife and in her appearance as a vamp with hour-glass figure, on high heels, with erect posture, signifying the rule of the phallus. Yet she also renders this image absurd. The gesture she expresses in her dress is one of contempt. She wears the grotesque wrappings as masquerade, suggesting their artificiality, and the freedom she had in choosing them. In her appearance alone, the Drinker questions the way women have been defined, questions the laws that established this definition, questions phallic discourse.

Chaos

In the sequence following the credits, the Drinker is descending on Berlin. We follow her plane's landing and taxiing, her entrance through the flight gate, and her walk through the terminal building--in search for a bar, as we are shortly told. The moment she appears at Customs, ready to walk through, a man's suitcase falls to the ground and its contents spill. Moments later, as she walks in the terminal, a bar car tumbles across the frame, tipping over in the lower left. A man carrying an attaché case and hand-cuffed is escorted by police into the frame from bottom right; he crosses the path of the Drinker, turns around, and runs wild. The Drinker's first encounter with the bag woman involves a near crash, during which the shopping cart gets tipped over. After their drinking spree at Café Möhring, the women scramble up a staircase, with the shopping cart spilling its contents. During the walk along Siegesallee, the Drinker drops her handbag, and in the final sequence, a crowd of people spills out of the corridors of the station, causing a gruesome end for the Drinker and her friend.

The many tumblings and spillings signify chaos. The Drinker brings chaos to those who cross her path, and she brings chaos to herself. She delights in upsetting the order of things, unconsciously as in the above instance, or wilfully, as during one of her initial bar stops, when she lifts a cognac glass, only to let it drop and break on the counter top. The angle is reversed, the camera very close, and the focus is on the broken glass. A similar breakage occurs when the Drinker and her friend stop by at Nina Hagen's bar. As a matter of fact, the two create some form of disturbance wherever they show up, and they are often evicted. Their unruly behavior is a signal of rebellion, an act of protest against being excluded. For neither the mythical foreigner nor the bag woman belong. They are outside of the social order, and they make this known by upsetting things. Law and order, however, are established by the phallic principle. Chaos is that which is excluded. In that sense both the Drinker and her friend are representatives of chaos and threats to the law.

Dreams

Dreams are signified by the appearance of the dwarf. This happens five times in the course of the film and allows the visualization of the Drinker's unconscious. The first time, he appears as she is leaving the airport, about to find herself trapped between two automatic glass doors. The second time, the dwarf is outside the taxi, as she transforms herself into the young man. The third time, the dwarf signals the first longer dream sequences. He invites her to drink from a medieval-looking fountain, then climbs the spiral staircase of a glass tower with her, serves her a drink in a Japanese pavilion amid a snowy landscape, and leads her to a pond with exotic flowers and greenery, where he picks one of the bright red flowers and offers it to her to drink from. The camera dwells on the image of her holding the flower to her mouth, signifying great sensuality through color combination and framing. The next appearance of the dwarf signals a merging of reality and fantasy, as the Drinker, a lone spectator in Berlin's Philharmonic Hall, witnesses the dwarf appear on a television screen, presenting a tray with a roasted goose, knife and fork in its back, which he deposits on a small round table. The camera leaves the television and pans to the right,

58

revealing that the television is situated in the Drinker's room, and that the same round table has a real tray and goose on top, dream and reality having merged.

The dwarf's final appearance introduces the longest dream section of the film, where the Drinker is alternately represented as Hamlet, an office secretary, a tightrope artist, an advertising consultant, a stunt person, and the young man in black business suit. In all these sequences, the Drinker has an audience, including the three social ladies.

These fantasy sequences are playful variations on the theme of social identity, of sexual identity, and they represent an opening of the film's narrative into the surreal. In the case of the middle fantasy, there is also occasion to reveal repressed aggression, a topic which will be discussed below.

Windows, Mirrors, Doubling

The Drinker is forever on the move. In the opening sequence, she traverses a stately room and climbs an equally stately set of stairs. After the credits, her plane moves her to Berlin. Once disembarked, she walks through the terminal. Later, we see her moving in elevators, climbing and descending more stairs, moving in planes, always to the click of her heels. There is repetition in the use of this motif, suggesting that the adventures are but variations on one theme, the theme of going somewhere, but ultimately to a dead end, to a barrier. These barriers are mostly windows, sometimes combinations of doors and windows, or combinations of mirrors and windows. They may signify entrapment, as in the first episode at the airport, where the Drinker is caught between the double glass doors and, for a moment, is bewildered as to how to open them. They also create spaces where the Drinker acts out her exhibitionistic drives to an onlooking public, as in the dream sequence which has her counsel the three social virtues in what appears to be a store front, with the public peeping in. Most importantly, windows merge interior with exterior spaces and allow for an extension of the Drinker's unconscious. This happens as the dwarf appears outside the cab window, in the dream sequence where the Drinker and the dwarf are climbing a spiral staircase in a glass tower, and, most significantly, as the Drinker experiences a doubling of herself in encounters with images of two women that are seemingly alien to her

59

self-image. Once, this happens at the airport between the double doors. In a medium shot, she has entered the frame from the front, the dwarf appearing in the background between the double glass doors and walking toward her. Their paths crossed. A medium shot has her turning around to the front, as she appears to hesitate, wishing to go back. A cut to another medium shot has her behind glass, with both hands touching, looking through the surface in front of her on which splashes of water appear. A reverse-angle close shot reveals a woman's face, hand, and cloth, as she cleans the window. The woman appears to laugh. The reverse has the Drinker turn around and go back, only to find herself at the glass door which at first does not open.

This motif is taken up again on her way back from the casino. In a long shot, she passes through the casino's glass doors, the camera panning with her to the left, where a taxi and the bag woman are waiting, the bag woman eager to help her in. In a cut to a close shot from inside the taxi, the bag woman is wiping the window with her sleeve; she blows, rubs, and laughs. The reverse angle has the Drinker watch in amazement, before the taxi leaves the frame. In both the airport and the taxi, she encounters an image of a lower-class woman, working, smiling, eager to please her. The glass between them signifies distance, but there is a hypnotic effect. The Drinker is caught with this image, there is no escaping. It helps her define herself, her otherness. Her cold, composed appearance is but one aspect of her self, one that is socially defined, whereas that which the two women represent is her unconscious, her libido, a hidden part of her which only surfaces in uncontrolled moments. In this sense, the bag woman represents the Drinker's repressed drives, a complement to her smooth and controlled woman image.

As the film progresses, the Drinker begins to see herself in a way that is similar to the way she experienced the images of the two lower-class women. The first time, this happens at Café Möhring, where she sits against a window, sees the bag woman outside, and waves her in. As she waves, we see a reflection of the Drinker in the window. After the bag woman has sat down next to her, she takes a glass of water and splashes it against the window, causing much commotion and her first eviction. The second, similar episode happens the morning after the Möhring incident. There is a close shot of a newspaper being shoved under a door, a cut to her in medium shot, as she rests in bed in pink silk, before

60

the camera pans with her as she gets up to fetch the newspaper. A close shot shows a newspaper article, with her photo, reporting yesterday's incident. A pan follows her to the right to a mirror in medium close framing. She compares herself to the image in the newspaper, takes a glass, drinks, looks again into the mirror, and splashes the image with her drink. A third similar confrontation takes place toward the very end of the film. She is in a public restroom of the Zoo Station, quite drunk. The attendant had to help her to a stall. In a close shot, we see her leaning toward a mirror from the right of the frame, doubling her profile during a very brief moment of rest. She then spits at herself, moves her fingers across the surface, blows, laughs, wipes, is amazed, laughs, and is pulled away by the attendant, leaving the empty mirror in the frame. In this very last instance, she repeated the actions of the two alter ego images to the point of mimicking them, implying an identification with the other, the previously alien images of her self. It would seem that at this point, she is ready to accept herself fully, to allow her unconscious to come forth, to rid herself of the image that had defined her as woman.

Violence

During the surreal sequence toward the middle of the film, the dwarf had presented the Drinker with a goose, knife and fork in its roasted back. As the drinker discovers the real goose on her night table, she pulls out the knife, lifts it toward the wall, and attacks the pinned-up photo of herself as young man. She does not destroy the photograph, but punctures the wall around it, in rhythmic stabs, first several times to the right, then to the left, and then again to the right. As she does this, she is seen in medium shot, approaching the picture from the right, and on the wall we see a clear outline of her shadow. This appears to be a quote from Oscar Wilde's Dorian Gray, where the protagonist had attacked a picture of himself, a portrait painted to capture his great beauty as a young man, allowing him to remain forever young and beautiful, while the portrait was growing old. Dorian felt haunted by this image to the point where he needed to destroy it, but, by doing so, ultimately destroyed himself. He was found stabbed to death, while the mysterious portrait had resumed its original beauty. It is questionable whether Ottinger meant more than a quote, a playful homage to Wilde's treatment of a similar theme (Wilde's novel is also

61

alluded to in the term "Bildnis" of the German title). The photograph disappears after this incident, and the wall above the bed where it used to hang remains empty. The Drinker resumes her identity and does not die till some time later. But her violent gesture implies ambivalence toward the image, and we may at least question whether this young man was perhaps her ideal self, or whether she saw herself changing into that identity.

The second violent incident occurs towards the end of the film. The Drinker has just been on the extensive drinking tour with the bag woman; they had walked along the Straße des 17. Juni, where she had dropped her purse. She was alone on an outing to a restaurant in the Europa Center where she had ventured onto a deserted ice rink, and the bag woman was seen with a man in an industrial setting, searching for a place to make love, winding up in a desolate glass shed, presumably a railroad shelter, champagne bottle in hand, drunk and happy. The following sequence represents another knifing attack, and, as it turns out, a shadow fight with the alter ego. In a close shot, a switchblade enters the frame from the right. A clear shadow is cast on the wall behind. The same is repeated from the left. A cut reveals the switchblade opening, from the right. Again, the same is repeated from the left. Following is a cut to a medium shot. The shadow of the open switchblade, of a hand and a lower arm in a veil-like sleeve enter from the right and move along the wall to the left, toward the bed, to the empty spot where the photo used to be. The shadow stabs the wall violently, to a strange metallic noise. The next cut has the shadow entering from the left, in close shot, but it turns out that the kife is real. The following medium shot represents the Drinker and the bag woman, both with knives, and in identical postures, with the bag woman toward the rear, hiding in the shadow of the Drinker. Both make aggressive stabbing moves toward the spot where the picture once hung. A reading of this sequence suggests aggression to the former image of the self, tentative aggression, however, since the attack happens in shadow. The doubling effect of the shadow and the unison of the two women's movements reveal a pending merger of their identities.

The Final Mirror Image

In the very last shot of the film, violence turns against the mirror. This is a variation on the theme of the opening shot, where a static camera, from an extremely low angle, had held the image of the Drinker's feet, in high heels, traversing a mirror-like, marble floor toward an opening in center frame. In the last shot, angle and framing are similar, again the camera is static, but significantly closer. The Drinker now walks into what appears to be an alley of mirrors. There are multiple reflections, as we see a detail shot of her heels stepping along a mirrored surface, framed on either side by slanted mirror walls. She walks slowly, as each of her steps crushes the mirror below into many tiny fragments. This shot is held a long time, and finally frozen, while the sound track plays distorted variations on a tarantella. This beautiful image has a cathartic effect. It provides relief from the somber pathos of the previous shot, where the crowd had overrun the Drinker and her friend. More importantly, however, it conveys a feeling of freedom. The crushing of the mirror signifies that the Drinker has chosen to turn her aggression not against herself, but against the system which has been oppressing her. In psychoanalytic terms, and in the framework of Luce Irigaray, this suggests an act of defiance against the system of representation, symbolized by the flat mirror, which had defined her as woman. Her rebellion leaves the single image, the clearly defined image as woman, shattered into many tiny fragments, providing a multitude of reflections that provide a truer representation of her self as woman.

To return to the theoretical framework of this paper, and to the question of how to discuss a feminine aesthetic, we wish to reiterate the danger involved in seeking to define, to offer clear-cut concepts of a feminine text:

> . . . the issue is not one of elaborating a new theory of which woman would be the subject or the object, but of jamming the theoretical machinery itself, of suspending its pretension to the production of a truth and of a meaning that are excessively univocal (This Sex, 78).

The issue, therefore, is not how to define feminine discourse, but to point to its otherness. In the reading of texts by women and men, for feminine discourse is not limited to texts by women, this involves looking for signs of disruption, for anything that might point to the fact that the dominant discourse is being subverted. In the words of Irigaray, texts of a feminine writing "work at 'destroying' the discursive mechanism" (76), they tend "to put the torch to fetish words, proper terms, well-constructed forms" (79). Ticket of No Return offers many instances of disruption. It questions the image of woman as fetish and offers alternatives. The Drinker's masquerade signals deliberation, and is an attempt at mimicry, which, historically, has been the way women were able to enter discourse:

> To play with mimesis is thus, for a woman, to try to recover the place of her exploitation by discourse, without allowing herself to be simply reduced to it. It means to resubmit herself--inasmuch as she is on the side of the "perceptible," of "matter"--to "ideas," in particular to ideas about herself, that are elaborated in/by a masculine logic, but so as to make "visible," by an effect of playful repetition, what was supposed to remain invisible: the cover-up of a possible operation of the feminine in language (76).

The masquerade hides the fact that the Drinker had to renounce her own desire in order to conform.[11] Her sexuality remains repressed, articulating itself in violence, and in dreams. Her search for different images of herself signals her unhappiness, and she ultimately destroys herself. She also destroys the mirror which defined her. Ticket of No Return, therefore, deconstructs the image of woman in phallic discourse. It is subversive, by challenging woman's definition as fetish, and by questioning the system which refused her presence, language, and desire.

Ulrike Ottinger has said that all of her films deal with prototypes, and that she felt it necessary to find ways to shock, both with regard to content and to the ways she expressed it.[12] The prototype of this film is the narcissistic woman as fetish, who is restructured to question the very system of representation in which she is defined as lack, silent, and devoid of desire. The film establishes her claim to sexuality and a voice of her own.

Notes

[1] Today, the leading journals in feminist film criticism are camera obscura and Frauen und Film. New German Critique has periodically dealt with the topic, as have Discourse, Screen, and Jump Cut.

[2] B. Ruby Rich has written an excellent review on both books in American Film, vol. IX, no. 3, Dec. 83, 68-75. See also the review of Kaplan's book, by Diane Waldman and Janet Walker, in camera obscura, nos. 13-14, pp. 195-214.

[3] Lauretis, p. 158; this is a reference to a term used by Audre Lorde, cf. "The Master's Tools Will Never Dismantle the Master's House," in: Sister Outsider: Essays and Speeches, Trumansburg, NY: The Crossing Press, 1984.

[4] Cf. Hélène Cixous, "The Laugh of Medusa," in: New French Feminisms, ed. by Elaine Marks and Isabelle Courtivron, New York: Schocken, 1980, pp. 245-64. Cixous mentions Kleist, and, among the French poets, Colette, Marguerite Duras, and Jean Genet. Cf. also Renate Fischetti, "Querelle bei Fassbinder und Genet," in: Akten des VII. Kongresses der Internationalen Vereinigung für germanische Sprach- und Literaturwissenschaft, Tübingen: Niemeyer, 1986, pp. 330-38.

[5] Voice-over narration during the landing and taxiing of the plane, reprinted in the Press Book for the film, courtesy Basis-Film Verleih.

[6] Only in the beginning do we hear her voice, as she orders the ticket, in Spanish, and later on again during one of the dream sequences, as she speaks the Hamlet lines, "to be or not to be. . . ."

[7] "Wanderer durch Jahrtausende. Ein Gespräch mit Ulrike Ottinger über ihren jüngsten Film," in: Der Tagesspiegel, 9/13/81, p. 62.

[8] Claudia Lenssen, "mit glasigem blick," Ilse Lenz, "die öde wildnis einer schminkerin," und Karin Reschke, "frau ottingers (kunst)gewerbe," in: Frauen und Film, 22 (December 1979), 23-25, 28, and 29.

[9] Hansen, p. 104; cf. p. 103: "The whole film attempts nothing less than to disentangle visual pleasure

from the voyeurism inherent in the codes of patriarchal cinema."

[10] "Ihre Pläne für einen narzistisch-pessimistischen Kult der Einsamkeit waren auf der kurzen Flugreise vertieft und bis zu jenem Punkt intensiviert worden, an dem sie sich in eben diesem Stadium befinden, in dem sie gelebt werden sollten." Press Book for the film, courtesy Basis-Film Verleih.

[11] Irigaray in This Sex, p. 133: "Psychoanalysts say that masquerading corresponds to woman's desire. That seems wrong to me. I think the masquerade has to be understood as what women do in order to recuperate some element of desire, to participate in man's desire, but at the price of renouncing their own."

[12] Interview in Press Book for Dorian Gray im Spiegel der Boulevardpresse, courtesy of Basis-Film Verleih; Ottinger made a similar statement in an unpublished interview with Renate Fischetti, summer 1982.

List of Works Cited

de Lauretis, Teresa. "Aesthetic and Feminist Theory: Rethinking Women's Cinema," New German Critique No. 34, winter 1985, 154-75.

de Lauretis, Teresa. Alice Doesn't: Feminism, Semiotics, Cinema. Bloomington: Indiana University Press, 1984.

Hansen, Miriam. "Visual Pleasure, Fetishism and the Problem of Feminine Discourse: Ulrike Ottinger's Ticket of No Return," New German Critique No. 31, winter 1984, 95-108.

Irigaray, Luce. Speculum of the Other Woman. Translated by Gillian C. Gill. Ithaca: Cornell University Press, 1985.

Irigaray, Luce. This Sex Which Is Not One. Translated by Catherine Porter with Carolyn Burke. Ithaca: Cornell University Press, 1985.

Kaplan, E. Ann. Women and Film: Both Sides of the Camera. London and New York: Methuen, 1983.

Kuhn, Annette. Women's Pictures: Feminism and Cinema. London: Routledge and Kegan Paul, 1982.

Re-Vision: Essays in Feminist Criticism. Edited by Mary Ann Doane, Patricia Mellencamp and Linda Williams. Los Angeles: The American Film Institute, 1984.

The illustrations are from materials courtesy of Basis-Film, and from the script to Madame X, Frankfurt a.m./Basel: Stroemfeld/Roter Stern, n.d.

Filmography Ulrike Ottinger

Laokoon & Söhne, 1972-74

Die Betörung der blauen Matrosen, 1975

Madame X, 1977

Bildnis einer Trinkerin, 1979

Freak Orlando, 1981

Dorian Gray im Spiegel der Boulevardpresse, 1983/84

China, 1985

The Absent Mother Makes an Appearance in the Films of West German Women Directors[1]

Jan Mouton

Members of the forties generation (born between 1937 and 1942), Helma Sanders-Brahms, Jutta Brückner, Helke Sander, and Margarethe von Trotta were too young to have grown up watching Zarah ("Achichhabesieverloren") Leander movies. For the same reason, they were spared the "glorious-German-past," Blut und Boden, and anti-semitic fare that rolled onto the silver screen during the Third Reich. By a quirk of fate, and under the name of "re-education" (in the ways of democracy), what was showing in West German theaters during the late forties and throughout the fifties were Hollywood movies: the great bulk of the 1933 to 1945 American production which had been banned by Hitler was brought up out of the vaults, at first subtitled but then routinely dubbed, and shipped out for German distribution.[2]

Eventually the generation of West German filmmakers working today did make connections with its own national filmic past--movies in the great UFA tradition of the twenties. As individuals and collectively these film-makers experienced the events of their own decades and responded to an immediate historical past. It is at the point of intersection formed by these different lines of experience that Sanders-Brahms, Brückner, Sander, and von Trotta are now making their films. It is at another point of intersection that we as viewers and critics receive--and participate in creating--the meanings of these movies, given our own past experiences with film and with history.

One distinctive feature of these directors' films, both startingly new and long overdue, is that contrary to all filmmaking traditions (in particular the Holly-wood and Weimar traditions) the figure of the mother has emerged as an autonomous subject. Stories of mother/daughter and mother/son relationships have been fore-grounded and treated as legitimate, authentic, and important. No longer are we forced to accept as "normal"

69

films without mother characters and films without so much as "mother-character space" (Hollywood's musicals and romances, Weimar's monster movies). No longer must we submit to the masochistic experience of viewing the devalued mother figures created within the confines of patriarchal film structures (the Hollywood woman's film, the German Kammerspielfilm, and street film).[3] No longer can we be satisfied with "alternative films" which present us with mother characters from the same patriarchal point of view as the mainstream films they were made to counter, such as the proletarian films Mutter Krausens Fahrt ins Glück (1929) by Piel Jutzi and Kuhle Wampe (1932) by Brecht/Dudow. At last we are able to view mother characters who are something other than objects, partial presences without a point of view, without a voice.

Such partial presences, film women who do not function as signifiers for a signified, but rather as a sign for something in the male unconscious,[4] are now being seen for what they really are. And the reason why we are able to look at them with new eyes is that we have of late been seeing a new kind of screen woman. These are the women--these are the mothers--who appear in Chantal Akerman's Jeanne Dielman (1975) and News from Home (1976), in Marguerite Duras's Nathalie Granger (1972), Michelle Citron's Daughter Rite (1978), and in the films of Sanders-Brahms, Brückner, Sander, and von Trotta to be discussed in this paper. In addition to the work of these filmmakers, we now also have a theoretical apparatus which provides us with a framework for understanding these new films, and in particular for understanding the kinds of relationships which exist between the filmmaker and her characters, between the spectator and those characters, and among the characters themselves. Among the voices contributing to this international feminist discourse are those of German women directors and film theoreticians (in frauen und film), Laura Mulvey and others in England writing for Screen, the French psychoanalyst feminist writers Irigaray, Kristeva, and Cixous, and a great variety of American feminist psychoanalysts, literary critics, and film theoreticians.

In an effort to understand how and why filmmaking by women differs from filmmaking by men, and how this in turn makes possible a very different kind of viewing experience for the woman spectator, I will draw on some of Nancy Chodorow's ideas about male and female personality. She holds that

70

> women's mothering produces assymetries in
> the relational experiences of girls and
> boys as they grow up, which account for
> crucial differences in feminine and mas-
> culine personality, and the relational
> capacities and modes which these entail.[5]

According to Chodorow, mothers identify more strongly
with female infants and see them more as extensions of
themselves, whereas they encourage boys to become separate and autonomous--thus causing the ego boundaries
between themselves and their daughters to be more fluid,
more undefined. Furthermore, since girls retain their
preoedipal attachments to their mother, later adding the
father-attachment, they come to define and experience
themselves as continuous with others. Boys on the other
hand, in breaking the motherbond in order to identify as
"male," see themselves as more separate and distinct.
The contrasting initial patterns, breaking one attachment to form another versus simply adding an attachment
to the one already present, result in a masculine sense
of self which is separate, and a feminine sense of self
which is connected to others.

The outcome of this for the male, then, is that he
sees the woman--the mother--as Other, as separate, perhaps as object, perhaps as ideal, but in any case as
something or someone different and distinct, and he perceives himself as independent, whole, and unique. For
the female the case is different. Just as mothers tend
to experience their daughters as more like and continuous with themselves, so, too, daughters grow up involved
in issues of merging and separation, and out of this
they develop a capacity for empathy and a tendency to
define themselves through social relationships. It is
this continual merging of self with other which accounts
for a woman's empathic literary and cinematic identification, including the intense and personal relationships
which form between the woman writer/filmmaker and her
characters, and the woman reader/spectator and those
characters.

In her article on female identity and writing by women, Judith Gardiner makes the point that "female identity is a process" and she sees this as having important
implications for women's writing.[6] In contrast to male
identity formation which is "a developmental progress
toward the achievement of a desired product, the
autonomous individual" [Erikson], the process of female
identity formation is more on-going; female personality

formation is cyclical as well as progressive [Chodorow]; and female identity is thus "less fixed, less unitary, and more flexible than male individuality" (353).

Because of these differences in identity formation, women writers and readers approach texts differently from men. As Gardiner puts it,

> . . . the woman writer uses her text, par-
> ticularly one centering on a female hero,
> as part of a continuing process involving
> her own self-definition and her empathic
> identification with her character (357).

The woman reader goes through a similar process, "shifting her empathic identifications and her sense of immersion in and separation from the text as she reads" (357). Thus we can see how the act of writing (and by extension, filmmaking) and the act of reading (i.e., viewing) involve the same relational issues which have defined female personality from the beginning.

Films by Sanders-Brahms, Brückner, Sander, and von Trotta will serve to show how these ideas function in particular instances. In terms of point of view, the films fall into three groups: the "daughter as film-maker" films in which we see the mother through the daughter's eyes; the "mother as filmmaker" examples in which she tells her story with her voice; and the "mother/daughter/sister/friend" kind of film in which the mother-role is shared by several women, regardless of whether they are "real" (i.e., biological) mothers. In terms of the intersecting lines of experience, the filmmakers are both responding to and working against the Weimar/Hollywood tradition of patriarchal filmmaking while at the same time reflecting in their work the struggle for a balance between separation and merging as regards their own historical and personal experiences.

In Helma Sanders-Brahms's Deutschland, bleiche Mutter (1979) the filmmaker-daughter presents both her own story as daughter and the story of her mother in so far as the daughter shared it with her or is able to reconstruct it imaginatively. This has the effect of emphasizing the problems of separation and merging between mother and daughter in the story itself. The film strongly invites empathic identification with both women characters, since the viewer is asked to participate with the daughter-filmmaker in the effort of imaginative reconstruction of the mother.

72

From the beginning Anna is faced with a special problem of ambivalence toward her mother, Lene, and toward her mother's story. Like all daughters she must seek an identity independent from her mother without denying the positive force of a strong motherbond. In addition, however, Anna is forced to judge her mother for her acquiescence in evil during the Nazi period, while at the same time she realizes she cannot take credit for her own innocence. At one point, for example, we hear Anna accuse her mother for failing to resist, but her accusation evolves into a self-examination. "What right do I have to accuse you? I am no better--except that I was born later." In this film, language functions both as a bond and a barrier between the women. Early on we see the mother in a medium close-up while we hear the daughter in voice-over speaking directly to her: "'Ich habe schweigen gelernt,' sagtest du." "Von dir habe ich sprechen gelernt, meine Mutter. Muttersprache." As the film continues, so, too, does the language struggle: the mother gradually withdrawing into a self-protective silence, the daughter probing and questioning, trying--through telling her mother's story--to define the boundaries of her own self and to continue the process of her own identity formation. In this film, and other West German films by women, the daughter's identity-establishing process is seen as necessarily including the mother's own process, just as in actual therapy sessions with women patients, much time may be taken up initially with description and analysis of the mother's history and problems.[7]

A further use of language in the film, and one which demonstrates the way literature can play a role in the process of female identity formation, is to be found in the Märchen-telling sequence.[8] When Lene tells Anna the tale of the Räuberbräutigam from the Grimms' collection, she is at once recognizing that there is evil in the world, horrifying beyond comprehension, and affirming the possibility that evil can be overcome. By using their wits and helping each other, the two Märchen women, "die Alte," and "das Mädchen," bring about the destruction of the wicked robber and all his band. As Anna listens to this Märchen and hears its timeless--and timely--message, she incorporates this into her sense of who she is and what the world is like. That she is later able to help save her mother from destruction behind the closed door, that ultimately she is able to make this film, suggests the importance of literary meanings for personal development. In viewing this film, and in identifying empathically with both women and with their

73

relationship to each other and to their times, we, too, are involving ourselves in our own identity-formation process.

Another film from the daughter's perspective is Jutta Brückner's Hungerjahre (1980), an agonized telling of struggle and denial and lack of understanding which characterize the mother-daughter relationship. Ursula is one of the daughters who sees her mother as having taught the very kind of compromise and self-hatred she is struggling to be free of, a daughter who finds it easier to hate and reject her mother outright than to try to look beyond to the forces acting upon her.[9] For the viewer, who is able to see beyond, empathic identification is nonetheless complicated and shifting, and alternates with feelings of anger and disapproval, whether toward the mother for her cowardly acquiescence in an oppressive patriarchal system or toward the daughter for her negativity and destructiveness. Especially disturbing is the way this film exposes the paradoxical position in which a mother finds herself in a patriarchal society. On the one hand she has been rendered powerless by a society whose values she had no voice in determining, while at the same time she is called upon--in the name of "good mothering"--to train her daughter to accept a similar position of powerlessness, to be willing in fact to "accept the uses to which others will put her children and to remain blind to the implications of those uses."[10]

As painful as this film is to watch, it is nonetheless a very good illustration of female identity-formation in process. The filmmaker as daughter engages her imagination and her memory in constructing and reconstructing Ursula's personal development, her mother's development, and that of their mutually hostile relationship. The viewer, overwhelmed with the sense that "things shouldn't be like this between mothers an daughters," also realizes that behind the pain and enmity in the relationship lie the damaging values of the dominant culture. This film thus furthers the viewer's identity-formation process on two levels: immediately through empathic identification with the characters, and by implication through engagement with the cultural dimensions of the mother-role problem.

It is again apparent in this film, as in Deutschland, bleiche Mutter and in the films by Sander and von Trotta yet to be discussed, that socio-political forces figure crucially in all private spheres. For these women

of the forties generation, the shadow of the Third Reich
and of its destructive power, particularly in the lives
of women--including the mothers of these filmmakers--is
ever-present and strongly felt. It is a shadow which, as
it merges with the cinematic and psychological patterns
also present in these women's minds, is reflected in the
complex and nuanced final forms their films take.

In the three Helke Sander movies released in the
United States--Die allseitig reduzierte Persönlichkeit
(Redupers) (1977), Der subjektive Faktor (1980), and Der
Beginn aller Schrecken ist Liebe (1983)--the protagonist
is a mother and a career women who in addition is shown
to have broader involvements with lovers and friends,
political causes and artistic projects. Der Beginn aller
Schrecken ist Liebe is a particularly interesting film
because it presents a mother/son relationship not from
the point of view of the son--or of the father--but from
the mother's point of view, making her the subject and
giving her the voice, instead of letting her be merely
the bearer of the male child, the sideline position
traditionally accorded her.

In this film we see Freya, the protagonist,
struggling to come to terms with a dissolving relationship with her lover at the same time that she struggles
to love her teenage son in such a way as to help him and
his generation avoid the kinds of "troubles with love"
(the English title of the film) that she and her generation have known. Furthermore, Freya and her generation
are shown to be struggling with the problems of history
inherited from the preceding generation, hoping that
their efforts will enable those who follow to inherit a
better world.[11]

In her book Of Woman Born, Adrienne Rich includes a
chapter "Mother and Son, Woman and Man," in which she,
like the Freya character, seeks a new understanding of
the mother/son relationship. She begins by challenging
the fundamental Freudian assumption that the two-person
mother/child relationship is by nature regressive and
unproductive, and that all a mother can do for the child
is perpetuate a dependency which prevents further development, whereas culture depends on the father/son
relationship, and on the boy's making his way into the
male world of patriarchal law and order. But having
challenged the idea that civilization means identification, not with the mother but with the father, we are
faced with the questions of how, in patriarchy, the
mother can represent culture, and how the male child can

differentiate himself from his mother without internalizing patriarchal values (198).

Without actually solving this problem, the movie does suggest that if a woman reaches out of herself as Freya does, contributing to political causes, caring about friends, working in a job she likes, and showing at the same time that she can take pleasure in the little details of life, then her son does not have to live under the burden of the unlived, unachieved in her life. As Rich says, he "ceases to be her outreach into the world because she is reaching out into it herself, he ceases to be instrumental for her and has a chance to become a person" (207). Toward her son Freya is attentive and loving in an intense, pure, and disinterested way. Iris Murdoch once referred to this kind of unselfish attention, claiming that in fixing our attention on others we learn how they "can be looked at and loved without being seized and used, without being appropriated into the greedy organism of the self."12 This rare film about a mother from a mother's point of view provides us with an especially immediate portrayal of a film character involved in the identity-formation process. The fact that Sander herself plays the Freya role only adds to the impact of the film, underlining the involvement of the filmmaker with her character in that process.

In the last category of films, those with shared mothering roles, I will be considering some of the work of Margarethe von Trotta, a director whose films have met with a modest share of distribution success in the United States. Her Schwestern oder die Balance des Glücks (1970) presents an interesting example of a person who, though not a mother, in fact mothers or tries to mother everyone around her: her sister, her employer, a younger secretary/colleague, even the man she is romantically involved with, and her own mother. The objects of Maria's mothering efforts react in various ways: her employer encourages and exploits her; Miriam, the secretary, feels threatened and flees.

It is within the sister relationship, however, that we see the full complexity of Maria's mothering behavior and the response it elicits. Presented first at the level of fantasy and of the unconscious through the telling of a fairy tale from their childhood, we are shown how over the years the older-sister/younger-sister relationship has developed into one which replicates

that of mother/daughter. One reason why this relationship fails is that there is no proper rhythm according
to which it can develop though a fruitful process of
merging and separation, bonding and self-definition such
as might occur in a healthy mother/ daughter relationship. Instead it becomes frozen, with each person's
needs serving as a check on the other's freedom of
action and decision, and the pattern which establishes
itself is one of mutually destructive need, dependence,
resentment, and rejection.

The brief scenes in which Maria's and Anna's real
mother appears are at first glance reminiscent of those
from the "filmmaker as daughter" films discussed earlier
in that the subject is a woman who over the years has
accommodated herself to an oppressive patriarchal system. But as we watch her and listen to her--and as von
Trotta shifts the point of view back and forth between
Maria and her mother as they mourn Anna's death--we
perceive that this character, too, is struggling with
her own identity-formation process. She reaches back
into her memory for the threads which she will continue
to weave into her life pattern: what Anna had been like
as a child, what she had been like as a mother to Anna,
what she could have done differently, what it would be
like if Anna were still alive. In this film and in those
that follow, von Trotta uses the realms of imagination
and memory to suggest ways in which women may be able to
mother each other and avoid the confining limits of the
role as it has been defined by patriarchy.

In Die bleierne Zeit (1981) and Heller Wahn (1982),
von Trotta continues to investigate patterns of mothering. In both films we see the real, biological mother as
an older woman, accustomed to being defined by traditional patriarchal limits. But like Maria's and Anna's
mother these women, too, have honest screen presences
and are allowed to be subjects in their own stories--
stories which they are now in the process of revising
ever so cautiously, helped along by their daughters'
experiences and influences. On several occasions we see
Juliane and her mother together, as the latter re-thinks
her past and realizes how she has allowed herself to be
positioned by the representatives of the patriarchal
order in their domestic, religious, and political
guises. To Juliane she is finally able to acknowledge
that women must question the limitations placed upon
them and she admits that she has always had difficulties
in doing this. Her relationship with Marianne is much
more troubled, and her daughter's sudden death leaves

her with painful unanswered questions and grievous un-
finished business. Although the words of the traditional
prayer she recites at the bier deny the value of
questioning, the whole structure of the film is in the
nature of a question whose force overrides the momentary
denial of that scene. It is the spectator, as she
identifies empathically with all these women, who must
continue to seek answers to these difficult questions--
and who must affirm that it is indeed our responsibility
to raise questions just as von Trotta is doing.

In this treatment of the relationship between the
sisters we see a great emphasis on motifs of merging:
shared experiences, shared memories, exchange of clothing, exchange of mother-role, and even merging of
physical identities in the facial-overlap scene.
Although Juliane struggles against it, and repeatedly
affirms her separateness and autonomy, she is called
upon to be both surrogate mother to Marianne's son and
stand-in for her own mother while visiting Marianne in
prison. Later as she seeks to establish the cause of
Marianne's death, she become consumed by an empathic
identification/merging with her sister.

The older-woman-as-mother role is somewhat less important in Heller Wahn than in the other two von Trotta
movies, though to the extent that Ruth's mother is present, she is so in a manner very like that of her two
predecessors: rethinking with her daughter the patterns
of her life in relation to patriarchy. It is among the
women of the daughter's generation, however--here the
friends Ruth and Olga, as previously the sister pairs
Maria and Anna or Marianne and Juliane--that we see the
primary manifestations of mothering and female bonding.
In this kind of nurturing, empathizing behavior we see
the possibility of positive, healing, life-giving effects as well as the threat of a negative, suffocating
outworking. It is one of the strengths of von Trotta's
films that she creates such complicated networks of relationships among her women characters, clearly demon-
strating her own personal involvement with those characters and very powerfully involving her audience in them.

In all of the films we have considered, we see
demonstrated Chodorow's idea of a feminine self which is
connected to others in contrast to a masculine sense of
self which is separate. Carol Gilligan has spoken of
women's relational experiences in a similar way, emphasizing the nonhierarchical nature of these connections
by using the image of a web.[13] The dual connotations of

this web image are also appropriate in suggesting the complexity of the relationships in these films: particularly between mothers and daughters, or between the mothering subject and the mothered object, we see both the interconnectedness and the entanglement. This points again to the centrality of the notion that "female identity is a process." Whether as filmmaker or as spectator, women are involved with each other in this process to which we bring our own personal and collective histories and through which, by a process of merging and separating, empathic identification and distancing, we continue to define ourselves. Thus involved, we strive toward what Adrienne Rich calls "courageous mothering." As she says,

> The most notable fact that culture imprints on women is the sense of our limits. The most important thing one woman can do for another is to illuminate and expand her sense of actual possibilities. For a mother, this means . . . that [she] herself is trying to expand the limits of her life. To refuse to be a victim: and then to go on from there (246).

Notes

[1] This paper was presented in somewhat different form at the Conference on Feminism and Psychoanalysis at Illinois State University in May 1986; an earlier version was read at the October 1985 Women in German Conference in Portland, Oregon.

[2] Not only were the Americans bent on exporting their cultural products, but at the same time their censors laid a heavy hand on the newly reconstituted West German film industry, thereby stifling domestic production efforts.

[3] This extremely interesting question regarding the position of the female spectator of the traditional film of male address (or even of "women's films" made by men) has been widely discussed by feminist critics. These include: Laura Mulvey, "Visual Pleasure and Narrative Cinema," Screen 16 (1975): 6-18; Mary Ann Doane, "The 'Woman's Film': Possession and Address," in ReVision: Essays in Feminist Film Criticism, eds. Mary Ann Doane, Patricia Mellencamp, and Linda Williams (Los Angeles: American Film Institute, 1984) 67-82; Judith Mayne, "The

Woman at the Keyhole: Women's Cinema and Feminist Criticism," also in ReVision, 44-66; Michelle Citron et al., "Women and Film: A Discussion of Feminist Aesthetics," New German Critique 13 (1978): 83-107 (especially the comments by Ruby Rich); Mary Ann Doane, "Film and Masquerade: Theorising the Female Spectator," Screen 23 (1982): 74-88; Gertrud Koch, "Warum Frauen ins Männerkino gehen: weibliche Aneignungsweisen in der Filmrezeption und einige ihrer Voraussetzungen," in Frauen in der Kunst, eds. Gislind Nabakowski, Helke Sander, and Peter Gorsen (Frankfurt: Suhrkamp, 1980) 15-29 (also in translation, "Why Women Go to the Movies," Jump Cut 27: 51-53; and E. Ann Kaplan, "Is the Gaze Male?" in Women and Film: Both Sides of the Camera (New York: Methuen, 1983) 23-35.

4 Kaplan, 30.

5 Nancy Chodorow, The Reproduction of Mothering (Berkeley: University of California Press, 1978) 169.

6 Judith Kegan Gardiner, "On Female Identity and Writing by Women," Critical Inquiry 8 (1981): 349.

7 This is particularly true when the therapist is a woman, since as Jane Flax points out, "patriarchal social relations and male psychological development require that the male therapist . . . deny the power of the mother," a denial that is often reinforced by orthodox forms of psychoanalytic training. "Mother-Daughter Relationships: Psychodymanics, Politics, and Philosophy," in The Future of Difference, eds. Hester Eisenstein and Alice Jardine (Boston: G.K. Hall, 1980) 36.

8 Although I differ with Angelika Bammer on this interpretive point, I would strongly recommend her fine article to anyone interested in a more extensive study of Deutschland, bleiche Mutter: "Through a Daughter's Eyes: Helma Sanders-Brahms' Germany, Pale Mother" in New German Critique 36 (1985): 41-55.

9 Adrienne Rich, Of Woman Born (New York: Norton, 1976) 235.

10 Sara Ruddick, "Maternal Thinking," Feminist Studies 6 (1980) 343.

11 The original title for the film, From Generation to Generation, highlighted these ideas.

12 Iris Murdoch, The Sovereignty of Good (London: Routledge & Kegan Paul, 1970) 65.

13 Carol Gilligan, In a Different Voice (Cambridge: Harvard University Press, 1982) 62.

Katharina Blum: Violence and the Exploitation
of Sexuality

Charlotte Armster

In 1974, Heinrich Böll's then recent novel Die verlorene Ehre der Katharina Blum was serialized in the
West German magazine Der Spiegel. The appearance of the
novel in the news magazine was notable, as it marked the
first time that Spiegel published a literary work in its
entirety. The novel's literary merit was not, however,
the reason the editors chose to make an exception to
their usual policies regarding what they print. Instead,
Böll's short novel was viewed as having actual news
value in that it possessed a direct tie to immediate
political events in Germany. In Spiegel's own words:
"Eine denkwürdige publizistische Affäre - Bölls Kontroverse mit 'Bild' über dessen Baader-Meinhof-Berichte -
hat ein aktuelles belletristisches Nachspiel: In einer
Erzählung mit dem Titel Die verlorene Ehre der Katharina
Blum oder: Wie Gewalt entstehen und wohin sie führen
kann attakiert der Kölner Literatur-Nobelpreisträger
'gewisse journalistische Praktiken' . . . ."[1]

To Spiegel editors, the publication of Die verlorene
Ehre der Katharina Blum was seen as the continuation of
a bitter public confrontation between Böll and the
Springer-controlled press. In January 1972, Böll had
written an article for Der Spiegel entitled "Will Ulrike
Meinhof Gnade oder freies Geleit?" It was in part a
response to an earlier story in the Bild, and its main
point was to call into question the role which the
Springer press had in escalating the violence exhibited
by both the German police and such radical groups as
Baader-Meinhof. Bild, and similar publications such as
Quick, immediately targeted Böll for public vilifica-
tion. In their pages he was repeatedly denounced and accused of latent and intellectual complicity with
terrorist groups. The stories had an effect. On June 1,
1972 the police surrounded and searched Böll's country
house in the Eifel region, believing it to be a possible
hide-out for Ulrike Meinhof.[2]

83

Other news articles, including ones in Die Zeit and Süddeutsche Zeitung, tended to stress the political aspects of the novel.[3] Böll himself, within the structure of the novel, seemed to invite interpretations which concentrated attention on the relationship between his narrative content and actual political events. "Sollten sich bei dieser Schilderung gewisser journalistischen Praktiken Ähnlichkeiten mit den Praktiken der 'Bild'-Zeitung ergeben haben," reads in part an ironic disclaimer at the beginning of the novel, "so sind diese Ähnlichkeiten weder beabsichtigt noch zufällig, sondern unvermeidlich." With these words, a comparison between the fictional world of the novel and Böll's actual experiences with the Springer press became inevitable.

In light of the political climate at the time, it is not surprising that many initial interpretations of Die verlorene Ehre der Katharina Blum were primarily concerned with obvious connections to the external world. Such an approach, however, obscured the sexual exploitation depicted in the novel (which is integral to the entire plot development) and concentrated almost solely on the political reality of West Germany. This is most readily apparent in the fact that these interpretations emphasized the importance of the subtitle: "How violence develops and where it can lead"--and neglected the importance of the primary title: "The lost honor of Katharina Blum." The sexual nature of "lost honor" and its connection to violence, as implied by the interplay between title and subtitle, was simply overlooked.

In the few early interpretations where sexual aspects of the novel's structure were noted, their significance was completely downplayed. Rainer Nägele, for example, criticized the ambiguity of Katharina's use of her vulgar word bumsen with the argument:

> Offenbar wollte Böll hier den Zusammenhang von Wort und Gewalt in Wortspiel zur Unmittelbarkeit verdichten. Das ist ihm einerseits zwar gelungen, jedoch mit bedenklichen Kosten: denn was das Wortspiel symbolisch verdichtet, löst es im Kontext der Handlung auf, indem es die Motivation verwirrt und den Schuß zur Reaktion auf eine sexuelle Attacke macht, womit die von der Recherche mühsam aufgebauten Motivationszusammenhänge gefährlich in Frage gestellt werden.[4]

84

In fact, the motivation for killing Tötges is not confused in the sense that Nägele believes. From the beginning, a misuse of sexual innuendo and sexual terms provides the basis for the subsequent violence in the novel.

The most extreme example of an interpretation which disregards the importance of sexual aspects in the novel was that of Marcel Reich-Ranicki. According to him, any sexual problems present in the story arose from the fact that Katharina Blum is frigid. ("Sie leidet . . . an ihrer Frigidität."[5]) For him, sexuality was totally irrelevant to the political concerns of the novel.

The concern with the political nature of Die verlorene Ehre der Katharina Blum has continued, but as events which related to the novel have passed, some literary critics have finally begun a more intrinsic examination of the work. Most frequently, these analyses have focused on structural aspects, including narrative perspective, genre form, and such elements as the symbolic significance of character names.[6] Yet, even these less political approaches to the novel have failed to explore in detail the sexual exploitation of the heroine. When the sexual tones dominant throughout the work have been touched, they have generally been relegated to minor significance. The notion of "lost honor" is viewed as "old-fashioned," or the characterization of Katharina Blum as a "prude" is accepted at face value, or her behavior is termed "romantically idealistic."[7]

The repeated attempt to exclude or to reduce the importance of the sexual implications in Die verlorene Ehre der Katharina Blum has meant that the political--and not the sexual--qualities of the novel are still generally considered to be primary to the novel's meaning. The fact that sexual stereotypes motivate much of the political action has simply been isolated from the novel's overall meaning. Yet, Katharina Blum, whose name is central to the title, is not simply an arbitrary figure made to serve the text as a convenient vehicle through which a political message is revealed or exemplified. Instead, her character as a woman is crucial for an understanding of the novel. "Lost honor"--referred to in the primary title--is a concept which denotes a loss of virginity or something sexual when applied to women. And it is this "woman's honor" which first must be comprehended in order to discern the connection with violence mentioned in the subtitle.

The reader learns almost nothing about Katharina Blum, including her honor, in a direct manner. Almost all information about her is derived from a variety of documents—newspaper articles, police reports, interviews—and these in turn are transmitted through a seemingly objective narrator who gathers facts much the way a journalist might. To a certain extent, the narrator (presumably male) serves as a counterweight to the actual journalist Tötges, from whom the slanderous newspaper accounts originate.

In part, Böll's use of this narrative structure serves to provide the text with a type of control against which the varying "fact-gatherers" in the novel are to be measured. Journalists and police, for example, supposedly serve as public fact-gatherers, and it could be assumed that their portrait of Katharina Blum would be based on the objectivity of facts. Yet, the factual evidence presented by the narrator makes clear that the supposed objectivity of the journalist Tötges and the police is distinctly biased. Their reports are deliberately distorted and serve interests other than objective fact-finding.

Despite the narrator's role as counterbalance to Tötges and the police, his presentation of the facts is not without bias. His own anger surfaces in ironic comments. "Hier ist endlich ein Gebiet, wo Kirchen und Gewerkschaften zusammenarbeiten könnten," he writes after a critical passage on the practice of tapping telephones. "Man könnte doch mindestens eine Art Bildungsprogramm für Abhörer planen. Tonbänder mit Geschichtsunterricht. Das kostet nicht viel."[8] Elsewhere, when mentioning Katherina Blum's organizational talents, he remarks that these abilities are received "als Schreckensnachricht durch alle Haftanstalten. Man sieht: Korrektheit, mit planerischer Intelligenz verbunden ist nirgendwo erwünscht, nicht einmal in Gefängnissen, und nicht einmal von der Verwaltung" (113).

Interestingly, the narrator's most open irony is directed toward bureaucratic targets. When presenting descriptions of Katharina Blum, there is no mockery—although the possibility exists. The categories used by others to describe Katharina Blum—the sympathetic as well as the hostile ones—are invariably sexual. The narrator makes no comment on this, but simply reproduces both in a seemingly objective manner. His supposed objectivity is a limited perspective, which does not allow him to comprehend fully the sexual nature of the conflict. Like many of the critics, his eyes are focused on the political implications.

From the moment the police storm Katharina Blum's apartment, the fact that she is a woman provides a special vulnerability. In an attempt to humiliate her in order to extract a confession, the police immediately categorize her night spent with Ludwig Göttens in the most vulgar of terms: "Beizmenne (the police inspector) soll die aufreizend gelassen an ihrer Anrichte lehnende Katharina nämlich gefragt haben: 'Hat er dich denn gefickt,' woraufhin Katharina sowohl rot geworden sein wie in stolzem Triumph gesagt haben soll: 'Nein, ich würde es nicht so nennen'" (18). It was a fleeting triumph, as verbal sexual abuse became the method by which Katharina Blum was attacked.

What the police began, the journalist Tötges continued and expanded. The discrepancy between the newspaper's statements about Katharina Blum and the facts which the narrator uncovers is readily apparent. Tötges altered, for example, the characterization of Katharina Blum as "eine sehr kluge und kühle Person" (32) to read that she is "eiskalt und berechnend" (33). The testimony "Wenn Katharina radikal is, dann ist sie radikal hilfsbereit, plannvoll und intelligent" is transformed into the quote: "Eine in jeder Beziehung radikale Person, die uns geschickt getäuscht hat" (38). Her mother's lament-- "Warum mußte das so enden, warum mußte das so kommen?-- is changed to: "So mußte es ja kommen, so mußte es ja enden" (91). Other alleged facts presented by Tötges are similarly falsified: her father is labeled a communist, her mother an alcoholic, and Katherina herself is said to be fully capable of committing a crime.

Tötges's distortions are obvious when viewed in light of the documentation provided by the narrator. In order to create a sensational story which will sell well, Tötges manipulates, falsifies, and even fabricates facts and quotes. What is not immediately apparent, however, is that the success of his slander depends upon specific public stereotypes of women. Before the labels of "radical" and "communist" assume emotional significance for readers of the newspaper, Katharina Blum must be degraded sexually and made into "that kind of woman" who would do anything. As with the police, Tötges's attack begins with verbal sexual abuse.

Eiskalt und berechnend is Tötges's first characterization meant to undermine Katharina Blum's reputation by attacking her sexuality. To label a woman "ice-cold and calculating" implies that she is someone without feelings who will do anything to achieve her ends, including using her own sexuality. To malign her further, Tötges then speaks (as do the police) of Herrenbesuche, intimating that she is a prostitute. In fact, everything Tötges writes about Katharina Blum presents the image of a woman of questionable virtue. By questioning publicly her sexual purity, he undermines her character in all respects so that readers will view her as a criminal with questionable political beliefs.

The direct connection between questionable sexuality and criminal behavior is made by Tötges when he writes about Katharina Blum's reputed long-term relationship with Ludwig Götten. He calls her a "Räuberliebchen" and a "Mörderbraut" (32, 35). A characterization is again made in sexual terms, but now in combination with criminal labels. Of course, Katharina Blum is neither a "robber" nor a "murderer." Her ostensible "crime" is being sexually involved with a "criminal." By associating sexuality with criminality in this way, Tötges succeeds in discrediting Katharina Blum doubly. Questioning her sexual virtue lent credence to the public depiction of her as a criminal. To discredit her politically then becomes easy.

That a woman's honor, and not a man's, can be attacked by sexual innuendo is underscored in the text by the figure of Alois Sträubleder. A prominent industrialist, Sträubleder functions as a minor counterpoint to Katharina Blum. In contrast to Katharina Blum, whose reputation depends upon her sexual virtue, Sträubleder indicates that public knowledge of illicit romance could not harm him. "Eine romantische Frauengeschichte bringt mich höchstens privat in Schwierigkeiten, nicht öffentlich. Da würde nicht einmal ein Foto mit einer so attraktiven Frau wie Katharina Blum schaden," he says (81). He even implies that his reputation as a man might be enhanced by a sex-linked scandal. His only worry is that such a story might suggest an association with criminals. Sexuality for Sträubleder is a private matter, not subject to public dishonor.

Because Tötges succeeds in dishonoring Katharina Blum by exploiting her sexuality in the public sphere of politics and journalism, it appears that she seeks revenge and kills him. On the surface, the motif of "lost honor" and revenge seems to establish the connection between the title of the novel and the violence

referred to in the subtitle. This motif, however, functions largely as cliché or stereotypical theme, masking
the fact that a different, more lethal type of violence
other than Katharina Blum's act of murder relates to
honor within the framework of the novel. As Wolfram
Schutte wrote in an early review: "Die Gewalt, von der
die Rede ist, geht von der Presse aus, und führt
Katharina Blum zum Mord."[9]

The violence which permeates the novel is foremost a
violence committed through the medium of language.
Violence occurs through the use of words as weapons
rather than guns. Words and language create a story
based on lies, innuendo, and misrepresentation. The
world is ordered linguistically in such a way that it is
destructive to the individual, and therein lies its
inherent violent quality. By the misuse of words, the
sanctity of the individual is violated.[10]

Although language can be made to impart a quality of
violence, it is not language per se which is violent.
Tötges does not succeed in his attack on Katharina Blum
solely because he distorts facts or misuses language.
The images he creates of Katharina Blum, though bound by
a certain inner consistency, do not have intrinsic meaning. Instead, they gain their meaning from a set of
rigid sexual stereotypes embedded in societal consciousness. To have meaning, his characterization of Katharina
Blum is in need of these specific referents. His images
do not represent any form of pure linguistic or artistic
invention, but are inventions in the form of distortions—and these distortions are meant only to give expression to a distorted, yet widely accepted view of
reality in which women and men are characterized and
judged in terms of sexual stereotypes and gender role
expectations.

The connection between language and reality is
underscored by Böll's disclaimer which prefaces the
novel. His disclaimer is purposefully unsubtle, as it
points a finger at the actual publishing concern of Axel
Springer. The reader is made aware of a real situation
outside the text, even if unaware of West Germany's
political climate. The result is a parody of what has
become a standard literary form—that is, a pro forma
denial that the fictional reality of a particular book
is in any way based on actual characters and events. For
Böll, the connection between fictional reality and our
social reality is implicit. Tötges and his manner of
reporting are not meant to be singular to him as a

89

particular (and in this case fictionalized) individual. Instead, his reporting is representative of a whole type of journalism. And the success of this reporting depends on preconceived gender expectations, which prepare the reader to accept as fact certain sexual stereotypes.

In the case of Katharina Blum, for example, her sucure financial situation is "explained" (by both the police and Tötges) by the supposition that she works as a prostitute. Her long solitary drives are first seen as trips to "gentlemen visitors," then as journeys to "case" a villa for her lover. Her divorce is reported as caused by adultery. Her mother's death is attributed to shock at her "loose" ways. And her reactions are consistently described as "analytical" rather than "emotional"--a characterization for a woman which immediately implies she is hardened and deceptive. This reduction of reality to sexual stereotypes--conveyed through language--is the initial violence in the novel.

Once a woman has "lost" her sexual "honor," there exists no possibility to reverse or halt the process which judges and condemns her. The terms used to censure and describe her are locked into place, and she is tainted for life. If the individual seeks recourse, revenge is the only choice. Katharina Blum's act of physical (i.e., "real") violence appears to form a part of this unvarying circle. In conformity with clichéd expectations, a woman's lost honor is avenged by the murder of the man who besmirched her reputation. The only break with the stereotype is the fact that Katharina Blum does not remain a passive female, dependent upon a man to revenge her honor. She herself becomes her own agent of revenge. Yet her act alters nothing. By killing Tötges, she becomes an outcast as a convicted criminal. This does allow her to join the world of her lover, but the reunion is only symbolic. Her violence is nothing more than an act of defiance, but not a genuine alternative.

But does Katharina Blum kill Tötges to avenge her lost honor? Although both title and plot seemingly portray the familiar theme of lost honor revenged, Katharina Blum is actually motivated to commit murder for reasons apart from a sense of lost honor. She shoots Tötges to protect the integrity and sanctity of her own inner world, rather than to defend a stereotypical idea of honor in which she does not believe. For her, a woman's honor is something other than her sexual purity.

90

Within the novel, a contradiction exists between the public image of Katharina Blum and her own private self-conception. Tötges and the police contribute most to the creation of the public image. As already noted, this image does not rest on actual facts, but is based on a set of sexual stereotypes. Katharina Blum's efficiency, thriftiness, and modest lifestyle--all of which enable her to buy her own apartment--are overlooked as qualities uncharacteristic for a woman. Instead, the assumption is made that a wealthy "customer" (or "customers") supports her.

This conception of Katharina Blum relegates her to a dependent position, similar to that of a child. At the first police interrogation, her sense of independence goes completely unnoticed. Commissioner Beizmenne, at first harsh and authoritarian, adopts a "fatherly" tone and condescendingly reassures her that it is acceptable for a woman in her position to receive "gentlemen visitors" (Herrenbesuch). Later, one of the policemen also suggests that she (the potential criminal) is in need of protection and should be jailed for her own safety.

It is this public portrait of Katharina Blum, based on repeated factual distortions and sexual stereotypes, for which the concept "lost honor" has meaning. Publicly, her sexual behavior is placed into question, thereby dishonoring her. Within her own private world, however, there is never a loss of honor in the same sexual sense. At no time does she understand her relationship with Ludwig Götten in terms of lost honor. Instead, she gropes for other categories to define her sexual relationships. Important to her is Zärtlichkeit as opposed to Zudringlichkeit.

Katharina Blum does not develop these categories. They remain private and personal, and are not understood in the public sphere. Nevertheless, they do point to an attempt on her part to define her sexuality in terms other than those implied in such stereotypes as "lost honor." And it is this attempt to articulate her own understanding of sexuality which creates conflict when she is confronted with established norms.

To a large extent, Katharina Blum is unable to make publicly clear her private values because they remain an unconscious part of herself. She in no way regards herself as different, although in reality she lives a life which is quite different from others. The life which she has created mirrors that of an average single woman. Her taste in books, her leisure activities, her condominium, and her friends are all evidence of a basically middle-class mentality. Yet, behind this seemingly average existence is something which makes her stand out. She possesses an unusual independence, as is made clear by her financial arrangements with the Blornas, her divorce, and her refusal to engage in meaningless sexual relationships. It is this uniqueness which the police and Tötges are unable to comprehend, as it does not conform to their preconceived stereotypes.

Honor in its conventional sense bears little real meaning for Katharina Blum. By maintaining her own private values, her personal sense of honor remains intact, even while she suffers a public loss of honor. But rapidly, the sexual stereotypes used to characterized her begin to undermine and threaten her private world. In a number of ways, the public smear campaign initiated by Tötges intrudes on Katharina Blum's private sphere. Obscene phone calls and sexual solicitations by unknown neighbors become common. Her private world is attacked, and is in no way protected--not even by her friends and close acquaintances. They, too, essentially perceive her in terms of sexual stereotypes.

The manner in which Katharina Blum's friends view her does differ from that of the police and Tötges, yet their characterizations are also primarily sexually based. Her employer and friend Hubert Blorna, for example, cannot describe her without sexual reference. Although he on occasion speaks of her modesty and efficiency, equally important to him is her physical attractiveness and what he considers her sexual prudishness. In his eyes, she is a helpless and vulnerable female.

The belief that Katharina Blum is sexually prudish is shared by most of her acquaintances, who repeatedly refer to her as "the nun." The image of Katharina Blum as a nun is interesting, because it is diametrically opposed to the one formed by the police and Tötges. Despite the contradictory nature of the two images, neither presents an accurate portrait of Katharina Blum. Neither recognizes in any way her private set of values or her personal identity, and both represent extremes frequently used to characterize a woman--a whore or a nun. Her values are consequently distorted by both, as she is perceived only in terms of sexual stereotypes. In the case of Tötges, her aloofness, which originates from the desire to find someone zärtlich, is misconstrued negatively in such as way as to depict her as eiskalt

<u>und berechnend</u>. For friends and acquaintances, this same quality is endearingly understood as sexual prudishness.

The fact that close acquaintances, similarly to the police and Tötges, view Katharina Blum only in terms of sexual stereotypes means that her private values and ideals receive no public recognition or articulation. Her defense is to kill Tötges. Nevertheless, she does not shoot him to gain revenge. Instead, as the conclusion demonstrates, she shoots Tötges only when he acts in such a way as to threaten what remains of her private world:

> "Er sagte "Na, Blümchen, was machen wir zwei denn jetzt?" Ich sagte kein Wort, wich ins Wohnzimmer zurück, und er kam mir nach und sagte: "Was guckst du mich so entgeistert an, mein Blümelein - ich schlage vor, daß wir jetzt erst einmal bumsen." Nun, inzwischen war ich bei meiner Handtasche, und er ging mir an die Kledage, und ich dachte: "Bumsen, meinetwegen", und ich hab die Pistole rausgenommen und sofort auf ihn geschossen (120).

> Ja, nun müssen Sie nicht glauben, daß es was Neues für mich war, daß ein Mann mir an die Kledage wollte - wenn Sie von Ihrem vierzehnten Lebensjahr an, und schon früher, in Haushalten arbeiten, sind Sie was gewohnt. Aber <u>dieser</u> Kerl - und dann "Bumsen", und ich <u>dachte</u>: Gut, jetzt bumst's (120).

> Ich dachte natürlich auch an den Erschossenen da in meiner Wohnung. Ohne Reue, ohne Bedauern, er wollte doch bumsen, und ich habe gebumst, oder? (121)

As these passages make clear, Katharina Blum shoots only when Tötges attempts to violate her personally. He is, in accordance with her personal values, <u>zudringlich</u>. To allow him to violate her in this manner would mean that he had finally destroyed her private sense of honor as well as her public honor. In actuality, then, Katharina Blum's act of violence is not so much revenge for a public loss of honor, as it is a defense of private integrity.

In the end, Katharina Blum's private definition of honor remains inaccessible to others, making it impossible for those around her to understand her motivations. Realizing that Tötges, as a man, is able to render sex an act of violence, Katharina Blum, in the only way possible for a woman, responds in kind by equating the sexual act with a violent one ("ich habe gebumst"). Her defense, however, ultimately remains unsatisfactory. An act of violence cannot redeem her public name, nor can it challenge the sexual stereotypes which have been used to undermine her individual values. Like her attempts to define herself in terms other than sexual stereotypes, her defense remains locked and isolated within a private world. As an act of rebellion, the shooting of, Tötges does not challenge the rigid stereotypes, nor does it free her from them.

Notes

[1] Der Spiegel, 29 July 1974.

[2] In 1972, Kiepenheuer & Witsch Verlag published a documentation entitled: Heinrich Böll: Freies Geleit für Ulrike Meinhof - Ein Artikel und seine Folgen. The book presented the many articles, interviews, defamations, and disagreements which were connected with Böll's Spiegel article.

[3] Wolf Donner, "Der lüsterne Meinungsterror: Ein Buch, ein Film, eine deutsche Krankheit," Die Zeit, 17 October 1975, p. 15; Joachim Kaiser, "Liebe und Haß der heiligen Katharina," Süddeutsche Zeitung, 10-11 August 1974, p. 76.

[4] Rainer Nägele, Heinrich Böll: Einführung in das Werk und in die Forschung (Frankfurt am Main: Athenäum Fischer, 1976), p. 162.

[5] Marcel Reich-Ranicki, "Der deutschen Gegenwart mitten ins Herz," Frankfurter Allgemeine, 24 August 1974.

[6] See, for example: Margit M. Sinka, "Heinrich Böll's Die verlorene Ehre der Katharina Blum as Novelle," Colloquia Germanica 14 (1981), 158-74; William S. Sewell, "'Konduktion und Niveauunterschiede': The Structure of Böll's Katharina Blum," Monatshefte 74 (1982), 167-77; Rhys W. Williams, "Heinrich Böll and the Katharina Blum Debate," Critical Quarterly 21 (1979), 49-58.

[7] Rhys W. Williams, "Heinrich Böll and the Katharina Blum Debate," 53; Margit M. Sinka, "Heinrich Böll's Die verlorene Ehre der Katharina Blum as Novelle," 164; J.C. Franklin, "Alienation and the Retention of the Self: The Heroines of Der gute Mensch von Sezuan, Abschied von Gestern, and Die Verlorene Ehre der Katharina Blum," Mosaic 12 (1979), 94.

[8] Heinrich Böll, Die verlorene Ehre der Katharina Blum (Munich: DTV, 1976), p. 90. All other quotations from the novel are from this edition.

[9] Wolfram Schutte, "Notwehr, Widerstand und Selbstrettung," Frankfurter Rundschau, 10 August 1974.

[10] Eberhard Scheiffele, in his article, "Kritische Sprachanalyse in Heinrich Bölls Die verlorene Ehre der Katharina Blum, in Basis, ed. Reinhold Grimm and Jost Hermand (Frankfurt: Suhrkamp, 1979), pp. 169-87, examines the language used in this novel. Although Sheiffele does not concentrate on the sexual aspects of the story, his analysis points to the elaborate language prefiguration and spectrum of stereotypes which color the reader's perception--specifically of Katharina--from the beginning.

Novellistic Representation of die Berufstätige during the Weimar Republic

Renny Harrigan

The flapper, an eternally young woman with Bubikopf and Cupid's bow on her slightly parted lips, has become a symbol for the entire decade of Germany's goldene zwangizer Jahre, if the picture on the cover of Thilo Koch's book of the same name is any indication.[1] The particular image of the flapper reflects what was certainly the most visible change in women's lives during the Weimar Republic: the emergence of the female white-collar worker in the newly created semi-skilled jobs of a bourgeoning service and sales sector. Insofar as the "career woman" aped the fashions of the culturally dominant middle class, she too can be called a flapper. Although women's lives were changing in other areas even more dramatically,[2] it is here that we have the clearest and most immediate break with tradition. The present study analyzes the image of the flapper personified sociologically by the white-collar worker in three representative novels of the Weimar Republic. Social history is used as a means of understanding the multifaceted reality of the period for women in both its emancipatory and its regressive aspects.

Political economists and sociologists have stated that the treatment of women--or anyone defined as Other by the dominant culture, I would add--can be used as an index of a society's respect for human and civil rights. A growing literature on Weimar history, politics, society, and culture written by a new generation of German historians has applied this principle to the short-lived Republic. Led by Renate Bridenthal, Claudia Koonz, and Tim Mason in the English-speaking world,[3] the traditional view of the Weimar Republic as one bringing great advances for women has been overturned. Thus, an important gap has been filled in the general literature which had already recognized Weimar liberalism as seductive, fragile, and lacking in substance.[4]

The issues which these historians raise are similar
to those which arise when reading the fiction of the
period. To what extent, for example, did the Nazi
victory reverse, to what extent did it continue, the
attitudes and expectations of the democratic republic
which preceded it? Certainly, women made progress during
this period but how do we reconcile our image of
increasing female liberation with our knowledge of the
anti-feminist policies of an increasingly popular Nazi
party during the Weimar period? This study demonstrates
that the independence of the flapper--here die Berufs-
tätige--was not quite what it appeared to be and
provides thereby but one indication of the direction we
must take to answer this question. An analysis of the
image of the flapper also begins to expose ideology
functioning at its deeper, unconscious level.

Walter Kiaulehn describes the optische Wandlung of
women during the Weimar Republic with the following
words:

> Sie waren leichter und luftiger geworden,
> vielleicht auch etwas kantiger, ersetzten
> aber diese fehlende Fülle durch eine neue
> Grazie. Ihrer alten Verspieltheit war ein
> neuer spöttischer Zug beigemischt. Bei der
> Berlinerin war die Verwandlung besonders
> verblüffend. Sie hatten alles Provinzielle
> abgestreift, . . . vor allem das stern-
> äugige Kokettieren mit Naivität und Ahn-
> ungslosigkeit. Die neue Berlinerin hatte
> klare Augen, und ihrer äußerlichen Sach-
> lichkeit stand die kleine Beigabe von Sar-
> kasmus gut.[5]

Kiaulehn's observations are concerned primarily with
the feminine externals under which he surmises a new
psychology. His urban women are no longer naive and
sentimental, but matter-of-fact and just a little sarcastic. These women apparently know what to expect and
are perhaps no longer in need of male protection. In an
even match, such an assumption would be of no import,
but can we assume the match is even?

There is certainly a marked difference between this
image of female beauty and that of the Victorian lady
who preceded her. According to Stefan Zweig, the latter's attire, "in jeder Einzelheit die Natur vergewal-
tigend," consisted of a corset, buttons to the neck, and
"außer ein paar Dutzend russischer Studentinnen [als

auch die ins Ausland vertriebenen deutschen Studentinnen, RKH] [konnte] jede Frau Europas ihr Haar bis zu den
Hüften entrollen."[6]

Zweig views the change for his definitely middle-
class woman as an advance in the name of sexual freedom
and independence. Kiaulehn places the transformation in
the context of a changing consciousness caused by
women's work during World War I and their receiving the
vote in 1919. Clearly, the almost revolutionary change
in fashion was but one symptom of the material changes
in women's lives, which extended far beyond the immediately obvious shortening of hair and skirts.

Women in the Weimar Work Force

The extent to which women actually left the traditional hearth between 1918 and 1933 has been exaggerated
in the cultural histories of the period. The working
woman undoubtedly impressed the public with both her
novelty and her visibility more than her actual numbers
warranted. In fact, 35% of all women worked according to
the 1925 census; this number was an increase of only 5%
since 1907 and composed 36% of the entire work force.[8]
In general, women of the middle class became completely
dependent on their husbands' salaries during the Weimar
Republic because of changes in both the economy and in
the family: family size decreased rapidly and indus-
trialization removed all productive work from the home.
Working-class women, no longer able to exist on their
husbands' wages, were propelled out of the home into the
unskilled industrial work force.[9] Although there was
much credence on both left and right given to the idea
that women were forcing men out of the job market, in
actual fact, women took only 23% of the one-and-one-half
million new jobs added to the economy between 1925 and
1933.[10] White-collar work was the _fastest_ growing area
of female employment, but it accounted for only one-
eighth of the work force.[11]

The sudden visibility of an apparently independent
woman in white-collar office work may account for her
exaggeration in the novels. The popularity of the fictional image, coupled with the historical fact that the
lowest _absolute_ number of women worked clerical, semi-
skilled white-collar jobs, has determined my particular
topic, for the contradiction between the image and reality admits the widest play of both ideology and
artistic imagination. Therefore, it should come as no

surprise that male writers seem to include the Berufs-
tätige--often as a peripheral figure, often in a negative light--more often than female writers,[12] with the
result that the picture becomes skewed. Most commen-
tators now agree that the "new women" attracted undue
attention:

> They were simultaneously seen as "guar-
> dians of morality" and as "chief agents of
> a culture of decadence. . . ." While the
> "new woman" did not signal female emanci-
> pation or the collapse of patriarchy, she
> did represent--to some--a moral crisis.
> The definition of the female in the Weimar
> period included images of women as victim,
> threat, and salvation. Thus the "new
> woman" captured the imagination of pro-
> gressives who celebrated her, even as they
> sought to discipline and regulate her, and
> of conservatives who blamed her for every-
> thing from the decline of the birth rate
> and the laxity of morals to the unemploy-
> ment of male workers.[13]

In addition to these considerations is my belief
that work is a necessary pre-condition for emancipation,
even where its exploitative elements in a class and
sexist society are also evident. Work cannot in and of
itself create emancipation, but emancipation surely will
not occur without it. This realization may also account
for the ambivalence and distortion of the image of the
Berufstätige, the "new woman," by those who feared her
eventual social ascent and her apparent "freedom."

Class Consciousness

The class position of the non-professional white-
collar worker was a product of individual consciousness
to a much greater degree than that of any group during
the Weimar period. Within the first two decades of the
20th century, the semi-skilled white-collar worker came
to comprise almost a majority of the work force.[14]
Although the salaries for such jobs were comparable to
proletarian wages, der neue Mittelstand had definitely
middle-class pretensions and an almost pathological fear
of being reduced to the level of a manual worker. The
clerical worker took the newer jobs created by emerging
industrial needs, yet this worker defined his or her
position according to preindustrial social values.[15]

This contradiction produced a psychology which was considerably more complicated than one of false consciousness. Ernst Bloch's theory of fascism provides a useful approach to the problem. Bloch's point of departure is both historical and psychological:

> Nicht alle sind im selben Jetzt da. Sie tragen vielmehr Früheres mit, das mischt sich ein. Je nachdem, wo einer leiblich, vor allen klassenhaft steht, hat er seine Zeiten. Ältere Zeiten als die heutige wirken in älteren Schichten nach, leicht geht oder träumt sich hier in ältere zurück.[16]

Bloch describes this phenomenon philosophically in terms of synchronous and nonsynchronous contradictions ("Gleichzeitigkeiten" and "Ungleichzeitigkeiten"). The little person of the middle class in the here and now experiences in the inflationary economy of the Weimar Republic complete alienation from work which had previously promised both security and individual advance. At the same time, a strong memory of things past is fueled by the subjective wish to avoid the exigencies of the present. A part of one's psyche has been conditioned by older relationships than those which exist in the modern economy:

> Eine verelendete Mittelschicht will zurück in den Vorkrieg, wo es ihr besser ging. Sie ist verelendet, also revolutionär anfällig, doch ihre Arbeit ist fern vom Schuß und ihre Erinnerungen machen sie völlig zeitfremd. Die Unsicherheit, welche bloß Heimweh nach Gewesenem als revolutionären Antrieb erzeugt, setzt mitten in der Großstadt Gestalten, die man seit Jahrhunderten nicht sah. Doch auch hier erfindet das Elend nichts oder nicht alles, sondern plaudert nur aus, nämlich Ungleichzeitigkeit. . . . Ältere Seinsarten kehren derart gerade städtisch wieder, ältere Denkart und Haßbilder dazu. . . .[17]

The individual experiences, on the one hand, what Bloch would call an objective contradiction simply by not wanting the present. This takes the form of anger. At the same time, there is a nonsynchronous remnant from the past which is very real in the present.

101

Such an appreciation for the phenomenon of pre-logical thinking points to the inadequacy of reason in explaining individual motivations for political activity and development of class consciousness. Bloch affirms both the subversive content and the false consciousness which coexist in the expressions of a striving for transcendence; by so doing, he reaffirms the emotional impact of the dialectic on the class or individual.[18]

A phenomenon in literature which parallels Bloch's ideas is the existence of traditional stereotypical features in characters who actually participate in and reflect society's emergent cultural and social trends. Women were relatively new recruits to the Weimar white-collar work force but their social background bespoke other class realities and society continued to value them in their traditional role of wife-as-mother. The sexually and economically independent "modern woman" owed her existence to emergent conditions of industrial capitalism yet she was accepted only when she proved herself willing to give up her modicum of independence and lead a life for which both she and society were no longer suited. The remnants of her pre-industrial past were (and continue to be) magnified in the type of nurturance and need-oriented relationships which have been for centuries the primary responsibility of women. A new life in the work force which is both more independent and less secure pulls against the rewards of the old one at home in an objective and synchronous contradiction. The desire of the female white-collar worker to return to the traditional sphere, which in actual fact has substantially changed, is subjective and nonsynchronous.

By her very existence, the white-collar working woman appeared to threaten the last "secure" realm of the individual, the family. The attitude toward her in the three representative novels is generally ambivalent even when it is intellectually sympathetic.

An Orientation to the Three Novels

Gilgi, oder eine von uns (1932[19]) was a first novel by twenty-one-year-old Irmgard Keun.[20] Within its first year it reached a printing of 30,000. Keun delineates the contradictions of Gilgi's life through a montage technique which most consistently employed "erlebte Rede." The title alone expresses her sympathy with her subject matter which is informed throughout by the continuing dialectic of sexual politics introduced to

102

the German public by a nascent women's movement in the 19th century.[21]

Martin Kessel (Herrn Brechers Fiasko, 1932[22]) is an intellectual whose sympathies rest clearly with the middle class as a cultural rather than a political force. He displays ambivalence and occasional hostility to the modern woman in by far the most stylistically ambitious novel of the three. The plot is episodic, consisting primarily of descriptions of the home and work lives of individuals employed by the "Propaganda Abteilung" at "Uvag" ("Universale-Vermittlungs-Aktien-Gesellschaft") in Berlin. The episodes are tacked on to major events such as a bombing at Uvag, a general strike, and Brecher's dismissal, all of which have less emotional impact than the conversations of Uvag's employees.

Rudolph Braune, as a socialist whose politics cause him to affirm the historical justice of working-class demands in Das Mädchen an der Orga Private (1930[23]), is the only one of the three novelists who expresses a conscious political position. He is militantly sympathetic to both the class and sexual exploitation of the female white-collar worker. His heroine, Erna Halbe, is a working-class woman who has taken her first white-collar job in Berlin in order to escape a life in the factory. Braune's presentation remains fairly abstract and the solutions he implies remain rooted in the sphere of production: class solidarity and a direct relationship to the means of production as a method of gaining eventual independence. Braune's programmatic position allows him to overlook the patriarchal and occasionally sexist nature of Erna's relationship to her machinist lover as well as his own objectification of female sexuality through the machinist in the narrative. The weaknesses of Kessel and Braune are avoided by Keun, whose strength derives from her lack of pretense, and her respect for her chosen subject.

My choice of novels was determined by several considerations. I preferred to use novels written during the Weimar period and set in the Weimar period in what I hoped would provide the simplest reflection of ideology. I thus eliminate the risk of trying to read too much into the female characterizations set at an earlier period. In addition, I needed novels which were most complete portrayals of the Berufstätige. All three of the novels I chose address a different type of reader; however, I do not mean to imply that they are the only novels which could have been selected.

Ideally, I had also wanted novels read by masses of the reading public but the runaway bestsellers of that period (among them such diverse works as Buddenbrooks, Im Westen Nichts Neues, Rudolf Herzog's Die Wiskottens, or even Margarethe Bohme's Tagebuch einer Verlorenen) simply didn't offer the kind of material I sought. There are also, of course, very few female writers whose works achieved such popularity, and there are even fewer-- Vicki Baum is the exception--who wrote of an urban, contemporary setting, although a complete analysis of the ideology must eventually include them. In the absence of popularity as a criterion, my choice here is somewhat arbitrary. It will be for the reader to decide if I do an injustice to her knowledge of Weimar literature.

General Economic Situation in the Novels

In all three novels, the females work together in a typing pool for subsistence pay, with no security and no chance of promotion, in one large office clearly separated from that of their employers. Two men, Brecher and Dr. Geist, also occupy this space in the Kessel novel, but they are copy writers rather than secretaries. Thus, both a functional division of labor (denoting class) and a sexual division of labor (denoting status) is preserved throughout the three novels. Both Keun and Braune state clearly that the salary of their protagonists (DM 120 to 130) is barely subsistence level.[24] Kessel, perhaps because he appears more sympathetic to the idea that white-collar work is preferred, no matter what its remuneration, is silent about the amount his characters earn. In the three novels, none of the female protagonists is able to live alone and survive economically except for Kessel's Gudula Öften, whose class origins have enabled her to furnish her studio but whose increasing age and unmarried state have called her inherited social position into question. A female at this time, according to Kessel, still needs the sponsorship of a male, either a father or a husband. In all three novels the workday is long, punctuated by a short lunch; the work itself is monotonous and there is no protection against immediate dismissal. In both Keun's and Braune's novels, a quota system prevails which destroys all pretense of middle-class professionalism. There is practically no chance of either a raise or a promotion, except in Kessel's grotesque depiction of an accident: the bombing of the Propaganda Abteilung at Uvag which eliminates its director and allows Dr. Geist

to ascend, bringing one of the Berufstätige with him. At
least here, "des Königs reitender Bote kommt."

Both Irmgard Keun and Rudolph Braune portray sexual
relationships of convenience between the secretaries and
their higher-ranking employers. The material gifts sup-
plied through these liaisons provide the women with the
wardrobe required by the job and an occasional frivoli-
ty. These relationships exist in secrecy side-by-side
with the "real" boyfriends and husbands. Braune, through
Erna's perspective, is quite critical of what he sees as
the corrupting influence of such relationships but he
draws a purely contrived distinction between working-
class and middle-class behavior:

> In der [Arbeiter]-Kolonie ging es manchmal
> nicht schön zu zwischen Jungens und
> Mädels, aber wenn eine ein Kind kriegen
> sollte, dann mußte eben geheiratet werden,
> sonst wäre es dem Täter schlecht ergangen
> (87).

Neither desertion nor the enforced marriage which Braune
advocates seems desirable or emancipatory.

Keun's Gilgi accepts society's standards, but only
with the proviso that she will not be ensnared either
emotionally or physically in an unwanted pregnancy: "Die
meisten versuchen natürlich ihr Glück, wenn ihnen ein
hübsches, junges Mädel in die Quere kommt - kann man
ihnen doch nicht übelnehmen. Oder? ich finde das ganz
normal and natürlich. Hauptsache: man versteht ihnen
geschickt auszuweichen" (86). Gilgi certainly uses her
charms to advantage but when her employer begins to
claim his due, she balks: "Sie hat keine Lust . . . ein
Verhältnis anzufangen, und sie hat keine Lust ihre
Stelle . . . zu vermurksen, sie eventuell zu verlieren"
(15-16). In the unequal situation of employer-employee,
Gilgi's admittedly calculated attempt to achieve the
upper hand remains inevitably short-lived.

The Typology of the Image

Mucki Schöpps in Kessel's Herrn Brechers Fiasko is
the prototype behind the image of the flapper as she
appears on the cover of Koch's Goldene zwanziger Jahre:

> . . . eine Dame mitte der zwanzig, an der
> Grenze jenes Alters, wo die Konvention

105

vorschreibt zu heiraten, vorausgesagt, daß
man nicht schon wieder geschieden ist, saß
seit fünf Minuten mit kühlen Armen und
ausrasierten Achselhöhlen im Empfangsraum
der Abteilung Progaganda. . . . Ein Bein
übers andere geschlagen, die Hände so
aufeinandergelegt, wie die Mode es vorschreibt, hegt sie in diesem Augenblick
nur die eine Befürchtung nicht natürlich
genug auszusehen (25).

Mucki is the fantasy creation of the clerical world
whose marriage will soon save her from her dreary work
just as convention dictates, at least in the literature.
The myth of a Prince Charming who will make the work
temporary for these young, attractive, well-clothed, and
well-coiffed women is attendant on the image of the
flapper. Siegfried Kracauer's sociological essay from
the same period substantiates the phenomenon:

Die Arbeiterin, besonders soweit sie noch
als junges Mädchen glaubt, die Berufs-
tätigkeit sei für sie nur eine vorüber-
gehende Erscheinung, träumt während der
monotonen Arbeit von Backfischromanen,
Kinodramen oder vom Brautstand.[25]

Mucki is the daughter of the widowed Frau Geheimrat
Schöpps who has been forced to sell the family villa in
Grunewald and send her daughter "ins feindliche Leben"
to work (180). The mother undoubtedly means to be
encouraging not only to Mucki but to herself when she
repeatedly says, "Es ist durchaus keine Schande" (180).
Mucki's identification, as a result of her personal
history, is hardly class based.

The two other office "girls" in Kessel's novel, who
together with Mucki provide us with a fairly complete
typology of the secretary, are Gudula Öften and Lisa
Frieske. Gudula, "eine reifere, ältere Dame" (16) with
"mehr als dreißigjährige[r] Erfahrung" (50), has worked
at Uvag as long as anyone can remember, a fact which
attests to the high turnover rate more than anything
else. Koonz and Bridenthal's research points out how
unlikely such "advanced" age is in such jobs and here
that would be doubly true since Gudula has a noticeable
limp.[26] "In der Regel," corroborates Kracauer, "spielt
das Äußere eine entscheidende Rolle" (222). Gudula is
the single woman whose work over the years has become

her life and she is the only character here who glorifies her job as a Beruf.

Gudula clearly considers herself of good enough stock to become a worthy friend of the widowed Frau Geheimrat Schöpps; however, she is part of the Besitzbürgertum only in its monopoly on high culture. She is heard to raise her voice only once in the "empörende[n] Verachtung des gebildeten Menschen" when her director gives concert tickets to the doorman and the elevator operator at Uvag rather than to secretaries like herself:

> Als ob Beethoven speziell für Wrampe [den Fahrstuhlführer] taub geworden sei! Als ob die Künstler alle . . . zu keinem anderen Zweck wahnsinnig geworden seien, als daß sich Portiers an Meisterwerken langweilten!

Gudula is oblivious to the irony of her situation in which an occasional concert ticket becomes prohibitive because her salary is too low. Simultaneously we see here the chasm which separates her from the worker despite their economic similarities. She proceeds here:

> Woran erkennen Sie einen Menschen, ja? An seinem Kulturbewußtsein! Wrampe in ein Klavierkonzert schicken ist Barbarei. Es ist ein Moment, wenn die Leutseligkeit in Snobismus ausartet. Verzeihung . . . das mußte gesagt sein (52).

Gudula is on intimate terms with all the women in the office; indeed, she is the maternal nurturer of the Abteilung Propaganda and her warmth derives partially from a need for vicarious experience. Only Brecher, the ultimate cynic, suspects "daß sie in Menschheit spekuliert" (41), an opinion which is not without basis. When Lisa Frieske comes to Gudula in anger and despair over an unwanted pregnancy--a pregnancy which Gudula had encouraged--the older woman listens to her tale while polishing her nails and correcting Lisa's grammar. Through such episodes Gudula is revealed as a self-deceptive humanist who as a female combines the stereotypical traits of the older, single, and thus, in Kessel's eyes, "unfulfilled" woman.

Fräulein Frieske's working-class family is described by the narrator as "kein täglich sich erneuerndes

Kunstwerk von Takt und guten Formen" where courtesy, rather than an accepted social form, is used as a weapon of sarcasm (184). Here too Kessel emphasizes the importance of mastering bourgeois cultural forms. Lisa Frieske is, however, blissfully unaware of any short-comings in this area. With the unstinting support of her mother she has managed to acquire a middle-class veneer through education and attention to fashion.

> Man muß sich nur einmal im Treppenflur aufgehalten haben, in den Minuten, da Lisa das Haus verläßt, um den feinen Geruch in der Nase zu spuren, der von ihr Kunde gibt, jenes damenhafte Überbleibsel. . . .

> Lisas Mutter ergötzte sich im Stillen an der Feenhaftigkeit ihrer Tochter, obwohl für sie wenig dabei heraussprang, war doch Lisa immer in Eile, immer außer Haus, in Sprachstunden oder in Schwimmanstalten, mit einem Wort, immer auf Ausbildung, immer unterwegs (184).

Lisa Frieske's perfume indicates that an acceptable wardrobe is a necessary bourgeois cultural accouterment. Because she is, in addition, the soul of responsibility and adaptability, she should survive; however, a pregnancy designed to manipulate her lover into a marriage proposal falls short of its aim. At the conclusion, her thickening body literally numbers her remaining days at the office.

Lisa's isolation has been prefigured already by her leaving home to rent a single room elsewhere in the city and by her treatment at the office. The reader knows before Lisa appears in the text that she has been entirely unsuccessful in concealing her proletarian origins. Brecher, who is Kessel's mouthpiece, pronounces the public verdict:

> Sie sitzt inmitten ihrer Karriere wie ein . . . Kutscher in einer Mistkarre. Ihre zwei Gäule heißen Tüchtigkeit und Gesundheit. Wenn es verstanden würde, könnte man sagen, gesund wie eine Schande. . . . Frieske ist ein Proletarier . . . nicht politisch sondern vital. . . . Man merkt's an ihrer Art Kaffee zu trinken. Bei ihr zu Hause steht der Kaffeetopf bestimmt von früh bis abends auf dem Herd (40).

Kessel's insistence on certain cultural forms is obvious, even in this gross caricature which ultimately criticizes the traditional bourgeois work ethic as well. Lisa--whose first name is omitted everywhere in the text except in the passages devoted to her home life--no longer has a psychological or social home.

Irmgard Keun's Gilgi and Rudolph Braune's Erna Halbe are similar to Lisa Frieske. They are all young, attractive, and industrious, and they all come from working-class--or in Gilgi's case, petty bourgeois-- homes. Gilgi is endowed with a savings account and a room of her own when the novel begins, acquired through private typing jobs in the evenings after work and previous rent-free living at home. Erna Halbe has attended business typing and stenography courses after working days in the factory, but here the similarities end.

Gilgi's young life appears calculated to the extreme when we meet her, and she lives it seemingly without contradictions. Her hold on middle-class respectability is shaken when she learns that she is adopted and that her real mother is an impoverished seamstress. Still later she discovers she is the daughter of a very wealthy and otherwise childless socialite.

In contrast to Gilgi, Erna Halbe arrives in Berlin endowed with only an incorruptible working-class consciousness. Braune is fond of proclaiming it in formulas such as the following:

> Sie steht allein in dieser Stadt Berlin, ein Büromädchen, eine schlecht bezahlte Tippse, ein kleines Mädchen von nicht ganz neunzehn Jahren, aufgewachsen in einer strengen klaren Arbeiterwelt, in der nie persönlicher Ehrgeiz geweckt wurde, in der alles den gewaltigen Gesetzen und dem unumschränkten Willen der Klasse unterstellt werden mußte. Aber sie wird sich nicht unterkriegen lassen von dieser verwirrenden Welt (67).

Clearly, Braune's appellation of working class is anything but criticism. Erna may be tiny, she may be young, she may be just a "girl," but she nevertheless manages to conquer not only Berlin but the apathy of her coworkers. She starts a strike among the secretaries to protest the dismissal of Trude, a colleague who has failed to meet the quota. Trude suffers from fever and

constant nausea produced by her primitive attempts to
stop an unwanted pregnancy. The co-respondent in the
matter is a completely uninterested member of the
management at the office. The strike lasts only two
days, Trude dies, and Erna is fired, but she leaves with
good references (management's only concession). Braune's
highly unlikely heroine protagonist is social realism's
stereotype of the positive hero(ine).

Sexual Politics and Emancipation

     The interconnections between social and sexual poli-
tics are evident in all three of the novels discussed
here. What is unique about the women in many of the
Zeitromane of the Weimar period is "daß sie wissend, oft
kalkulierend (das) Risiko eingehen"[27]; however, like
their predecessors of the 19th century, they continue to
be society's sacrificial lambs. The Weimar woman may
knowingly use her attractiveness for the purpose of
exploiting her antagonist's weakness but she continues,
just like her earlier sisters, to pay the costs. Lisa
Frieske's comparison with Mucki Schöpps in the Kessel
novel is not only a matter of class, as the following
commentary between Brecher and Geist indicates:

     "Mucki ist ein Naturell, Frieske eine
     Naturalie", sagt Brecher, und Geist, der
     ewig Abhängige, fügt hinzu: "Frieske ist
     Blut und Leberwurst, Eisbein mit Sauerkohl
     sozusagen, Mucki dagegen ist . . ."

     Statt eines Wortes wirft Doktor Geist, in-
     dem er Mittelfinger und Daumen pikant auf-
     einandersetzt, eine Art Kuß durch den
     Raum, einen Kuß, der etwas Knallendes hat
     (40).

Understanding how Kessel uses the comparison between the
two women is crucial to understanding how he views
women's sexual and economic independence. Mucki fulfills
the office "girl's" dream (as expressed in Kracauer and
in Braune, 86) by marrying Geist after his promotion.
Lisa Frieske is expendable as soon as she becomes
pregnant. Mucki as "Naturell" and Frieske as "Naturalie"
ultimately means that Lisa pays dearly for the physical
expression of her love. Mucki, on the other hand, flirts
outrageously and meaninglessly with everyone in the
office, "ihrer schmetterlingshaften Art entsprechend.
Sie brauchte dieses Fluidum. . . . Dieser flirtende

110

Dauerstand hatte sich frühzeitig herausgebildet. Und so versucht jeder Kollege auf seine Art damit fertig zu werden" (122). Mucki is the quintessential coquette who remains unattainable until her legal possession in marriage. Success, such as it is, is hers in the novel.

This conclusion complements the hollowness of the few phrases in the novel which encourage women's independence. Gudula Öften describes the general situation in her diary:

> So seien die Männer alle. Erst ermutigen sie die Frauenwelt sich beruflich zu engagieren, förderten auch die Frauenemanzipation, wo sie könnten, aber als Mann schlechthin, als Privatmann, ließen sie, statt die Konsequenzen zu ziehen, die öffentliche protegierte Frau sitzen zugunsten des Gretchentyps (134).

Gudula is at best a naive spokeswoman for women's emancipation. Her distinction between the private and public, the personal and the political, is certainly one which radical feminists of the previous decades in Germany would criticize. And the juxtaposition of Gretchen with the modern woman attests only to the strength of the unspoken ideology which supports the traditional patriarchal family. Gretchen's simplicity and domesticity, coupled with her relationship to the dominant, egotistical male were not a threat to the domestic status quo. Yet, even if we can say Gretchen's love breaks the boundaries of conventional bourgeois standards, the irony of the comparison should be obvious to the Kessel reader, since her position is hardly very different from Lisa Frieske's.[28] The juxtaposition posed by Gudula is falsely antagonistic.

One might also question if the emancipated working woman really was the "öffentlich protegierte Frau," for women's paid work was viewed as a temporary phase by the fictional characters as well as by the society in which they lived as the Demobilization Decrees after World War I and the conservative, Catholic, and Nazi attacks on women's employment after 1929 attest.[29] Furthermore, there was little progress made with the creation of day care centers which would have allowed women to work outside the home or family allowances which would have helped the woman at home. Finally, the much vaunted sexual independence of the "modern woman" occurred at a time when contraceptives were not permitted public

111

display (Paragraph 175) and abortion was a criminal offense (Paragraph 218).[30] As early as 1976, Tim Mason commented, "It would be worth investigating the hypothesis that the growth in the employment of women wage earners and white collar workers between 1925 and 1929 was sufficiently sharp to activate the anti-feminist resentments which were so powerful during the subsequent years of economic crisis."[31]

These observations are consistent with Kessel's novel for he is compelled to discredit Gudula throughout the novel. Twice he implies she is lesbian (136, 262) but her real defeat comes when she spends the night with Brecher. The two enact a familiar scene of male dominance and female submission about which she writes later in her diary, "Ich hätte mich morden lassen" (456). Thus is Kessel's only critic of male prerogative silenced.

Irmgard Keun's protagonist, Gilgi, is a stranger to the rhetoric of the women's movement but she is conscious of the many facets of sexual politics at the workplace. She knows that her youth, her attractiveness, her professionalism, and her unmistakable flirtation are indispensable ingredients for her success as a secretary along with her business skills. Gilgi's appraisal of one of her competitors indicates why she and not the competitor is the one who has had success:

> Die hat ja die gleiche Chance gehabt. So?
> Hat sie? Mit dem krunkligen, alten Gesicht, der latschigen Haltung, mit den matten blicklosen Augen und den häßlichen Kleidern??? Wer nimmt die denn noch? (72)

Gilgi's genteel air of prosperity and professionalism is also crucial to her success, along with her understated but unmistakable flirtation:

> Daß sie ihre eigene Maschine mitbringen wird, hat sie über die anderen Bewerberinnen siegen lassen. Vielleicht auch, daß sie ein bißchen verheißungsvoll mit den Augen gekudert hat. So niedlich Von-unten-nach-oben Blicke wirken bei Männern über fünfzig fast immer. Ferner ist's gut, an Beschützerinstinkte zu appellieren, im richtigen Augenblick solides Bewußtsein durch kleidsame Hilflosigkeit zu ersetzen. Man muß das alles verstehen. Gilgi

versteht es. Auf die Arbeitgeber ist man
nun mal angewiesen, und ganz ohne Mätzchen
ist ihnen nicht beizukommen. Können allein
entscheidet nicht, Mätzchen allein entscheiden nicht--beides zusammen entscheidet meistens (71).

Gilgi's calculated appraisal of the situation expresses
both sides of the dialectic for the Weimar woman. Clearly, she is more independent than her 19th century sister
but "auf die Arbeitgeber ist nun mal angewiesen" and exploitation, though certainly more diffuse, nevertheless
exists. Jobs are awarded on the basis of ability and
appearance; the job seeker thus behaves with her sexual
marketability in mind, yet she is still vulnerable since
she is dependent on the whims of her employer.

Female Subjectivity

The foregoing analysis of the female white-collar
worker has concentrated on her exploitation. To understand fully, however, the force of the dialectic, we
must also understand the source of her strength. The
middle-class in Germany failed to ally with the left
historically, among other reasons because the left
viewed the situation simply as a problem of false consciousness, rather than as an expression of subjective
and nonsynchronous contradictions as well. The difference between the portrayal of female subjectivity in
Erna Halbe and Gilgi Korn illustrates this distinction.

Rudolph Braune defines Erna's sense of solidarity
with the working class as her strength. Her ideological
convictions are unshakeable throughout the novel, as the
following excerpts from a conversation with an older,
more sophisticated friend reveal:

Meine Wünsche sind bescheidener als eure,
ich weiß ungefähr was man erwarten darf.
Ich bin losgefahren, weil Berlin mich
gelockt hat. . . . Ich dachte, hier mehr
Aussichten zu haben.

. . . Ihr seid mir in vielen Dingen vor-
aus, ihr wißt mehr, und habt keine
Illusionen, aber manche von euch tun mir
trotzdem leid.

. . . Ich wunsche mir nicht zu viel und
werde nie vergessen, daß es Tausenden noch
dreckiger geht als mir. Und wenn ich hier
ausrutsche, fahre ich wieder nach Hause
(102).

Erna's comments are prompted by her unwillingness to
sacrifice her belief that sexual relationships should be
motivated by love. These are the modest wishes to which
she refers. Although Braune has taken care to portray
Erna as a fearless strike leader, the resignation which
sounds in her words here belies the narrative. She
sounds so accepting of the status quo, we could hardly
imagine a cry for revolution. Erna wears her consciousness, like armor ("sie weiß . . . was man erwarten
darf"). She is completely impervious to the lure of
material luxuries which are attainable here through the
sexual liaisons because of her identification with the
"clear, harsh, working-class world" Braune has described
previously. Erna's colleagues are unwilling to give up
their middle-class dreams, a fact which makes them vulnerable to sexual exploitation which is present whether
they "profit" from it or not. Erna's idea of returning
home is an idealization of the proletarian family,
although we know that her country home is an
impoverished colony of over-populated "Dreckbarracken"
(101) and shot-gun marriages. Erna's view of her home as
a haven of working-class goodness in a heartless world
(32) is undoubtedly synonymous with Braune's, but the
more discriminating reader recognizes that Erna allies
herself with the forces of conservative patriarchy as
well because of the tacit assumptions about her life as
wife and mother there.

Erna's modest wishes are seemingly synonymous with
her needs. Their proper antagonist appears to be, perhaps unintentionally, the city itself. This is clear
early in the novel:

Eine rauschende und doch stille, eine
gleichmäßige Flut geht durch die Straßen.
Erna ist mitten drin. Ihr Herz klopft
heftig. Sie kennt nun schon ungefähr die
Richtung. Aufmerksam betrachtet sie alles,
überall sind neue Dinge, die ihr fremd
waren. Junge Mädchen laufen eilig dahin
mit kunstvoll gemalten Gesichtern unter
schiefen, schicken Hüten. Sie treffen sich
mit den jungen Männern dieser Stadt, sie
verschwinden in Cafés, aus den Cafés tönt

114

Tanzmusik, sie fahren mit den Autobussen,
ihre knappen geschmackvollen Frühjahrs-
kleider leuchten im Gewühl auf. Erna hat
sich noch nie sonderlich um ihre Kleider
gekümmert, sie ist nicht eitel und schon
gar nicht anspruchsvoll, an diesem einen
Tag aber beginnt sich plötzlich ihre
kleine Welt zu ändern. Sie wünscht etwas
anderes anzuziehen (66).

The city is almost atomized here, its enticements are
clearly the luxury items of consumption and beauty of
the young people who use them. Erna is portrayed, on the
one hand, as being "mitten drin" but she is also an
observer, a newcomer. This phenomenon allows Braune to
describe the scene with words which negate what we are
meant to understand as its charm for Erna. The faces are
"kunstvoll gemalt," the hats are "schief," the dresses
are a "Gewühl" of material. Braune implies that nothing
is simple, straight, or honest.

Braune seems to equate middle-class consciousness
throughout with the desire for luxuries which are
slightly degenerate. Despite the growing sophistication
of marketing skills during the Weimar Republic--it is no
accident that the setting for one of the novels is a
Propagandaabteilung--Braune believes that wishes should
easily be separable from needs. Erna, as a result of the
urban street scene described above, succumbs to the
dictates of its needs and stays up all night in order to
remodel her coat. This is her only concession to bourgeois high fashion.

Erna's attention to fashion is similar here to that
of the other secretaries discussed: Gudula wears one
stylish article of clothing each day, however small;
Lisa Frieske consults Gudula before she buys anything;
Gilgi sews to defray expenses; Mucki, the model of high
fashion, is constantly and seriously in debt. The sus-
ceptibility to middle-class tastes has a dual source:
the split consciousness of an alienated white-collar
work force caught between proletarian working conditions
and middle-class aspirations, and the belief in women's
paid labor as temporary, terminated by attraction of a
providential mate. Here we see both the synchronous and
nonsynchronous contradictions at work.

Erna alone never loses sight of the ideological
totality, i.e., the objective situation and its contradictions for the individual. We know that she has come

to Berlin because it fascinates her but, since we never
see her succumb to its charms, we must take her words on
faith. Her argumentation is always logical; she experiences no contradictions. When one has been educated
to the interests of the class, Braune seems to say,
bourgeois social forms will wither away.

When we compare Gilgi's character with Erna's, we
begin to understand from another perspective why historically the new middle class did not join the left.
Keun's ability to understand her character's subjective
wishes and desires is, I think, simply a product of the
respect she has for her subject. Women are not, as in
Braune's novel, objects in the strategies of others, but
subjects in their own spheres. Gilgi's aspirations are
real, sometimes irrational, sometimes contradictory, but
always personalized. In the following passage, Gilgi is
described in the single room where she is sovereign:

> Sie bezahlt es, und es gehört ihr. Die
> Wände hat sie mit braunem Rupfen bespannen
> lassen. Die Möbel: Diwan, Schreibtisch,
> Schrank, Stuhl hat sie allmählich Stück
> für Stück angeschafft. Alles ist eigen
> erworbener Besitz. Die kleine Erika-
> Schreibmaschine und das Grammophon sind
> mit Überstunden verdient worden (19).

Here Gilgi is in control, it seems, just as Erna was.
She has created a modest escape hatch here through hard
and careful work. She knows what to expect from the city
and what she can take from it. Her sense of security,
however, also allows her to relax her guard, and the
passage continues in a curious mixture of pragmatism and
fantasy, competence and vulnerability:

> Sie zieht von neuem das Grammophon auf: es
> geht alles vorüber. . . . Hat man's nicht
> zu was gebracht? Man wird es noch weiter
> bringen. . . . Zwölfhundert Mark hat sie
> bis jetzt gespart. Noch ein Jahr weiter,
> und sie wird auf drei Monate nach Paris
> fahren, drei Monate nach London und drei
> Monate nach Granada. . . . Alles ist genau
> ausgerechnet und beschlossen. Wenn man
> drei Sprachen perfekt kann, ist man gegen
> Stellungslosigkeit gesichert. Vielleicht
> wird sie auch eines Tages überhaupt nicht
> mehr aufs Büro gehen. Sie hat noch andere
> Möglichkeiten. Hat ein Talent, Kleider zu

116

entwerfen und zu nähen wie bald keine. Wenn die kleine Dame Gilgi abends ausgeht, sehen ihr Männer und Frauen nach, und wenn sie erzählt, sie kauft bei Damm oder Gerstell - man würde ihr's vielleicht glauben. . . . Vielleicht wird sie später mal in Paris oder Berlin ein kleines Modeatelier aufmachen, vielleicht - vielleicht -, auch, sie ist noch jung, und außer Ehe, Filmschauspielerin und Schönheitskönigin zieht sie jede Existenzmöglichkeit in Betracht (19).

The monotony of Gilgi's daily life pales to insignificance here beside the power of her dreams. Bolstered by her concrete successes so far, Gilgi's fantasy has no boundaries. She mixes both realism and fantasy to such a degree that our impression is one of her naiveté rather than her competence: Gilgi's savings account is a source of pride and self-confidence, but her travel plans are grandiose; the learning of three languages perfekt would certainly be an admirable achievement, but there is no evidence in either fiction or non-fiction that anything protects an office worker from being fired; three months must seem like a long time in a foreign culture to the non-traveler, but it is hardly long enough to learn a new language thoroughly; finally, Gilgi may be an excellent seamstress but the knowing eye would not mistake the source of her creations. Gilgi's fantasy, however, soars; her possibilities for self-actualization are limitless.

It is precisely the daily monotony of Gilgi's existence which sets her mind and her semi-conscious free to dream.[33] Until these dreams and aspirations can be channeled, understood, and directed, all attempts to educate a consciousness perceived as false are in vain. Bloch's theoretical insights are evident: subjective aspirations may not be progressive or even liberating, yet they provide a subversive critique to daily reality. Gilgi's portrayal reaffirms the emotional impact of the dialectic. Consciously she believes in a Puritan work ethic and is aware only of the escape provided by her dreams. These psychological mechanisms whose source is embedded in her daily social reality make her all the more susceptible to revolt when it presents itself.

Within a matter of weeks after the passage quoted above, Gilgi has discarded work and independent life for an impossible love. The man is patronizing, patriarchal,

117

and sexist, but urbane, experienced, and many years her senior. Gilgi's revolt is individual, personal, and, as such, it must fail. Her determination not to burden him isolates her even more and ultimately absolves him of all responsibilities. At the conclusion, she is almost destitute and three months pregnant, on her way to her friend Olga in Berlin. The situation demonstrates the impossibility of sexual, and thus social, independence for women in a society where women were at a material disadvantage and where a double standard dominated. If Braune's protagonist experiences no contradictions, Keun's protagonist exposes them and Gilgi, unlike Erna, cannot return home. Although Keun may appear to mirror contradictions shamelessly,[34] learning is indeed a slow process.

Despite Gilgi's naiveté and misfortune, Keun does not treat her only as a victim. Perhaps more important, Gilgi rejects the prevailing male models of sexual independence: objectification, infidelity, irresponsibility. True, Gilgi uses what she can but consistently refuses the sexual exploitation inherent in a relationship of convenience. In addition, Keun has introduced her to sources of strength which derive from the female's experience of the underside of life in Western society where the white male has been the historical subject. A proletarian friend who loves and hates her husband at the same time for his inability to find employment and his responsibility for her third pregnancy states the objective side of the problem: "Schaff dir Selbständigkeit und Unabhängigkeit - dann kannst du einen Mann lieben und dir dir Liebe erhalten" (179). The subjective source of strength is expressed in the words of Gilgi's beautiful, free-spirited, and apparently emancipated friend, Olga:

> "Ich habe doch Männer als solche wirklich gern - aber komisch ist's und mißtrauisch macht's, daß man keine wirkliche Freundschaft von Männern untereinander mehr findet, kein ehrliches selbstverständliches Zusammenhalten, keine unbedingte Solidarität vor allem. Gibt nur noch 'Kollegen' oder 'Parteigenossen' - herzlich wenig das. . . . Ist dir nicht auch schon aufgefallen, Gilgi - daß wir in einer Zeit leben, wo's mehr wirklich Solidarität unter Frauen gibt als unter Männern? Das macht uns überlegen" (171-72).

118

I interpret Olga's remarks not only about the absence of male friendship but also of male solidarity as an implied critique of the rationalization of life during this period. Olga defines men in their work lives and through their Party memberships, where they too function to a great extent as objects in the grandiose strategies of others. Olga hints also that females, at a point of even greater discrimination and oppression, by virtue of their completely outside stance, have succeeded in creating an autonomous sphere of communication, a primäre Öffentlichkeit.[35] Despite the fact that Olga's point of comparison is male, her sentiments already transcend the male model. Here we begin to see the creation of the preconditions for an autonomous women's subculture and public sphere. Her words are all the more remarkable given the state of disarray in which the women's movement found itself by this time, with the brief exception of the Communist-led campaign against Paragraph 218 in the late 1920s.[36]

Conclusion

The analysis of female characters in these novels reveals a contradictory reality for women during the Weimar Republic. The flapper is indeed a reality but she is not as modern and independent as the conventional perception of her would have us expect. All three novels show women's lives as somewhat more independent, yet in all they are the victim of class and sexual exploitation to a greater or a lesser degree. The particular ways in which sexual and social politics intersect for the white-collar female worker are evident in the content of all three novels: youth and beauty help secure the job, along with the appropriation of middle-class cultural norms, both of which are most often expressed in the attention to fashion. Sexual liaisons are expected in exchange for the right to work, although they appear more subtle in Kessel. Sexual independence comes at a price which denies both freedom and equality. Kessel further sabotages his portrayal of women by imbedding it in anti-feminist rhetoric and Braune subsumes his vision of female emancipation under the banner of class struggle which ignores the complicated issues of sexual and family politics. Keun's portrayal is significantly different.

Most importantly, Gilgi rejects both the Father and the Husband, and the patriarchal authority which they represent. Keun's explicit narrative certainly limits

119

Gilgi's choices; however, the implicit message is confirmed by the scenes with Olga, who is otherwise a
gratuitous addition to the plot. In addition, Keun's
recognition of female subjectivity and female desire
aids us in understanding the history of female progress
as a group. Keun's comprehension of the female subject
avoids a portrayal of the Berufstätige merely as victim,
although she is also that. By giving us a more complicated picture, Keun supplies some mechanism for
understanding the dialectic of historical progress. This
novel alone illustrates the real break with tradition,
representative of the period precisely in its rarity.

If we really want to discover what female daily
life, female subjectivity, and female possibilities were
like during the period, the author's gender may be an
overriding factor. Based on my reading thus far, I would
cautiously contend that female writers are more likely
to give us answers, but certainly not the same ones as
Keun's in many cases. Keun is admittedly the perfect
foil and, although there are other women writers like
her, they are, relatively speaking, few and far between.
Even those who wrote the bestsellers of the period,
those whom the passage of time cannot conceal, are
outnumbered by the men one hundred to one.[37] We are
already familiar with the few women who will be preserved for posterity by the current standards of literary canonization, but there are so many other female
writers whose single volumes are still waiting to
provide us with a re-vision of the period. The choice of
novels in this paper simply reflects the character and
the quality of what is there and gives an indication of
what we might find if we look further.

Notes

[1] Thilo Koch, Die goldenen zwanziger Jahre, unter
Mitarbeit von Juergen Suess (Frankfurt/M: Akademischer
Verlagsgesellschaft, 1970).

[2] The most dramatic change was the falling birthrate
and the emergence of the small family in this generation. See Tim Mason, "Women in Germany 1925-1940: Family, Welfare and Work," Pt. I, History Workshop no. 1
(Spring 1976), pp. 82-83. Renate Bridenthal and Claudia
Koonz also mention the falling birthrate in "Beyond
Kinder, Küche, Kirche: Weimar Women in Politics and
Work," in Liberating Women's History, ed. Berenice Car-
roll (Urbana, IL: University of Illinois Press, 1976),

p. 45. This article is reprinted, with few changes, in _When Biology Became Destiny: Women in Weimar and Nazi Germany_, ed. Renate Bridenthal, Atina Grossmann, and Marion Kaplan (New York: Monthly Review Press, 1984), pp. 33-65.

[3] In addition to the titles in note 2, there are also: Bridenthal, "Beyond Kinder, Küche, Kirche: Weimar Women at Work," _Central European History_ 6 (1973), pp. 149-69; Bridenthal, "Something Old, Something New: Women between Two World Wars," in _Becoming Visible: Women in European History_, ed. Bridenthal and Koonz (Boston: Houghton Mifflin, 1977), pp. 424-44.

[4] See for example, Kurt Sontheimer, _Anti-demokratisches Denken in der Weimarer Republik: Die politischen Ideen des deutschen Nationalismus zwischen 1918 und 1933_ (Munich: Nymphenburg, 1962); Klemens von Klemperer, _Germany: New Conservatism_ (Princeton, NJ: Princeton University Press, 1969); Walter Struve, _Elites against Democracy: Leadership Ideal in Bourgeois Political Thought in Germany 1880-1933_ (Princeton, NJ: Princeton University Press, 1973).

[5] _Schicksal einer Weltstadt_ (Munich and Berlin: Biederstein, 1958), pp. 540-41.

[6] Stephan Zweig, _Die Welt von Gestern_ (Stockholm: Bermann-Fischer, 1944), p. 74.

[7] Bridenthal and Koonz, "Beyond Kinder . . . ," p. 310.

[8] Bridenthal and Koonz, "Beyond Kinder . . . ," p. 312.

[9] For information on changes in women's work and the family, see Annemarie Tröger, "Die Dolchstoßlegende der Linken: Frauen haben Hitler an die Macht gebracht," in _Frauen und Wissenschaft: Beiträge zur Berliner Sommeruniversität für Frauen Juli 1976_ (Berlin: Courage, 1976), pp. 324-55; Gisela Böck and Barbara Duden, "Arbeit aus Liebe — Liebe aus Arbeit," in _Frauen und Wissenschaft_, pp. 118-99.

[10] Bridenthal and Koonz, "Beyond Kinder . . . ," p. 313.

[11] Bridenthal and Koonz, "Beyond Kinder . . . ," p. 315.

[12] My statement is an impression left by the research and should be tested statistically. Such a phenomenon may result from the fact that so few of the female writers, relatively speaking, are available to us. Several exceptions (of those who wrote Zeitromane) are: Vicki Baum, Marieluise Fleißer, Gabriele Tergit, Maria Gleit, Christa Brück, Hilde Kraus, Anna Seghers, Irmgard Keun, and Hanna Forster's Die Privatsekretärin (1916), which I would like very much to locate. Content considerations, their previous use in another paper of mine, and the attempt to provide a representative sample allow me to use only Irmgard Keun here.

[13] "Introduction," When Biology Became Destiny, ed. Bridenthal, et al., p. 13.

[14] Walter Struve, "Hans Zehrer as a Neoconservative Elite Theorist," American Historical Review 50 (1965), p. 1038. His source is Theodor Geiger Soziale Schichtung des deutschen Volkes (Stuttgart: 1932), pp. 72-73.

[15] Hermann Lebovics, Social Conservatism and the Middle Classes in Germany, 1914-1933 (Princeton: Princeton University Press, 1969), p. 31 ff.

[16] Erbschaft dieser Zeit (Frankfurt/M.: Suhrkamp, 1962), p. 105.

[17] Bloch, p. 108-109.

[18] See Anson Rabinbach's "Unclaimed Heritage: Ernst Bloch's Heritage of Our Times and the Theory of Fascism," New German Critique (Spring 1977), pp. 5-21, for an excellent discussion of Bloch's ideas.

[19] The cited edition is Gilgi, eine von uns (Düsseldorf: Droste Verlag, 1955).

[20] Keun's birthdate is variously given as 1905 and 1910 in different sources.

[21] There are various accounts of German feminism: Richard Evans, The Feminist Movement in Germany: 1894-1933 (London & Beverly Hills, CA: Sage, 1976) is an account of the Bund Deutscher Frauenvereine, its failure and that of German liberalism; Barbara Greven-Aschoff, Die bürgerliche Frauenbewegung in Deutschland 1894-1933 (Göttingen: Vandenhoeck & Ruprecht, 1981); Marielouise Janssen-Jurreit, Sexismus: Über die Abtreibung der Frauenfrage (Munich: Hanser, 1976); Jean H. Quataert,

Reluctant Feminists in German Social Democracy, 1885-1917 (Princeton, NJ: Princeton University Press, 1979); Werner Thönnessen, Frauenemanzipation: Politik und Literatur der deutschen Sozialdemokratie zur Frauenbewegung 1863-1933 (Frankfurt/M: Europäische Verlagsanstalt, 1969).

22 The cited edition: Berlin and Frankfurt/M: Suhrkamp, 1952.

23 The cited edition: Frankfurt/M: Societätsverlag, 1930.

24 Siegfried Kracauer, Die Angestellten in Schriften I (Frankfurt/M: Suhrkamp, 1971), pp. 214-15.

25 Kracauer, p. 231.

26 Bridenthal and Koonz, "Beyond Kinder . . . ," p. 316. They are speaking primarily of the saleswoman rather than the secretary. Kracauer quotes the Afa-Bundezeitung of February 1929 which says that "auffallende körperliche Mängel . . . machen den . . . sozial Schwachen vorzeitig zum unfreiwilligen Arbeitsinvaliden (222).

27 Unpublished manuscript by Helene Szépe, "Zur Diskussion der 'neuen Frau' im Zeitroman 1919-1933," p. 3. Szépe, however, believes that women "als bloße Opfer der verderbten Gesellschaft" ceased to exist after the 19th century.

28 Andreas Huyssen, "Das leidende Weib in der dramatischen Literatur vom Empfindsamkeit und Sturm und Drang," Monatshefte 69 (1977), pp. 159-73, has a reinterpretation of the Gretchen figure along these lines.

29 Mason, p. 93.

30 See Atina Grossmann, "Abortion and Economic Crisis: The 1931 Campaign against Paragraph 218 in Germany," New German Critique (Spring 1978), pp. 119-37; also available in When Biology Became Destiny, pp. 66-86.

31 Mason, pp. 81-82.

32 Christopher Lasch's phrase in Haven in a Heartless World: The Family Besieged (New York: Basic, 1977). He must be read critically.

[33] For the following discussion I am indebted to Oskar Negt and Inge Negt and the New German Critique study group during the winter of 1978-79. See also Negt and Alexander Kluge, Öffentlichkeit und Erfahrung: Zur Organisationsanalyse von bürgerlicher und proletarischer Öffentlichkeit (Frankfurt/M: Suhrkamp, 1972) and Ulrike Prokop, Weiblicher Lebenszusammenhang: Von der Beschränktheit der Strategien und der Unangemessenheit der Wünsche (Frankfurt/M: Suhrkamp, 1976).

[34] Bertolt Brecht's term in Gesammelte Werke 20 (Frankfurt/M: Suhrkamp, 1967), p. 166.

[35] Oskar Negt's term, "Wallraffs Untersuchungsarbeit in Bereichen der 'unterschlagenen Wirklichkeit,'" in Keine Demokratie ohne Sozialismus (Frankfurt/M: Suhrkamp, 1977), p. 318.

[36] The earlier generation of radical feminists had been largely inactive after the failure of pacifism. The socialist women's movement remained close to the Socialist and Communist Parties, the limitations of which Atina Grossmann has pointed out (note 30). The bourgeois women's movement, with its ideal of woman as the moral guide, "meandered through the early twentieth century with an ideological profile so low as to bring its feminist credentials into question" (Renate Bridenthal, "'Professional Housewives': Stepsisters of the Women's Movement," in When Biology Became Destiny, p. 154.

[37] Based on the information compiled by Donald Ray Richards, The German Bestseller in the 20th Century: A Complete Bibliography and Analysis: 1915-1940 (Berne: Lange, 1968).

124

From the Crown to the Hammer and Sickle:
The Life and Works of Austrian Interwar Writer
Hermynia zur Mühlen

Lynda J. King

On her sixtieth birthday in 1943, Hermynia zur
Mühlen was honored by a London B.B.C. broadcast, a
P.E.N. Club gathering, and several articles in emigré
periodicals for her socially critical writing and for
her courageous personal antifascist stance.[1] Reviewing a
zur Mühlen book a short time later, one critic predicted
that in postfascist Austria this book could become a
standard for an entire generation, and in 1948 well-
known Communist literary figure Eva Priester called zur
Mühlen "the best known progressive woman author writing
in the German language.[2]

But despite such promising opinions and the re-
publication from 1945 to 1950 of several zur Mühlen
works of the interwar and exile periods, the Austrian-
born writer's name soon disappeared from public view.
Recently, however, more and more readers have been re-
discovering zur Mühlen's writings. This interest has
been so great that one librarian at the Deutsche Bib-
liothek was prompted to call her the new Dauerbrenner,
and she has become so respectable in the scholarly world
that a Magisterarbeit about her was accepted in 1986 at
the University of Vienna. Both the disappearance and
reappearance of zur Mühlen's works are tied intimately
to cultural politics and scholarly trends, as well as to
audience tastes, making the circumstances surrounding
her works nearly as interesting as the works themselves.

Much of the blame for the disappearance of her works
can be placed on conservative cultural politicians and
critics who established a restaurative Traditionalismus
as the dominant trend on the Austrian cultural scene
after 1950.[3] Writers of conventional fiction in a
conservative Austrian tradition (Max Mell, Karl Heinrich
Waggerl, or Josef Weinheber) were supported by influential men of letters like Hans Pertner and Rudolf Henz,
but also by critics like Friedrich Torberg and Hans

125

Weigel. These same men made it difficult for writers such as zur Mühlen, Jura Soyfer, or Daniel Spitzer to be recognized or published. In zur Mühlen's case there were two reasons for this. On the one hand her works represented a leftist ideology the conservatives opposed. In addition, the books spotlighted certain issues of the interwar period which the men did not regard as the correct subject of literature, or which they did not wish to be forced to confront.[4]

Throughout her career Hermynia zur Mühlen understood herself as a socialist writer. She always considered literature primarily as an instrument for revealing the injustices of existing capitalist society and for lobbying to replace it with a new order based on socialist principles. However, exactly how she proposed to achieve these goals through her literary works did change from her earliest writings to her later works.

In the early 1920s she was closely aligned with the K.P.D. (Kommunistische Partei Deutschlands), and her works were correspondingly radical in their demands. She joined the K.P.D. in 1919 and during the early-to-mid 1920s wrote the stories and novels she would later label propagandistic because of their Party-line politics.[5] Zur Mühlen's proletarian-revolutionary fairly tales, to be discussed below, were her contribution to the larger search by Communists for literary forms suited to the Party's goal of promoting world revolution. By 1927 her relationship with the Party had eroded, a fact underscored by an attack on zur Mühlen in that year by K.P.D. literary leader Johannes R. Becher, who accused her of writing texts which did not adhere to the Party's precepts.[6] This attack demonstrates that she was embroiled in the increasingly acrimonious arguments among members of different leftist factions about correct literary form and content and about the Party's role in setting literary policy.[7]

Zur Mühlen was not accused of conducting formal experiments, as writers like Brecht were, but rather of being too independent. A review defending how she wrote her 1929 autobiography, Ende und Anfang, discloses how much quality was opposed by some Party leaders. The review was written by Henri Guilbeaux for Die Weltbühne, a left-intellectual journal opposed to the Party's rigid policies.[8] Guilbeaux wrote:

Sie hat nichts gemein mit kommunistischen
Funktionären, die mechanisch und bureau-
kratisch ihre tägliche - achtstündige -
Pflicht erfüllen . . . so ist sie doch von
einer großen geistigen Unabhängigkeit. . . . Daher wird sie auch nicht sehr
von Leuten geliebt, die vielleicht zuerst
unbeträchtliche Chansonniers oder patrio-
tische und religiöse Reimschmiede waren
und später Revuen inszenierten, um dann in
unintelligenter Weise diejenigen zu kriti-
sieren, die keine Demagogen sind. Für
diese Herren zählt sie nicht. . . . Sie
betet keinen Katechismus blind nach. Sie
ist also nicht interessant.

Zur Mühlen's works of the late 1920s and early 1930s
expressed her personal observations of the world, as
well as a more personal vision of social and political
problems and their solutions. But she still affirmed
that individualistic solutions did not work and never
gave up the principle of solidarity. In fact, it was
probably this principle which forced her to break with
the K.P.D. Although no direct evidence exists, it is
probable that she left the Party because she thought
their denunciation of sympathizers who were unwilling to
submit unqualifiedly to Party doctrine and discipline
could only undermine the solidarity that was needed to
combat the growing threat of National Socialism.

Zur Mühlen was, then, part of the political left in
the interwar period, but this position was not the only
factor which made her distasteful to post-World War II
conservatives. A further reason was that many of her
works revolve around women and their role in pre-World
War II society. In postwar Austria and Germany, so-
called "women's literature" was not highly valued by
those in control of the literary scene.

Before joining the K.P.D. zur Mühlen did not belong
to a women's movement, and there is no evidence that she
later was identified with any women's group, nor that
she ever used any term equivalent to feminist to
describe herself. First and foremost she was dedicated
to the goals and principles of the socialist movement as
she understood them. But one socialist principle stood
high on her list of priorities: Women's position in
society had to be changed. Her writing was a tool for
increasing public awareness of the issues vital to
women. As will be shown below, her novels consistently

spotlighted the limitations women faced in existing society and their struggle to change their own lives and the face of society. The author also used literary works to suggest possible new roles for women in a society restructured along the lines of her socialist beliefs.

As zur Mühlen's idea of socialism evolved during the course of her life, so too did her stance on and portrayal of women's concerns. Early in her career her position on the interrelationship of socialism and women's issues echoed the position of the K.P.D., i.e., that women had to subordinate their needs to the greater cause of bringing about the socialist world revolution. After capitalist society had been eliminated, women's problems would be solved because their causes would no longer exist in the new order.[9]

In her earlier works centering on female characters, for example in the 1922 novel Der Tempel (see Bibliography), zur Mühlen expressed no doubts that before the inevitable revolution women would begin their fulfillment by working within Party structures. Later, pessimism crept into her writing as she becamse skeptical that emancipation could be gained in this way. The personal note in her feminism increased, but again she did not abandon the principle of group action, certain that only through systemic change could true emancipation be achieved.

In the past five years zur Mühlen's works have been "rediscovered." Scholars have been attracted to zur Mühlen's interwar writings in the wake of the shift toward examining literature in relationship to an historical context and exploring the interaction of textual and extra-textual elements intersecting in the literary work. The scholarly world has also recognized that women's participation in German literary history, and indeed in German life, was larger and more significant than had been assumed in the past.

My readers have perhaps already recognized another reason for the renewed interest in zur Mühlen: her own life's story. Her life up to joining the K.P.D. after World War I is the subject of her engrossing memoirs, Ende and Anfang. Born in Vienna in 1883, the future author was christened Hermine Isabella Marie Foilliot de Crenneville-Poutet, a name befitting the offspring of one of Austria-Hungary's highest aristocratic families. From her somewhat unorthodox family zur Mühlen learned lessons she continued to value later, like an appreciation for beauty and certain traditions, and a sense of justice. But her upbringing also instilled in her some negative qualities which she had to fight against consciously later, like haughtiness and a disdain for practicality. Two other qualities rooted in her upbringing, stubborn individualism and independence, got her (like her main characters) into trouble with authority figures more than once. But neither the author nor her characters ever renounced these qualities for long.

Crucial in forming her convictions about the injustices in society, particularly in relation to women's role, were zur Mühlen's late teens and twenties. As a young female aristocrat she was expected to marry another aristocrat and settle down to a round of tennis matches and charity functions, interrupted only by the birth of children. This independently-minded woman did not want to settle for such a future and decided to seek a fulfilling career outside the family, first by training as a teacher, then by taking an apprenticeship in a bookbinder's shop. Problems arose, including the opposition of her parents, and she eventually gave up. Despite her intentions, she was completely unprepared to accept life in the classroom or in a shop, both of which she admits she found tedious.

So she chose a different avenue out of her world by marrying Baron Victor zur Mühlen in 1908. This marriage was another attempt at independence since it upset her Austrian Catholic family almost as much as a career would have. Victor lived in the "wilderness" of the Baltic region; he was a German and a protestant; and he was only a baron, meaning a step down on the aristocratic ladder for the young countess. Baroness zur Mühlen discovered she had made a mistake by marrying Victor, but not for the reasons her family had imagined.

Victor was one of the colony of German landowners in the Baltics who for centuries had exploited native laborers on their lands. As his wife, zur Mühlen came face to face with abject suffering when she witnessed the conditions under which his laborers had to live. Outraged, she fought long verbal battles with Victor over the inhumane treatment of the farm workers. Also while living in the area, she learned that a revolutionary movement was growing in Russia. Although she did not make contact with revolutionaries, she began vaguely to comprehend the need for revolutionary change.

On the farm she tried to help allievate the workers' sufferings but was largely unsuccessful. From the perspective of the 1920s when writing her memoirs, zur Mühlen judged that these attempts had been doomed to failure. She was only one individual treating the symptoms of a disease whose cause lay in the social structure itself. But in the Baltics in 1910 or 1911 (she does not make the dates clear), she had not yet understood that she could take part in a mass movement to change society. Because of her lack of success, this attempt to do something worthwhile with her life by helping the workers ended the same way her venture into the work world had: She just stopped caring. Isolated already from the rest of the German community for her iconoclastic views and for her failure to fulfill her function as a wife by having children, zur Mühlen withdrew into her home. An illness eventually necessitated a trip to Davos, Switzerland, and she left Victor's home around 1914, never to return.

Once in Switzerland she cured her illness and her apathy. Zur Mühlen reassessed her marriage and decided to divorce Victor. She wrote in the memoirs that she never disliked Victor, but that she could not live in the repressive environment of his farm. In Switzerland she was also exposed to the ideas of exiled revolutionaries and reassessed her convictions about the state of European society. When she decided to return to her Austrian home during the hostilities of World War I, her eyes were opened to the realities of wartime. She had reentered the world after her period of withdrawal and had learned lessons which prepared her to accept a basic change in her life. When she heard about the Russian revolution, she decided to join in the Bolshevist movement, having realized that only through collective effort could the wrongs she had observed be righted. Once the First World War was over, she renounced her earlier life, moved to Germany, and joined the K.P.D.

Since the memoirs stop at this juncture, an outline of zur Mühlen's life for the period after 1919 has to be pieced together from scattered sources. Some time in the early 1920s she married Stefan Klein, a Czechoslovakian translator, and they lived in Frankfurt. Zur Mühlen (she retained this name) was forced to work constantly, for one reason because she was without the financial resources of her family. Her productivity was astounding, for she often translated several novels and stories (from English, French, and/or Russian) per year along with writing many articles and stories of her own, not to mention completing her longer works.

During the early twenties, her work was completely dedicated to the K.P.D. She was quickly recognized for translations of leftist writings, especially of Upton Sinclair's works, and soon her own works also began to attract attention as she became a regular contributor to Communist and leftist periodicals. Her novels and story collections were printed by several leftist publishing houses, most notably by Malik. Her dedication to the Party also earned her a police file, for, like Johannes R. Becher and other communist literary figures, zur Mühlen was the target of official persecution. According to police documents she was placed under police surveillance in 1921 not only because she was a vocal member of the K.P.D., but also for being so radical as to live with Klein without being married to him. In 1924 charges of literary high treason were brought against the story Schupomann Karl Müller. The charges were eventually dropped, but a memorandum in zur Mühlen's file warned that the story was dangerous because its author so effectively used literary weapons to motivate readers to direct political action.[10]

Zur Mühlen earned fame in the twenties through her proletarian-revolutionary fairy tales, which combined social criticism, fantasy, and a moral in keeping with Communist Party teachings. Within the K.P.D. literary strategy, zur Mühlen's tales were designed to awaken class consciousness in young readers, while heightening identification with the Party and dramatizing working-class solidarity. Zur Mühlen's contribution to German socialist children's literature was recognized as early as 1962 in the German Democratic Republic, and her stories are mentioned in all subsequent studies of this topic along with those of Berta Lask and Alex Wedding. An Austrian scholar recently labeled zur Mühlen's fairy tales "miniature works of art," which "were among the best and most original of the proletarian-revolutionary literature of the twenties."[11]

With the National Socialist takeover in 1933, zur Mühlen was forced into exile, fleeing first to Vienna, then Prague, and finally to England. In late 1933 she was embroiled in another controversy, this time surrounding the anti-Nazi journal, Die Sammlung (1933/34-1934/35), edited by Klaus Mann. Mann had solicited contributions from several leading writers, including his father. When officials from the ministry in charge of literature in the newly founded Third Reich discovered the articles, they pressured the writers through their publishers to proclaim publicly their regrets at having had their work published in such an "anti-German" journal. Wieland Herzfelde, no friend of Thomas Mann's, contended in his Prague-based exile journal, Neue Deutsche Blätter, that the elder Mann had capitulated to this pressure. As a counterexample he cited zur Mühlen. She had not published in Sammlung, but she had been pressured by one of her German publishers, Engelhorn, to renounce her earlier K.P.D.-influenced writings. She refused in an eloquent letter which Herzfelde printed under the rubric "Briefe, die den Weg beleuchten," noting that zur Mühlen's precarious finances made her stand even more courageous.[12]

During her remaining exile years, zur Mühlen published several novels (some originally in English), contributed to exile periodicals, wrote radio plays, and continued to translate, managing just to keep her head above water financially. After World War II zur Mühlen did not return to Austria or Germany, probably not only because of her ill health, but also because of her disappointment over the negative reception of her works in the German-speaking countries. Hermynia zur Mühlen died near London on 19 March 1951.

As noted above, zur Mühlen's career entered a new phase after she turned away from the K.P.D. From 1932 to 1935 she penned a series of largely autobiographical novels set against the historical backdrop of the first third of the twentieth century. Zur Mühlen wrote them with two goals in mind. Each proffers a sensitive and discerning vision of the challenges, possibilities, and goals of women's emancipation during that time. Each is also a political novel, what is sometimes called a Tendenzroman. Since zur Mühlen believed that personal emancipation was ultimately a political issue, the process of emancipation within a personal, domestic environment is always blended with issues of party politics even in the novels of this period.

One of the novels, Reise durch ein Leben (1933), will serve here as a basis for understanding the series and as an introduction to zur Mühlen's oeuvre. Like all of her novels, Reise deals with women's lives in and outside the home; in this case the main character moves among three separate environments. The first two are the domestic settings in which most women lived their lives:

the parental-dominated family and the husband-dominated family. The third environment is that of a political movement, thus a public one. Each setting has its own power structure and set of conventions which erect barriers designed to limit women to pre-established behavior patterns.

Like most of her other novels, Reise is written in the mode of the nineteenth-century realistic novel. The thrust in the novels as in all of her writing is on presenting an unambiguous content in a manner accessible to a large reading public. As far as narrative structure is concerned, the narrator generally remains hidden behind the main character, Erika. That is, most events are transmitted to readers from her point of view, and her thoughts and emotions are almost always at the fore. This pattern is broken only occasionally by the narrator's commentary on her actions or motivations. These comments are few because the author is intended to stimulate readers to consider and think about Erika's actions, not dictate to them the correct response.

Certain characteristics of Erika's personality interact with conditions in her three environments to affect the quality of her sojourns in each. Open, curious, and intelligent, she possesses a streak of independence which allows her to recognize the shortcomings of each setting. But openly expressing what she has recognized makes her a social outsider, which in turn stimulates an intense need for security and belonging. The conflict between her independent nature and the longing for security reduces her ability to make decisions to actively change her life. Having had no training, guidance, or role models in her youth that could have suggested viable alternative lifestyles, Erika founders, unable to make the final break from the roles she is expected to play. Most often she remains passive, submitting to the authorities and conventions of each environment until stimulated, even compelled to do otherwise by outside forces.

Erika's first world is the isolated glasshouse-like villa of her aristocratic grandmother. Although her grandmother has the best intentions in raising Erika, her horizons are also limited by conventions, and she raises Erika to fulfill the traditional role of young female aristocrats. Independent enough to realize the stifling future this promises, the young countess dreams of a different, more interesting and fulfilling life. But having no guidance in that direction from within her world, she turns to a source of information about an exciting outside world, "harmless" romance novels. Following their lead, she marries a man from the "exotic" middle class, whom she believes she loves madly, and moves into his world, the second of her environments. One of the most significant parts of Reise starts here, as the author explores why women read romance novels and the results reading them can have.

Zur Mühlen did not include the theme of romance novels by chance. Her treatment of romance novels in 1933 was built in part on theories she propounded in a 1919 article printed in the Communist journal Die Erde. First damning those in the power structure who used this literature not to provide young souls with the ideals and guidance they eagerly sought, but rather to mold them with "amoralischer Dreck" into "das Idealbild der deutschen 'Heldenfrau und Mutter,'" she continued:

> Kein menschlicher Ton wird in diesen Büchern angeschlagen, der Horizont ist von einer erschreckenden Enge. . . . Eine niederträchtige, kleinliche, spießbürgerliche Welt wird als einzig gute aller Welten dargestellt, die Pflichten der Frau existieren bloß der Familie gegenüber, ihre verderbliche, angeborene Engherzigkeit wird gefördert und gepriesen.[13]

Seen in one way, the 1933 novel echoes this view of romance novels which stresses their function as a weapon used by bourgeois capitalist society to help indoctrinate women and thus limit their freedom. This view is well represented in current research on romantic women's fiction, one example being Günter Waldmann's study of the function of Frauenschicksalsromane. According to Waldmann, the novels provide solutions to uncertainties and conflicts women encounter: After learning that active protest against the negative circumstances of their lives is useless, the novel's characters find a substitute "durch die Annahme bestimmter Regeln eines bestimmten sozialen Rollenspiels," which takes the form of pure, asexual love of "reine Hingabe und verhaltene Innigkeit," around which the fictional world revolves. It is shown repeatedly that the only way to receive this fulfilling love, and to feel secure and happy as a member of the social in-group, is to accept and internalize the traditional female function of servant to husband and family.

134

Reise's depiction of Erika's move through marriage from the aristocratic world to the middle-class world can be seen in this context. She feels a need for change, but she also needs security denied her because of her outsider position in the aristocracy. The novels seem to offer a solution to this problem in "an ideal marriage in which a woman achieves independence, dependence, excitement, and nurturance all at the same time."[14] After leaping into marriage based on the novels' promise, she realizes that she has simply exchanged one set of barriers for another, as will be discussed further below.

Zur Mühlen's treatment of romance novels in _Reise_ suggests less obvious aspects of the reading process than she expressed in the article, however. The important difference lies in the perspective, for _Reise_ shows why the main character chooses to read romance novels _from her own perspective_. Although she never consciously realizes it, the readers can see that her romance novel reading represents a protest against the circumstances of her life. Their bourgeois values and ideology appeal to Erika because they are foreign to her world. Reading them and constructing her own version of their message gives her a sense of rebelling against her surroundings. From her perspective, she eventually does break out of her first world by marrying into the middle class, and one could say that she used the novels as a basis for this semblance of rebellion. Seen in this way, the novels exert a kind of positive motivation, and thus their influence is not singularly negative.

On further consideration, it could also be said that it is Erika's use of the novels that is the positive force, not the novels themselves. That is, Erika as responder constructs her own version of the story based on the texts available.[15] An important question is, what would happen if they were not available? Would Erika create her own solutions for her dissatisfaction and thus really change her life? Or would she do nothing, not even rebel in the small way on the novels' basis? After these questions have been asked, another question presents itself: By relying on the novels to prompt a form of rebellion, is the woman also likely to accept the novels' message about women's role in society, or at the least base her expectations on their picture of society? These questions bring us back to the negative view of romance novels stated by zur Mühlen in her article. The next section of her novel addresses the problems Erika has when she moves into her new environment full of expectations prompted by her novel reading.

Before turning to this part of Reise, it is interesting to note some striking similarities between zur Mühlen's two-pronged treatment of romance novels and Janice A. Radway's 1984 study of the romance reading process, Reading the Romance, Women, Patriarchy, and Popular Literature. After asking a group of female readers why they read romances, Radway analyzed their responses from two perspectives. She used the perspective of the readers themselves to understand what they believed to be gaining through the reading process. Then, assuming the more traditional external perspective of the scholar, Radway aimed at revealing how the reading of romances and the readers's self-understanding "have tacit, unintended effects and implications" (211).

From their own view, which is very similar to Erika's, Radway's readers saw the act of reading positively, as "oppositional and contestative," using it to "thwart common cultural expectations and to supply gratification ordinarily ruled out by the way the culture structures their lives . . ." (211). Radway's external scholarly perspective focuses on the more negative concept that the women's leisure time withdrawal into the novels' fantasy world is a protest that does nothing to alter the social system which created their problems. Indeed, if their needs are fulfilled completely through fantasies, the women's ability to change actively the conditions of their lives might be obviated. Radway concludes that the feminist critic has to approach the reading of romances in a different way than scholars have done in the past. Feminists must learn to validate the limited protest the novels represent for their readers and also to identify the dissatisfacton from which their protest stems. She continues that strategies must be developed

> for making that dissatisfaction and its causes consciously available to romance readers and by learning how to encourage that protest in such a way that it will be delivered in the arena of actual social relations . . . we might join hands with women who are, after all, our sisters and together imagine a world whose subsequent creation would lead to the need for a new fantasy altogether (220).

136

In her 1933 novel, zur Mühlen recognized this protest in her representation of romance novel reading. By writing her novel, she was also making the causes of this woman's dissatisfaction available to her readers, as well as encouraging them to protest in another way by showing the romance solutions to be useless in eliminating the causes. Her basic pessimism when writing Reise did not allow her to offer countersolutions, for she could not longer accept the simplistic vision of her earlier, Party-line books, nor did she have a different alternative solution.

In Erika's first environment, the novels represented her protest and the inner perspective dominated the narrative. In the next environment, zur Mühlen stresses the other, external perspective as Erika is confronted with the reality zur Mühlen believed lay behind several of her expectations as aroused by the novels, Radway's "unintended effects and implications." Having married middle-class Georg and moved to Germany, she almost immediately runs into difficulty fulfilling the role of perfect wife. Despite the fact that she consciously wants to fulfill the role--she tells herself again and again that she must do as Georg wants, she must please him and her in-laws--she never can give up her independent attitude. Submission is not in her personality, no matter how much she has been conditioned to want the prize promised for submission, a sense of belonging and security.

One example of Erika's problem is in the increased freedom she expects as a married woman. In her reading of the novels, the wife became freer in marriage because once one had perfect love, one had complete freedom. But the illusion of greater freedom disappears quickly as she senses early that Georg only wants to erect higher walls around her. This exchange is a good illustration:

> "Bist du gar eine Frauenrechtlerin?" neckte er sie.
> "Ich weiß nicht, Georg. Aber ich glaube, ich müßte mehr davon wissen."
> "Eine Frau soll sich um ihr Heim, ihren Mann und ihre Kinder kümmern, und das andere den Männern überlassen."
> Erika schwieg. Es war ihr plötzlich zumute, als wüchsen auf allen Seiten Mauern auf: so weit darfst du dich bewegen, aber auch keinen Schritt weiter. Und sie hatte doch immer gedacht: wenn ich

einmal eine verheiratete Frau bin, so
werde ich alles wissen, mich um alles küm-
mern dürfen. . . . Sie blickte zu Georg
hinüber; wahrscheinlich hat er sie nur
necken wollen und gar nicht im Ernst ge-
sprochen. Aber sein schönes Gesicht war
ganz ernst, und er sah aus, als habe er
eben das Natürlichste von der Welt gesagt
(148).

Another example of her problems is in her expec-
tation of what the sexual experience would be like. She
trusted the novels' promise that she would feel the
ultimate sense of belonging and oneness, but she missed
the implicit loss which accompanied this gain: that she
as the woman had to surrender herself in "pure submission" (to use Waldmann's words) to her husband's
domination. The following quotation demonstrates the
link between the novels' promises, Erika's expectations,
and her actual experiences:

Erika fiel ein Roman ein, den sie gelesen
hatte. Sie erinnerte sich genau an die
Stelle: "Und Mara gab ihm aus übergroßer
Liebe das Opfer ihres jungen Leibes. Beide
wurden eins und genossen das höchste
Glück, das es auf Erden gibt. . . ."
"Beide wurden eins. . . ." Auch das hatte
sie nicht gefühlt. Da war immer Georg und
sie, zwei Menschen, die einander sehr
liebten, aber immer zwei Menschen, ein
jeder für sich. Sie hatte ein Wir erwartet, ein völliges Vergessen des eigenen
Ichs, aber dieses Ich war geblieben: ich
und du, nein, du und ich, denn zuerst kam
Georg (137-38).

Once again, even though she thinks she wants to submit, to give up her difficult self, she actually has too
much regard for herself to do this, as her many vocal
arguments with Georg show. Neither is her freedom
expanded, nor do her sexual experiences provide her with
a sense of belonging, and she is left unhappy, confused,
and more alone than ever.

These hopes are gone, yet she does not leave Georg
because she has been brainwashed by Georg's family, by
the doctor, and by her novels that she is an hysterical,
spoiled woman to feel as she does. If she does not
fulfill the role of obedient servant, she does not

deserve to be secure and happy, and the failure of her relationship is her failure alone. At this point zur Mühlen introduces three strong female characters who were born into the middle class but who now lead unconventional lives. Through them Erika begins to see that the conventions of bourgeois society are actually responsible to a large degree for the "failure" of her once-idealistic quest for a meaningful life within its confines. As in her aristocratic surroundings, Erika has again become somewhat aware of her present world's limitations, but this time she can go a step farther toward personal liberation by trying to emulate the role models she is exposed to. At the same time her personal limitations and conditioning counteract her strides, stopping her short of directly challenging the authority figures in her life when they tell her to return to conventional behavior.

Instead she compromises again by attempting to modify another aspect of the traditional female role to suit her own idealized goals. She decides to have a baby. According to her plan, since the child is hers, she can raise him to be loving and sensitive (as his father is not). In addition, she and the child will automatically belong together. Thus she will have an outlet for her energy and receive the nurturance and sense of belonging missing in her relationship with Georg. But the environment proves stronger again, and her motherly devotion does not produce the results she expected. Although Erika's views on education and child-rearing are influenced by her romantic nature, the alternative of having Georg control his son's upbringing is far worse. Even when Erika is involved in her son Wilhelm's education, however, the child's environment is Georg's and it molds the boy into an egotistical, hateful little terror in a uniform who adores playing war and despises his mother for trying to teach him to value beauty and love.

By finally forbidding his wife to play any part in Wilhelm's education, her husband pushes Erika into impulsively leaving him. After several detours she ends up in Switzerland, alone and trying for the first time to determine her own future without outside intervention. Now she is outwardly free of conventional restraint, but the conditioning of a lifetime remains to influence her decisions. Conditioning tells her to do what other rich, aristocratic women in her position do by using her wealth to pursue personal pleasure. She does not make

139

this decision easily and does try to think of alternatives. But the combination of lack of guidance, conditioning, and a strong strain of egotism overcome her
need to find a more fulfilling goal for her life.

Pursuing personal pleasure was not zur Mühlen's idea
of a positive life's goal--as her own life proved--so
she does not allow her heroine to put this plan into
action. The events of World War I shake Erika out of her
obsession with personal problems. The anti-romance
section of Reise ends here, as emphasis is shifted from
private to political concerns when she stumbles into her
third major environment, the world of revolutionary
socialists.

Erika's relationship with Marfa, the Russian revolutionary socialist leader, convinces Erika that working
for the revolution is the goal she needs. She recognizes
in Marfa the qualities she would like to have and in
Marfa's lifestyle the life she would like to lead.
Whereas she met the other strong women while still in
the middle-class environment, she is now separated from
the conventions of the middle class and could gain by
emulating Marfa. A logical, disciplined, and optimistic
woman, Marfa leads a completely goal-oriented existence.
Her life is the revolutionary movement, which tells her
what to do, when to do it, and rewards her with a sense
of belonging and working for justice and social change.
Erika's attraction to Marfa demonstrates that Erika
still needs an authority and longs for group identification. Yet the author illustrates that these qualities
can be positive (if funneled in the correct direction
with group support) by making clear that Erika could
make a vital contribution to bettering the world if two
conditions were met. Erika must commit herself whole-
heartedly to the cause, and the leaders of the cause
must allow her to commit herself in her own way by
finding the role she is best suited for.

Erika is willing, but Marfa is not. The revolutionary leader rejects the aristocrat as an unfit
comrade because of the movement's own set of conventions. These submit that class and upbringing completely
determine one's qualification for participation in the
movement. Marfa tells her:

Wir haben keine Zeit, um einzelne zu
trauern. Der Mensch, das Ich, ist nichts,
die Sache, das Wir, ist alles. Aber das
werden Sie nie begreifen können. . . . Sie

140

sind ein lieber Mensch, Erika, ein guter
Mensch, aber Sie haben zu viel Gefühl und
zu wenig Verstand. Das ist das Un-
glück. . . . Sie möchten hinter einer weh-
enden Fahne herlaufen und Ihr Leben aufs
Spiel setzen. Sie täten es auch, davon bin
ich überzeugt. Aber die tägliche Klein-
arbeit, die ermüdet und langweilt, das ist
nichts für Sie. Und gerade auf die kommt
es an. . . . Seien Sie nicht traurig.
Vielleicht finden Sie noch einen Platz im
Leben, wo Sie arbeiten und etwas leisten
können. Vielleicht (324-26).[16]

Another door has been slammed in her face by an
authority figure whom she is not strong enough to challenge. Erika ends up a wasted resource for the socialist
cause, and her journey returns to its starting point in
the useless isolation of her grandmothers' villa.

Reise gives a differentiated, but pessimistic rendi-
tion of vital political and sociological issues which
affected all women's lives with special emphasis on
their effect on women like Erika, the representative
type. Strong female characters do populate the novel,
but they are presented in such a way that the reader is
led to feel that Erika (and other women like Erika)
could never base the quest for a fulfilled life on their
example. Either these strong women are extraordinary
personalities, and thus can overcome barriers of middle-
class conventions on their own, or they are lucky enough
to be born into the correct supportive environment, here
the proletariat.

The reasons for zur Mühlen's pessimism were rooted
not only in her assessment of the prevailing social
situation; after all, as a socialist she would hardly
have placed her faith in bourgeois society's welcoming
emancipatory urges. The deeper cause for her bleak
vision lay in her disappointment with the K.P.D., as
mentioned earlier. Thus while the first part of Reise
durch ein Leben represented zur Mühlen's vision of the
workings of romantic fiction and of the limitations of
personal attempts at emancipation, the last part emphasized political issues. It represented her disappointment with destructive Communist Party policies in the
late 1920s and early 1930s that had contributed and even
led to the Nazi victory in 1933. Comparing the author's
life to her character's makes this disappointment with

141

the way the Party developed between 1919 and 1933 more evident. Zur Mühlen was welcomed into the movement in 1919, but Erika, who was so much like the author, was rejected for not being suitable in the 1933 version of the same journey.

Zur Mühlen was not the only writer who gave fictional vent to her disillusionment around this time. Once the Nazi victory had become a reality, a wave of pessimism broke among writers with views and beliefs like hers, and a number of works were written with a similarly negative bent as Reise. Adding to zur Mühlen's distress was her conviction that personal fulfillment for most women could be achieved only through identification with the Party. Yet despite her reproach of Party leaders and their policies, zur Mühlen never questioned the justness of the cause or the fulfillment it could offer. So when the Party began to show signs of a more conciliatory position, she became more optimistic.

This position was the cornerstone of a new K.P.D. strategy being evolved among exiles. Already in late 1933 leading Communist literary figures like Becher and Wieland Herzfelde were laying the groundwork for the Volksfront, a concept aimed at combating the causes of the defeatism, disunity, and the fascist victory. The Volksfront was designed to unify intellectuals and artists of all viewpoints, so long as they were antifascists.[17] Although some non-Communists like Heinrich Mann were among its leaders, the K.P.D. and its Moscow-based advisors believed Volksfront activities should be directed by the K.P.D., and for this and other reasons it was never a broad-based success. Nonetheless its very existence prompted many authors to use their writing to propagate its message in hope of a better future.

Under this influence, zur Mühlen composed two more novels in the autobiographical series which combined a renewed hope for the antifascist cause with a more optimistic view on personal emancipation for women. Unsere Töchter, die Nazinen (1934-35) and Ein Jahr im Schatten (1935) challenge readers to fight against oppression in an idealized vision of the actual historical circumstances. In Unsere Töchter, serialized in 1934 in the exile newspaper Deutsche Freiheit and printed in book form in 1935, strictly personal issues remain in the background and behind political party concerns of a specific time and place—1933-34 in a German village on the Austrian border. As Gauß points out, this was one of several contemporary accounts of Nazi Germany authored

142

by recent emigrés that were intended to enlighten readers about the true nature of the National Socialist regime. Living outside Germany and writing about issues they had been forced to confront personally, the authors often had difficulty making their works more than static descriptions.

> . . . die nicht vom Werden, sondern nur vom endgültig Gewordenen, nicht vom Prozeß und von der Bewegung, sondern allein von dem als selbstverständlich vorausgesetzten Ergebnis ausgehen und so nichts über den Weg zu sagen haben, nur über das Elend, in das er führte . . . (Gauß, 26).

In such works characters react, each in their own way, as cogs in the historical machinery, and neither they nor the readers achieve an overall perspective on the process which led to this end, thus diminishing their value. In Unsere Töchter zur Mühlen sought to avoid this by focusing specifically on the process in a manner that would give comprehensible dimensions to an extraordinarily complex historical situation. To do so she chose three young women, representing three different classes. She laid bare their concrete reasons for participating in the National Socialist movement by spotlighting their involvement in the same series of pivotal village events. In order to supply readers with a multidimensional vista over these events—and the overall historical situation—zur Mühlen abandoned the third-person narrative from the heroine's perspective used in Reise. She employed instead three first-person narrators, the mothers of the three women who chronicle their daughters' actions. Despite the different points of view, the author did not aspire to be objective by giving good arguments for the actions of all three women. Whereas the author sympathetically portrayed the aristocratic and working-class women, predictably the middle-class representative is egotistical and materialistic, a flat and uninteresting character.[18]

Through the two nonbourgeois daughters, zur Mühlen exhibits her explanation for the attraction of National Socialism for idealistic young women. Both turn to the Nazis after being disillusioned with other attempts to find their lives' goals: Working-class Toni rejects the infighting and broken promises of the leftists, and aristocratic Claudia, a character much like Erika, embraces Nazism as a surrogate religion. Toni's and

Claudia's personal reasons for joining their revolutionary movement are similar to those Erika displayed in choosing the socialist revolution. As the ultimate authority (with the consummate authority figure in the Führer), National Socialism has enormous appeal for the women confused and disappointed by their earlier lives. Since zur Mühlen's disenchantment with the Party did not extend to socialist ideals, the parallels between the two revolutionary movements soon are shown to be superficial when the barbarism of Nazism is revealed to the women. Wanting to stimulate resistance with the novel, zur Mühlen makes these two women stronger than Erika, and after weighing logically the evidence of Nazi evil, they consciously decide to pull away from this environment and choose another. Fulfilling the phophecy of Marfa's words to Erika, Claudia dies for the now-united leftist front, while through day-to-day struggle within Party ranks, Toni contributes tangibly to the overthrow of Nazi tyranny and becomes influential in the Party. Even though the novel stresses that it is most important to live for the cause, the aristocratic woman's sacrifice is not disparaged; on the contrary, the point is made forcefully that all decent persons of good will (which seemed to exclude the middle class in this novel written before the Volksfront gained momentum) must contribute to the victory with the weapons available to them.

The clear-cut delineation of the interaction between women and the revolutionary movements is certainly the strong suit of this novel. Other aspects suggest conclusions which in retrospect must be called illusory or utopian because they were out of touch with historical reality. For example, studies have proved that leftist parties in Germany and Austria never allowed any significant number of women to gain influential positions in their structures, despite egalitarian rhetoric, so Toni's type of fulfillment was very unlikely, especially for the average woman.[19] Also, the novel's implication that the Nazis would be defeated very soon by the unified leftist front was an overly optimistic view zur Mühlen shared with many compatriots outside Germany. These and other examples indicate that if it is judged according to its value as a historical document, the novel is flawed, but zur Mühlen certainly did not have this goal in mind when she wrote it. It was designed as a novel of commitment, and, judged in this respect, the best gauge of its value was its effect on readers. The novel could have been especially significant for the antifascist cause since it targeted women readers, an

audience seldom addressed so directly in a political
novel. It is difficult to assess what the novel's impact
was on a general audience, but the Austro-Fascist
authorities took its propaganda value seriously, just as
Weimar officials had done in confiscating Schupomann
Karl Müller in 1924. Almost immediately after its book-
form appearance in Vienna in 1935, the novel was banned
for its "social revolutionary propaganda," because the
Austro-Fascists feared that its illumination of everyday
life under National Socialism too easily could be
extended to their form of fascism, the "Corporate
State."20

The third novel in this series, Ein Jahr im Schatten
(1935--released in Switzerland) is obviously influenced
by Volksfront optimism, for the issues of the united
leftist front are deemphasized in favor of instilling in
readers the concept of an antifascist front. Zur Mühlen
returns to the perspective of one Austrian aristrocratic
woman, Martina, but she retains a time frame closer to
Töchter than Reise by spanning one year from mid-1931 to
mid-1932 in the novel. The interrelationship between the
overriding historical events and individual women's
lives is clearer than in Reise, as Martina becomes conscious of her own value, then of the fact that her hard-
won independence is threatened directly by fascism. In
the face of that threat Martina wavers but does not
capitulate; zur Mühlen is on the offensive, demon-
strating the power of positive values and how much an
ordinary woman and other ordinary people can achieve in
combatting evil.

At the end of Ein Jahr, when Martina is reunited
with her husband, they choose to throw their united
strength into the fight against fascism. There is no
hint that they might not be accepted into that battle,
even though they are aristocrats. This novel is composed
so that Martina can consciously choose her goal and be
sure of acceptance and success in the movement because
of two elements of her life and environment missing in
Reise. One element has to do with Martina's sense of
self-worth as she establishes her independence. Forced
to separate from her husband, she first believes she
cannot cope with life alone but comes to realize that
she can survive, even thrive, if she learns to differentiate and understand her own talents and strengths
as a separate person from her husband, i.e., away from
her life's dominant authority figure. Through her
reflections the reader finds out that years before, when
they had lost their money, her husband looked for

145

emotional and financial stability to Martina, who unwillingly played the dominant role. Now she comprehends how strong she had been (however unwillingly), and the negativism of Erika's situation is reversed as Martina uses her new awareness to influence positively her own environment. The social hurdles the author placed before Erika have been greatly lowered for Martina, who is placed in an environment of support Erika never had, in keeping with zur Mühlen's new positive message.

The second reason Martina succeeds is that she escapes her isolation by finding people of good will to share her life. Her new relationships are not based on traditional male/female liaisons, which the author criticizes, though not so vehemently as in Reise, through Martina's recollections of her marriage. Looking back on her "happy" marriage, she concludes that her isolation was caused by the exclusivity of her devotion to her husband, and when he left her, she had no contact with the world around her. She now builds contacts, and the persons she seeks and finds help her, but Martina's feeling of being needed by them expands her sense of self-value and leads her consciously to understand the concept of solidarity among decent people. This solidarity begins with the characters' helping each other to confront private problems and is then extended to the fight against fascism, making the connection between the private and public spheres more comprehensible than in Reise. Reflecting People's Front Ideology, these people from all social groups (even from the middle class) become united in their resolve to combat fascism wherever they find it. Through Martina's stirring words, the author endeavors to kindle readers' own resolve—if they hold together, fascism will be defeated:

> Aber ein solcher Zustand kann nicht lange
> dauern. Es gibt doch überall anständige
> Menschen, die das nicht dulden wer-
> den. . . . Es werden ihrer viele sein,
> alles, was geistig ist, die Dichter, die
> Künstler, die Gelehrten. Und alles, was
> einen anständigen Instinkt hat, die
> Arbeiter, die Bauern. Sie werden zusammen-
> halten . . . und an Niedertracht zerschel-
> len (357-58).

In opposition to her earlier novels, zur Mühlen places most of the decent people outside political party structures, and by removing the necessity of political organization and showing that ordinary people can fight fascism in their personal circumstances, zur Mühlen presents positive role-models and goals accessible to almost all readers. But she also sidesteps the issue of party conventions, a strategy similar to providing Martina with a supportive environment to defuse criticism of social conventions present in Reise.

For 1980s Germanists, feminists, and teachers seeking suitable texts and material for courses delineating and analyzing women's role in life and literature of the interwar period, the current zur Mühlen renaissance is a boon. From a purely organizational standpoint this is true because several of her interwar texts have been or will be reissued in inexpensive editions, allowing them to be incorporated into course work.[21] Zur Mühlen's memoirs, Ende und Anfang, which provide so much engrossing information about her life, were reprinted in the German Democratic Republic in 1976 and are also readily available through interlibrary loan. Along with several of her novels, the memoirs were also translated into English.

Reading and studying zur Mühlen's oeuvre can be a fascinating and illuminating experience for us and our students for a number of reasons. Seen synchronically, her works can fill gaps in our perception of interwar history and literature in a way no other writer's can because they blend what seem to be mutually exclusive elements from her life. Influences from her Austrian aristocratic upbringing and from the socialism she adopted as an adult give them a perspective on the interwar period different from that of the works of other already "rediscovered" progressive female writers of the 1920s and 1930s like Irmgard Keun, Maria Leitner, Marieluise Fleißer, Anita Brück, or Paula Schlier. These writers' works often revolve around the struggles of women of the proletariat or middle class to control their lives within their postwar roles as employed women. Since many of zur Mühlen's main characters are born aristocrats, they come from the other end of the socio-economic scale. They have to deal with what is outwardly a different set of problems than their counterparts in the other novels.

A brief comparison of all these novels, however, reveals similarities in the basic nature of the female characters' problems. That is, although many of zur Mühlen's women at least initially live in an

147

aristocratic environment, they are forced to struggle with limitations placed on their freedom and independence by the conventions of their world. The actual barriers might be different, but the results are the same: Women are denied the right to control their own lives, and they must struggle long and hard to attain any sort of freedom. An indepth study comparing zur Mühlen's works with those of several other progressive interwar female writers would help our understanding of the structure of modern society, for it could help establish whether the problems were (and are) due to a class-oriented power structure or to a patriarchal power structure. This kind of investigation could also be part of a university class on interwar or twentieth-century German-language literature.

Zur Mühlen's works are also valuable to the study of twentieth-century literature in another way. Especially the texts written in the 1930s can be seen in a diachronic sequence with works of postwar female writers such as Christa Wolf or Ingeborg Drewitz. Like these writers, zur Mühlen portrays the individual experiences of women during the fascist era and poses important questions about the responsibility of women in resisting National Socialism and other forms of fascism. In addition, the personal and public struggles of zur Mühlen's women continue to be relevant to women in the 1980s, for neither have the barriers to personal emancipation she portrayed been fully dismantled, nor have women yet been fully integrated into the power structure of political parties or society in general.

On another level the three zur Mühlen novels mentioned here illustrate a thorny literary problem often encountered by writers committed to socio-political change through their art. Should they portray existing society realistically (including its limiting structures) and risk suggesting resignation to readers, thus sacrificing the emancipatory message? Or should they create positive role models in circumstances not strictly realistic in order to stimulate reader activity, but possibly sacrifice credibility and thus again risk not achieving their goal? Exploring these difficult questions, as well as the many other issues I have touched upon, through Hermynia zur Mühlen's oeuvre is an experience which should not be missed.

Notes

[1] Rudolf Popper, "Hermynia zur Mühlen zum sechzigsten Geburtstag," Zeitspiegel 11 Dec. 1943: 7-8. W. St., "Hermynia zur Mühlen sechzig Jahre," Freie Tribüne Dec. 1943: 8-10. See also: W. Sternfeld, "Hermynia zur Mühlen: Zu ihrem sechzigsten Geburtstag," Freies Deutschland 3 (Jan. 1944): 28. Concerning B.B.C. telecast, see: Zeitspiegel 18 Dec. 1943: 7.

[2] Rev. of Kleine Geschichten von großen Dichtern, Zeitspiegel 9 Dec. 1944: 8. Eva Priester, "Hermynia zur Mühlen zu ihrem fünfundsechzigsten Geburtstag," Österreichisches Tagebuch 3 (Dec. 1948): 28.

[3] See: Sigurd Paul Scheichl, "Weder Kahlschlag noch Stunde Null: Besonderheiten des Voraussetzungssystems der Literatur in Österreich zwischen 1945 und 1966, Vier deutsche Literaturen, Vol. 10 of Kontroverse, alte und neue. Akten des VII. Kongresses der Internationalen Vereinigung für germanische Sprach- und Literaturwissenschaft, 11 vols., ed. Albrecht Schöne (Tübingen: Niemeyer, 1986), 45.

[4] In immediate postwar Austria, two leftists, Viktor Matejka (Viennese city councilman for cultural affairs until 1948) and Ernst Fischer attempted to influence the cultural-political life of the country. Matejka especially worked to get exiles to return to Austria and to have their work recognized as that of a different tradition in Austrian literature which had been suppressed during the Austro-Fascist era in the mid-1930s. Publications of these writers' works by the Communist Globus Verlag—among them zur Mühlen's—are examples of his dedication to these goals. However, his actions created a backlash among the conservatives who soon took control, and the writers he had supported were militantly discriminated against.

There were other, less politically oriented attempts at opening Austrian literature to a new beginning. The most prominent was Otto Basil's literary journal Plan, founded in 1945. However, literary figures like Pertner and Heinz, themselves intimately linked to the Austro-Fascist regime, gained control and backed writers who shared their cultural and political point of view. These certainly did not include zur Mühlen. For more information see Scheichl. See also Hilde Spiel, "Die österreichische Literatur nach 1945," in Die zeitgenössische Literatur Österreichs (Zürich and Munich: Kindler, 1976), pp. 49-62.

The author herself believed the problems her works
had in Austria during the postwar period stemmed largely
from their critical focus and complained bitterly about
official response to them--including censorship--in a
letter to Matejka, writing, "Jetzt weiß ich endlich ganz
genau, was man im 'neuen' Österreich unter Förderung der
österreichischen Literatur und jener Schriftsteller, die
nicht bereit waren, dem Nationalsozialismus Konzessionen
zu machen, versteht!" Letter from zur Mühlen to Matejka,
9 Mar. 1948. Cited in: Herbert Staud, "Zum hundertsten
Geburtstag von Hermynia zur Mühlen," Mitteilungen des
Instituts für Wissenschaft und Kunst (Vienna), 38, No. 4
(1983), 96.

[5] Hermynia zur Mühlen, "Eine Bio-Bibliographie," Das
Wort 2 (April/May 1937): 184-85.

[6] Johannes R. Becher, "Bürgerliche und proletarisch-
revolutionäre Literatur in Deutschland," Publizistik I,
vol. 15 of his Gesammelte Werke (Berlin: Aufbau, 1977),
624-26.

[7] The parting of the ways among leftists began
around mid-decade, and the debate was especially pro-
nounced among the members of the Party-sponsored
B.P.R.S. (Bund proletarisch-revolutionärer Schriftsteller, founded 1927), like Becher, and between the
B.P.R.S. writers and independents like Bertolt Brecht.
See Franz Schonauer, "Die Partei und die schöne Literatur. Kommunistische Literaturpolitik," Deutsche Literatur in der Weimarer Republik, ed. Wolfgang Rothe
(Stuttgart: Reclam, 1974), 114-42. Helga Galas, Marxis-
tische Literaturtheorie. Kontroversen im Bund proletarisch-revolutionärer Schriftsteller (Darmstadt and
Neuwied: Luchterhand, 1969).

[8] Henri Guilbeaux, Rev. of Ende und Anfang, Weltbühne 26, No. 2 (1930), 68.

[9] See Arbeiterinnen kämpfen um ihr Recht. Autobio-
graphische Texte zum Kampf rechtloser und entrechteter
"Frauenspersonen" in Deutschland, Österreich und der
Schweiz des 19. und 20. Jahrhunderts, ed. Richard
Kluesaritz und Friedrich G. Kürbisch (Wuppertal: Hammer,
1977).

[10] Zur Mühlen mentions this case in her memoirs, but
only recently have the files on the case been located by
G.D.R. research Manfred Altner in the Central Archives

in Potsdam. Dr. Altner kindly made his finding available to me in a letter of 20 Oct. 1984.

[11] Karl Markus Gauß, "Der lange Weg nach Hertfordshire: Zum hundertsten Geburtstag von Hermynia zur Mühlen," Wiener Tagebuch (Dec. 1983), 23-24. For more information on this type of children's literature, see: Edwin Hoernle, "Etwas über Erzählungen, Fabeln und Märchen," Das proletarische Kind 2, No. 1 (1922), 16-19. "Die proletarisch-revolutionäre Jugendliteratur," Proletarisch-revolutionäre Literatur 1918 bis 1938: Ein Abriß (Berlin: Volk und Wissen, 1962); Hanno Möbius, "Revolutionäre Märchen der zwanziger Jahre," Kürbiskern 1971, No. 2, 267-70. Ingmar Dreher, Die deutsche proletarisch-revolutionäre Kinder- und Jugendliteratur zwischen 1918 und 1938 (Berlin: Der Kinderbuchverlag, 1975). For a more specific analysis of zur Mühlen's role, see: Bernd Dolle, "Hermynia zur Mühlen," vol. 3, Lexikon der Kinder- und Jugendliteratur, ed. Klaus Doderer (Weinheim and Basle: Beltz, 1979), 861-63.

[12] Wieland Herzfelde, "Briefe, die den Weg beleuchten, Neue Deutsche Blätter 1, No. 3 (1933-34), 129-39.

[13] Hermynia zur Mühlen, "Junge-Mädchen-Literatur," Die Erde 1 (Aug. 1919), 473-74.

[14] Janice A. Radway, Reading the Romance. Women, Patriarchy, and Popular Literature (Chapel Hill and London: University of North Carolina Press, 1984), p. 221.

[15] I am aware that this statement opens up questions debated by reader response critics and I cannot go into them here. The Radway book cited above gives a good introduction to the question of reader constructions in relation to romances.

[16] Marfa's words to Erika are strikingly similar to Johannes R. Becher's description of the revolution in his autobiographical novel, CHCL=CH 3 AS (Levisite) der Der einzig gerechte Krieg (1926):

> Denn Revolution bedeutet nicht nur gefühlsmäßige begeisterungsflammende Hingabe an das revolutionäre Ideal . . . , Revolution bedeutet auch kleine zermürbende Parteiarbeit. Revolution ist auch die Klebekolonne. . . . Die Kampfmaschine der Revolution: sie treibt einen ungeheuren

Verschleiß an Menschenzahl und Menschen-
kraft. Revolution ist gründlichstes exak-
testes Wissen: sie ist das härteste,
gewagteste, furchtbarste Lebenstraining
dieser Welt; sie fordert deine Disziplin,
deine Ausdauer, sie fordert dich hinein
bis zur letzten Nervenfaser; sie fordert
dich ganz.

Quoted according to Hans-Albert Walter, Deutsche Exil-
literatur 1933-1950, Vol. 1 (Darmstadt and Neuwied:
Luchterhand, 1972), 130-31.

[17] This was actually not a new idea, since many
leftists had been trying to form a united front for
several years. The K.P.D. only threw its support behind
the idea after 1933. Also, the People's Front was an
international movement, of course, and its ideas were
not exclusive to German-speaking intellectuals. But the
German section had a special set of circumstances, if
for no other reason than because Germany was the home of
National Socialism. For more information on the German
section, see Manfred Lefevre, Von der proletarisch-
revolutionär zu sozialistisch-realistischer Literaturtheorie und Literaturpolitik (Stuttgart: Akademischer
Verlag Hans-Dieter Heinz, 1980).

[18] For other novels of the same period, like Nora
hat eine famose Idee (1933) or Ein Jahr im Schatten, to
be discussed next, the author created positive middle-
class characters, but Töchter is the most polemically
antibourgeois of her post-1932 works.

[19] See: Lynda J. King, "The Woman Question and Politics in Austrian Interwar Politics," German Studies Review 6, No. 1 (1983), 75-100.

[20] Friedrich Achberger, "Österreichische Literatur,"
Deutsche Literatur. Eine Sozialgeschichte, Vol. 9, ed.
Horst Albert Glaser (Reinbek bei Hamburg: Rowohlt,
1983), 333. See also: Staud, 96.

[21] See Bibliography below. A monograph on zur Mühlen
is being prepared by G.D.R. scholar Manfred Altner, and
Persona Verlag in Mannheim is planning to reissue Ein
Jahr im Schatten as soon as rights to the novel are
obtained.

Zur Mühlen Bibliography

The following is a list of zur Mühlen works of special interest. A more complete list is available from the author.

Was Peterchens Freunde erzählen, illustrated by George Grosz. Berlin: Malik, 1921. Vienna: Globus, 1946. Leipzig: Edition Leipzig, 1979.

Die Tempel. Berlin: Vereinigung Internationaler Verlags-Anstalten, 1922.

Schupomann Karl Müller. Berlin: Vereinigung Internationaler-Verlags Anstalten, 1924. (Serialized in Die Rote Fahne, 8 Mar. to 14 Mar. 1924.)

Ende und Anfang: Ein Lebensbuch. Berlin: Malik, 1929; S. Fischer, 1929; Aufbau, 1976. (The Runaway Countess. Trans. Frank Barnes. New York: Cape and Smith, 1930.)

Das Riesenrad. Stuttgart: Engelhorn, 1932. Vienna: Österreichische Buchgemeinschaft, 1948. (Serialized in Die Woche (Vienna), 22 June to 14 Dec. 1947.) (The Wheel of Life. Trans. Margaret Goldsmith. London: Barker, 1933. New York: Stokes, 1933.)

Nora hat eine famose Idee. Berne: Gotthelf, 1933. Vienna: Saturn, 1937. (Serialized in Das Kleine Blatt (Vienna), 6 Nov. 1932 to 14 May 1933.)

Reise durch ein Leben. Berne: Gotthelf, 1933. (Serialized in Der Bund (Berne) Aug. to Sept. 1933.) (A Life's Journey. Trans. Phyllis Blewitt and Trevor Blewitt. London: Jonathan Cape, 1935).

Ein Jahr im Schatten. Zurich: Humanitas, 1935. (A Year under a Cloud. Trans. Ethel K. Houghton and H.E. Cornides. London: Selwyn and Blount, 1937.)

Unsere Töchter, die Nazinen. Vienna: Gsur, 1935. Berlin: Aufbau, 1983. (Serialized in Deutsche Freiheit (Saarbrücken), 20 June to 16 Aug. 1934.)

Came the Stranger. London: Muller, 1946. German: Als der Fremde kam. Vienna: Globus, 1947. Berlin: Aufbau, 1979.

Der kleine graue Hund und andere Märchen, illustrated by
Karl Holz. Oberhausen: Asso, 1976.

Der Spatz: Märchen, illustrated by George Grosz. Ed.
Manfred Altner. Berlin: Kinderbuchverlag, 1984.

The "Odd" Woman as Heroine in the Fiction of
Louise von François

Linda Kraus Worley

Louise von François writes to Conrad Ferdinand Meyer in 1881 of a mutual friend, "Frl. Doctor" Druskovitz:

> es ist ein braves, tapferes Mädchen und ihre Stellung zur Gesellschaft, präciser ausgedrückt die Existenz-frage sehr zweifelhaft. Noch gilt in Deutschland das Schillersche Frauenideal und vom Standpunkte des Geschlechtes Nummero Eins aus betrachtet, gewiss mit Recht. Nur daß den vielen Unbegehrten und den wenigen nicht Begehrenden nicht der Raum versperrt werden darf, auf eigenen Füssen zu einem würdigen, menschlichen Ziele zu gelangen (Bettelheim, François-Meyer 26).

François (1817-1893) was one of the few writers of fiction in the nineteenth century deeply concerned with the existential problems encountered by the "vielen Unbegehrten" and the "wenigen nicht Begehrenden." Therese Huber had dealt with similar problems in works such as Die Ehelosen (1829) as had Friederike Helene Unger earlier, but the situation of such women was by no means a popular theme. This relative neglect is all the more astonishing in light of the fact that approximately fifty percent of all German women were unmarried in mid-century (Twellmann-Schepp 27-29).

The British novelist George Gissing focused on the lives of unmarried women in his novel The Odd Women published in 1892. The heroine of his novel remarks on the fact that there are half a million more women than men in England: "So many odd women—no making a pair with them. The pessimists call them useless, lost, futile lives. I, naturally—being one of them myself— take another view. I look upon them as a great reserve" (37). Annis Pratt, very likely referring to Gissing's novel, uses the term in Archetypal Patterns in Women's

Fiction to refer to fiction in which the heroine tries to live on her own. The heroine is "odd" because she is not half of a couple and therefore does not fulfill a set function in a nuclear family (113-14). The term can be profitably extended to include all women, even those eventually pairing up, who do not fulfill the functions in the nuclear family set by the strict nineteenth-century norm of appropriate female behavior.

By the middle of the nineteenth century, the ideology of complementary gender-based character traits, _Geschlechtscharakter_, was firmly entrenched. Traits such as passivity, emotionality, dependency, sensitivity, and _Anmut_ were hypothesized as being specifically "female." In _Complaints and Disorders_, Barbara Ehrenreich and Deirdre English document how doctors, psychologists, and anthropologists in the latter part of the nineteenth century attempted to prove "scientifically" that these traits were anchored in woman's very biology. Any deviations from this prescriptive norm were decried as contrary to nature. By mid-century, earlier models for women such as the _Gelehrte_ had long since become figures of either derision or horror. After the Industrial Revolution had caused the strict separation of the workplace from the home, middle-class women were literally confined to the isolated and isolating realm of home and family, to the roles of wife and mother. There was no place in this rigid socio-cultural matrix for the unmarried woman.

Louise von François never directly attacked the dominant ideology of gender-based character traits, the "Schillersche Frauenideal." In _Die andere Frau_ Renate Möhrmann documents how the women writers of the _Vormärz_ spoke up against this ideology by stressing women's right to a profession and the emancipation of the heart. Their overt calls for social change were almost completely silent by the 1850s when François began publishing. Feminists such as Louise Otto-Peters and Hedwig Dohm were notable exceptions to the tendency surfacing in the _Nachmärz_ to concentrate on "Bestätigungsliteratur anstatt Tendenzpoesie, Verinnerlichungsbemühungen anstatt Veränderungsbestrebungen, Comfort des Herzens anstelle intellektueller Mobilität . . ." (Möhrmann 151). Yet within this specific historical constellation, François's concern for the "odd" woman opens up a fruitful line of inquiry, one that may modify the prevalent view of women's literary history as well as the common view, held even by feminist critics, of François as a "conservative" author.[1] François's achievement in creating

156

"strong" female characters such as Hardine von Reckenburg, the heroine of François's deservedly most successful novel, Die letzte Reckenburgerin, has long been
recognized by some critics and literary historians.
There has been a tendency, however, to focus on François's historical fiction, a predilection reflected in
the selections made by Insel Verlag for the five-volume
set of François's Gesammelte Werke published in 1918.
Such editorial and critical selection has meant that
many of François's "odd-woman" stories have been
ignored, although approximately half of her ouevre con-
centrates on the conflicts faced by an unusual woman.[2]

The "odd" woman as heroine is most readily recog-
nizable in early works such as Die letzte Reckenburgerin
(1870, but completed by 1865), "Eine Formalität" (1857),
"Eine Gouvernante" (1859), and "Judith, die Kluswirtin"
(1862), where the female protagonist is a strong, active, rational woman--all traits at odds with the
nineteenth-century feminine ideal. These women face
difficult existential problems: how to live in a world
whose ideal of womanhood varies radically from one's
sense of self, in a world which relegates women exclusively to the realm of love and emotions. Having learned
to define themselves outside of the "feminine" sphere--
an often painful process--these women also learn to
adhere to their own rigorous ethical code, living, to
use the motto of the Reckenburgs, a life "in Recht und
Ehren." Hardine von Reckenburg, aware that she is far
from the ideal of feminine beauty and grace as embodied
by her girlhood friend Dorl, must see Prince August
choose her as a trusted and admired friend, but Dorl as
his lover. Hardine has the strength to take on the
responsibilities of managing her aunt's estate and even
of arranging for the care of Dorl's illegitimate son.
Using her immense energies productively, she is finally
able to carve out a satisfying realm of action for
herself as head of the Reckenburg, bringing prosperity
to its inhabitants. Cornelie Wille, the heroine with the
telling name in "Eine Gouvernante," towers above other
women by virtue of her energy, self-control, and organizational ability. Precisely because she has learned
"unter strenger Zucht," to subordinate "ihre Neigungen"
to "gewissen Grundsätzen," she doubts if she is
"liebenswürdig" (685)--capable of being the "zarte,
schmiegsame, willenlose" (687) woman a man can love. She
eventually chooses to remain single, utilizing her
talents within a broad realm of action as head of an or-
phanage. The heroine of "Eine Formalität," Constanze von
Hohenheim, refuses to go along with her new husband's

157

questionable financial dealings, dealings which could endanger the inheritance (and thus future) of her ward. By placing her sense of duty to her ward, her strict code of ethics, above her love for her husband, Constanze must hear the damning accusation that she is a "Weib ohne Herz" (420) as well as lose her partner.

Not all of François's "odd" women fit the model of the rational, strong woman.[3] Laurentia, the heroine of "Geschichte einer Häßlichen" (1858), is one example. Her extraordinary ugliness and extreme emotionality set her apart from the accepted image of femininity. As the story progresses, Laurentia comes to realize the extent to which her ugliness and socially inept behavior embarrass and repel her father. Reacting to her father's rejection, Laurentia, the ugly outcast, insists with all the implacable energy of a Storm-and-Stress hero on being accepted and loved for what she is. After retreating into madness, she nevertheless eventually achieves her goal when an atypical, "feminine" man gives her the unconditional love she demands while not denying her her autonomy. Eleonore von Fink, the heroine of "Der Posten der Frau" (1857), is, at first glance, by no means an "odd" woman—she is beautiful, married, a mother, and prone to indulge in fantasies of love. Indeed, the title of the story suggests that it may be François's definitive statement concerning a woman's post: she is, as King Frederick II of Prussia tells Eleonore in the story, to remain at home with her child. However, beneath this surface, a strong oppositional subtext traces Eleonore's development away from daydreams, wherein her "phantasiereiche" (222) imagination envisions her loving and belonging to a male hero, and towards a reliance on self, a mature acceptance of duty, wherein she utilizes her "stolzen, energischen Willen" and "kluge, umsichtige Art" (222) to act in the "real" world. After François has Eleonore's Saxon husband conveniently leave home to avoid the victorious Prussian army, Eleonore takes over the administration of the estate. She is now "wearing the pants," which, as King Frederick tells her, "passen Ihnen gut" (226).[4]

The tendency to judge François's "odd" women with respect to their success or failure in love has been strong from their first appearance in print to the present. Gustav Freytag, who praised Die letzte Reckenburgerin highly in 1872, notes a "Ton von Trauer und Entsagung" in the novel (300). Susan Cocalis and Kay Goodman write in 1982: "Where a woman is able to establish a productive life owing to her own competence, as

158

in Louise von François's Die letzte Reckenburgerin
(1871), it follows a history of personal defeat in love
and resignation to one's fate" (222). In this rather
traditional context, François's heroines must, for the
most part, be seen as heroines of renunciation.

The underlying, masked impulse of these stories is,
however, not eros, but power.[5] Barbara Watson discusses
power and the literary text: "The definition of power as
dominance covers one range of uses. The definition of
power as ability, competence, and the closely related
definition of power as energy, cover another, much wider
and more interesting cluster of meanings" (113). Referring to Watson's line of thought, Nancy Miller
postulates that the "repressed content" of much of
women's fiction is "an impulse to power, a fantasy of
power that would revise the social grammar in which
women are never defined as subjects . . ." (41).
François's heroines may renounce love, but they achieve
primacy and authenticity. These heroines are "odd"
within the norms established by the nineteenth-century
ideal because they are subjects, not passive objects defined only with respect to men. François's "odd" women
are in this sense heroines of fulfillment who are given
access to a realm of ethical behavior linked to the
highest values of the Western world, a realm which had
previously been in (male) theory reserved for men. Her
self-defining heroines follow the dictates of the cate-
gorical imperative. They achieve Würde by placing duty--
duty towards others and towards self--above inclination.
From a modern perspective this Kantian emphasis on duty
is recognized as a two-edged sword, for it prevented
François from imagining heroines who emancipate themselves from "duty," as defined by nineteenth-century society. Nevertheless, within François's world view (and,
it may be added, the world view of many leaders of the
middle-class women's movement), observance of duty was a
necessary step for women towards attaining authenticity
and full human status.

François never gave automatic, unquestioned pre-
dominance to romantic love in her "odd-woman" fiction.
In the story "Glück" (1871), the heroine Katharina
Peterson realizes that marrying the man she loves would
mean subordinating her liberal beliefs to his strictly
orthodox, authoritarian religious beliefs. Katharina
recognizes that she would have to place "seine Liebe
allein an die Stelle jedes theuren Zusammenhangs, seine
Wahrheit allein an die Stelle aller Heiterkeit und
Schönheit meines bisherigen Lebens" (255). She chooses

to retain her primacy; she remains single. Some of François's "odd" women do marry, but they marry an atypical man, one who will not deny them their autonomy. François's unmarried heroines also can find love; they experience maternal love from their relationship to wards or orphans. Thomas Fox points out that François rewards Hardine in Die letzte Reckenburgerin with an androgynous solution to the conflicting tensions in her life--she has the opportunity to pursue "manly" activity and experience "female" motherly love (236).

There is a potentially subversive thrust contained in the "impulse of power" found in François's stories: the very act of defining woman as subject implies a threat to male dominance, a dominance predicated on viewing woman as the "second" sex. Consciously or unconsciously, François felt compelled to submerge the disturbing content of her fiction in order to defuse potential reader-criticism and placate her own internal self-censor, a self-censor rooted in and formed by the prevailing culture. (An "odd" woman herself, François--unmarried, poor, a member of the déclassé nobility, a writer largely isolated in the tiny town of Weißenfels a. d. Saale--was most careful in her own life to mask any dis-ease with her lot.) François was quite successful in her masking endeavors for, despite their subversive potential, her imagines were never met by howls of protest, even though her "odd-woman" heroines were certainly "unnatural" deviants within the nineteenth-century context.

François avoided open conflict by never issuing a call for radical, universal change. There is no directly aggressive tendency in her fiction--each story tells the tale of only one unusual woman. Her "odd" women cannot be decried by the reader as "unnatural" since François posits basic human character as a given. Hardine von Reckenburg reflects this stance when she says "Wie die Natur uns gepflanzt hat, so müssen wir einander hegen--oder meiden" (230). Parallel to the main plot tracing the life of the unusual woman is often a secondary plot focusing on a "feminine" woman whose life follows a traditional course. The "odd" woman never attacks the validity of the lifestyle of the "feminine" foils; indeed, she often praises the "feminine" ideal. Realizing that her own unique fate, education, and God-given nature have combined to make her an unusual woman, an anomaly, François's heroine avoids proselytizing, avoids attempting to nurture similar traits in other women, who may in fact not have the inner resources needed to cope

with outsider status. François always ends her stories
on a conciliatory note; most often she provides barely
veiled atonement for any deviation from the nineteenth-
century code of the appropriate by engaging her "odd-
woman" heroine in some sort of social work, thus re-
establishing a link to the traditional female sphere.

Gender-related adjectives such as männlich and weiblich abound in François's fiction; she employs such vo-
cabulary strictly in keeping with contemporaneous usage.
However, she sets these adjectives loose from their
biological base. By never turning her "feminine" men and
"manly" women into objects of condescension or derision,
she extends the sex-role possibilities for men and
women. Similarly, François values motherhood highly, but
does not limit mothering to biological mothers. There
are "bad" biological mothers who neglect their duty (cf.
Dorl in Die letzte Reckenburgerin and Lorenza von
Leiseritz in "Der Katzenjunker") as well as excellent,
conscientious foster mothers throughout François's
ouevre. In her fiction, François most often employs a
traditional, conservative narrator who at times defends
patriarchal tyrants by providing possible reasons for
their actions. Author and narrator may, however, clash
as is the case in "Geschichte einer Häßlichen," producing disjunctions between the rather lame ration-
alizations proffered by the narrator and the obviously
heartless actions of the heroine's father. (In this
instance the author exacts revenge--the father dies.)

Some of these masking strategies can be linked to
unsatisfying elements of François's craft, components by
no means unique to her work. The attempt to end the
"odd-woman" stories on a conciliatory note often seems
forced; the conclusion too often becomes a melodramatic
dénouement. A discomfortingly strong chain of coinci-
dence tends to propel the plots along. Perhaps the
strongest criticism of François's work is similar to
criticism she herself levied against her contemporaries.
In a letter to Marie von Ebner-Eschenbach written in
1880, François writes that "Unsere besten Schriftsteller
werden langweilig, wenn sie einen edlen Menschen zu
schildern beginnen, machen daraus ein verschwommenes
Idealgebilde ohne Blut und Sinnen, das nicht wirkend
irrt und nicht kämpfend strauchelt" (Bettelheim, "Ebner-
Eschenbach" 112). All too rarely does the reader experience first-hand the "odd" woman struggling as she
"wirkend irrt" and "kämpfend strauchelt." In many of
François's "odd-woman" stories, a distanced third-person
narrator tends to summarize the action while merely

describing the personality of the characters. The reader remains on the outside. One factor that contributes greatly to the excellence of Die letzte Reckenburgerin is that Hardine is allowed to tell her own story. Such criticism of François's craft is not new. Gustav Freytag's comments in his review of Die letzte Reckenburgerin touch on similar points: "in jenen [the stories] beeinträchtigte ein Vorwiegen der Reflexion über die warme Erfindung und ein Zusammenfügen der Charaktere aus allzu künstlichen Voraussetzungen den vollen Genuß . . ." (295). There is the distinct possibility, however, that such a cool, distanced style of narration may be tied to fear of revealing too much, especially of an antisocial nature.[6]

Despite these reservations, we must not underestimate François's efforts in portraying the "nicht Begehrten," the "nicht Begehrenden," and other "odd" women, or her achievement in creating heroines who succeed in being something other than a literary embodiment of the "Eternal Feminine." The study of François's "odd-woman" fiction reveals that portrayal of "die andere Frau," to use Renate Möhrmann's term loosely, did not end with the failed revolution of 1848. François did not overtly attempt to extend the possibilities for woman with respect to occupational opportunities or sexual freedoms as had the women writers of the Vormärz and the few remaining publishing feminists after 1848; she did, however, succeed in extending the range of possibilities for women well beyond the normative "feminine ideal," according her "odd" women full human dignity. There is thus less of a caesura between the committed women writers of the Vormärz and the writers of the resurgent women's movement of the late nineteenth century than is presently assumed.

Notes

[1] Cf., for example, Ruth-Ellen Boetcher Joeres, "Self-Conscious Histories," 184-85. The enduring view of François as "conservative" does not, however, prevent Joeres from noting that François's short biographical sketch of George Sand was "both opinionated and forcefully self-confident" (185) or that apart from "the stress that she placed on the image of Sand as mother, the need to verify her subject's femininity is not strongly felt, nor is the advertising of marriage as an essential part of a woman's life particularly noticeable" (185).

162

² It is worth noting that in the stories and novels concentrating on the fate of a male hero finding his way in the world, François assumes an almost male-imitative stance, tending to reproduce the traditional images of the "Eternal Feminine" pre-formed by generations of male writers. In Frau Erdmuthens Zwillingssöhne (1872), for example, the male narrator sings a hymn of praise to Frau Erdmuthen, the ideal embodiment of motherliness (a motherliness which proves conspicuously ineffective at preventing the growing animosity between the twin brothers.)

³ Edith Wendel's dissertation "Frauengestalten und Frauenprobleme bei Louise von François" (1959) attempts a typology of François's female characters. Wendel distinguishes characters who are "strong-willed," "weak-willed," "motherly," "childish," and "intellectual." Since Wendel does not put these types into any sort of context, be it a larger socio-historical context or even the fictional context of the work in question, her work remains minutely detailed, but uncritical, unable to discern underlying structures.

⁴ For a detailed feminist analysis of Die letzte Reckenburgerin see Thomas Fox, "Louise von François: Between Frauenzimmer and A Room of One's Own"; for detailed analyses of "Der Posten der Frau," "Geschichte einer Häßlichen," "Eine Gouvernante," and "Eine Formalität," see my dissertation, "Louise von François: A Reinterpretation of Her Life and Her 'Odd-Woman' Fiction," Diss. U. Cincinnati, 1985.

⁵ A small number of female characters, none of them the main focus of the plot, are strongly connected with the erotic. They are portrayed quite positively if they take charge of their own lives and that of their dependents (cf. Eva Findling in "Des Doktors Gebirgsreise," 1860), but negatively if they ignore their duty to themselves and society (cf. Liszka in Frau Erdmuthens Zwillingssöhne, 1872, Lorenza von Leiseritz in "Der Katzenjunker," 1879, and Dorl in Die letzte Reckenburgerin). Yet even Dorl, as Fox has pointed out, is presented by François as both victimizer and victim (212-14).

⁶ François expressly posited a non-emotional, non-sentimental style for herself, a style based on "Not, der Reflektion und Reminiszenz" (Schwartzkoppen 197). François in essence distances herself from the sentimental style of "Dichterblüten" (Schwartzkoppen 197) so often linked to Frauenliteratur.

Works Cited

Bettelheim, Anton, ed. Louise von François und Conrad Ferdinand Meyer: Ein Briefwechsel. 2nd ed. Berlin: de Gruyter, 1920.

----------. "Marie von Ebner-Eschenbach und Louise von François." Deutsche Rundschau 27.1 (Oct. 1900): 104-19.

Cochalis, Susan L., and Kay Goodman, eds. Beyond the Eternal Feminine: Critical Essays on Women and German Literature. Stuttgarter Arbeiten zur Germanistik 98. Stuttgart: Heinz, 1982.

Ehrenreich, Barbara, and Deirdre English. Complaints and Disorders: The Sexual Politics of Sickness. Old Westbury, NY: The Feminist Press, 1973.

Fox, Thomas. "Louise von François: Between Frauenzimmer and A Room of One's Own." Diss. Yale U., 1983.

François, Louise von. "Eine Formalität." Gesammelte Werke. Ed., Karl Weitzel. 2 vols. Leipzig: Minerva, 1924. 2: 406-33.

----------. "Glück." Erzählungen in zwei Bänden. 2 vols. Braunschweig: Westermann, 1871. 1: 177-289.

----------. "Eine Gouvernante." Morgenblatt 28-31 (1859): 649+.

----------. Die letzte Reckenburgerin. Vol. 1 of Gesammelte Werke in fünf Bänden. 5 vols. Leipzig: Insel, 1918.

----------. "Der Posten der Frau." Gesammelte Werke in fünf Bänden. 5 vols. Leipzig: Insel, 1918. 4: 181-266.

Freytag, Gustav. "Ein Roman von Louise von François." Rev. of Die letzte Reckenburgerin by Louise von François. Im Neuen Reich 2.8 (1872): 295-300.

Gissing, George. The Odd Women. 1982. New York: Stein and Day, 1968.

Joeres, Ruth Ellen Boetcher. "Self-Conscious Histories: Biographies of German Women in the Nineteenth Century." German Women in the Nineteenth Century: A

Social History. John C. Fout, ed. New York: Holmes &
Meier, 1984, 172-96.

Miller, Nancy K. "Emphasis Added: Plots and Plausi-
bilities in Women's Fiction," PMLA 96 (1981): 36-48.

Möhrmann, Renate. Die andere Frau: Emanzipationsansätze
deutscher Schriftstellerinnen im Vorfeld der Acht-
undvierziger Revolution. Stuttgart: Metzler, 1977.

Pratt, Annis. Archetypal Patterns in Women's Fiction.
Bloomington: Indiana University Press, 1981.

Schwartzkoppen, Clotilde von. "Louise von François: Ein
Lebensbild." Vom Fels zum Meer 10 (1894): 193-98.

Twellmann-Schepp, Margrit. Die deutsche Frauenbewegung:
Ihre Anfänge und erste Entwicklungen 1843-1889.
Meisenheim am Glan: Athenäum, 1972.

Watson, Barbara Bellow. "On Power and the Literary
Text." Signs 1 (1975): 111-18.

Wendel, Edith. "Frauengestalten und Frauenprobleme bei
Louise von François." Diss. U. Vienna, 1959.

Three Late Eighteenth-Century Women's Journals: Their Role in Shaping Women's Lives

Helga Madland

The eighteenth-century discussion concerning the role of women grounded its assumptions in "nature." Since the Graeco-Roman period, women had been perceived as inferior to males in the social hierarchy; the enlightened supposition, however, that no "man" has the "natural" right to dominate another propounded by political theorists beginning with Hobbs (1588-1679),[1] saw the emergence of arguments extending the implications of these new democratic ideas to women. The advocates of natural law argued that there is "a law which antedates all human and divine power and is valid independently of such power" (Cassirer 239). In practical terms it meant that women should have equal rights to education (and subsequent participation in the public sphere),[2] an idea suggested as early as 1505 by the philosopher Agrippa von Nettesheim[3] but not really becoming a serious issue until the late seventeenth and particularly the eighteenth century.[4] To contest these claims a sustained and successful enterprise, whose primary objective was the establishment of "scientific" evidence attesting to women's "natural" inferiority, took place. For example, in France and Germany, anatomists' "depiction of a smaller female skull was used to prove that women's intellectual capabilities were inferior to men's"[5] thus justifying their social inequality. Similarly, "the larger female pelvis was used . . . to prove that women were naturally destined for motherhood, the confined sphere of hearth and home" (Schiebinger 43). These efforts were successful, for German women remained excluded from participation in the public sphere, the arena of discourse concerned with politics, throughout the eighteenth century and well into the twentieth century.[6]

Since education was a central concern of the Age of Enlightenment, however, the voices supporting the notion that women too had the potential to be educated were not totally silenced. During the early decades of the eighteenth century, the idea of "weibliche Gelehrsamkeit" became fashionable and was postulated in, among other literature, Gottched's journal Die vernünftigen Tadlerinnen.[7] The best-known treatise in support of women's education written by a woman is Dorothea Christiane Leporin's dissertation "Gründliche Untersuchung der Ursachen die das weibliche Geschlecht vom Studieren Abhalten" published in 1742. Leporin, the first woman to be awarded a doctoral degree from a German university, unmasks arguments against the education of women as prejudices and demands that women be permitted to attend universities, a right German women did not gain until 1900 although, as in the case of Leporin, there were occasional degrees awarded to women. During the second half of the eighteenth century, the notion of the intellectual female fell into discredit and women who aspired to a scholarly education became objects of ridicule (Bovenschen 158). While the concept of "Bildung," the idea that women should be trained in the "feminine" arts and letters, which included the study of French, English, painting, and music, remained influential, abstract knowledge, that is knowledge for its own sake such as Latin and philosophy, which would not contribute to the formation of a delightful and entertaining bourgeois wife, was discouraged.[8] Educational policy for women during this time was strongly influenced by Rousseau who in his Emile (Emile ou de l'education, 1762) projects the properly educated female to be a woman who has been trained to be a passive and subordinate appendage of her husband. At the same time, the redefinition of the house as a "haven from the hostile world" placed greater value on the woman as a beautiful and erotic object[9] who was expected to have a serene temperament and an inviting exterior.[10] The women's journals, a source accessible to middle-class women,[11] played a major role as an educational medium filling the "vacuum" created by the early discontinuation of a young girl's limited education. Evident in all the journals is their manipulation of women, their attempt to shape them into passive and decorative objects, and their lack of respect for women's viewpoints. It is particularly well illustrated by two letters discussing the wearing of corsets printed in the Journal des Luxus und der Moden. The arguments presented in these two letters, together with relevant fiction and editorial comments in Flora and the Leipziger Taschenbuch, are the concern of this article.

The Journal des Luxus und der Moden, first published in 1786 by Müller and Kiepenheuer and edited by F.J. Bertuch and G.M. Kraus, was a magazine intended for the affluent segments of society who had sufficient leisure and wealth to pursue an interest in and inclination for fashion and luxury.[12] The other two journals discussed here are the Leipziger Taschenbuch für Frauenzimmer zum Nutzen und Vergnügen first published in 1784 and edited by Franz Ehrenberg (it was also called the Frauenzimmer-Almanach zum Nutzen und Vergnügen) and Flora, first published in 1786 and edited by C.J. Zahn and L.F. Huber. Joachim Kirchner has identified eighty-five women's magazines published between 1700-1800.[13] Of these, only three adopted a new tone and attempted to formulate a more independent image of women: Gottsched's already-mentioned Vernünftigen Tadlerinnen, Sophie von La Roche's Pomona, and Marianne Ehrmann's Amaliens Erholungsstunden.[14] Of these three, Marianne Ehrmann was the most outspoken in her attempts to induce women to think for themselves.[15] Her journal consciously covers topics of historical, political, and cultural interest in contrast to the majority of other women's journals (a few of which were edited by women; Krull 193) which focus primarily on household and beauty hints and sentimental, didactic fiction, although the Journal des Luxus und der Moden also featured articles on the theater and music and political essays of an anti-feminist nature (Schumann 159-60). Sabine Schumann summarizes the female image presented in the women's journals as follows: "Die Frau wird in den Zeitschriften durchgängig in der Rolle der Passivität definiert, d.h., sie kann sich nicht als selbständig handelnde Person begreifen: Schönheit, Sanftheit, Bescheidenheit, hausfrauliche Tugenden, Triebverzicht sind die Elemente ihrer Existenz" (163). Woman is defined as the polar opposite of man according to the concept of "Geschlechtscharakter," a notion which evolved during the eighteenth century (Hausen 363). The three journals discussed here are typical in their support of this definition of women. While others could have been selected, these are representative and therefore appropriate for an analysis of the clever and sustained manipulation of women basing its arguments on the philosophy of nature (Cassirer 37-92).

A major goal for the editors of the Journal des Luxus und der Moden was the expansion of their readers' appreciation of luxury. In their introductory essay initiating the first volume of the Journal, they therefore discuss the pivotal role luxurious living plays in the economic and moral life of the German nation. Disclaiming allegiance to the two popular views of luxury regarding it as either a plague which consumes the profits and energies of a nation or as a blessing which serves as the almighty catalyst of industry and trade, they seek to arrive at their own morally and politically acceptable definition. Ingeniously, they isolate three stages of luxury: "Wolleben, Hochleben und Ueppigkeit."[16] "Wolleben" and "Hochleben" are regarded as a major driving force in the economy, indeed a sacred obligation the wealthy bourgeoisie and the aristocracy owe the state. Basing their views on Johann Georg Büsch's "Abhandlung von dem Geldsumlaufe,"[17] they write: "Er [der Aristokrat] muss nicht nur wolleben, er muss hoch leben, damit das ihm reichlich zufliessende Geld wieder in Umlauf komme" (Journal 25). "Ja es ist ihm gewissermassen Pflicht gegen den Staat, in dem er lebt" (24). The luxurious living enjoyed by the wealthy burghers and the aristocrats is morally justified as "eine der grossen Puls-Adern in jedem Staatskörper der Leben und Kräfte hat" (25). Our eager advocates of luxury do not, however, refrain from issuing a didactic and moralistic warning:

> sobald der Mittelmann das auf Wolleben wendet, was er noch zum Lebensunterhalt brauchte, und der Reiche mehr auf sein Hochleben, als seine Einkünfte nachhaltig erlauben, sobald wird Luxus Ueppigkeit; und wer wird noch läugnen, daß er dann dem Wohlstande der Staaten so wie seiner Familie schädlich werden kann (25).

The editors' reasoning is calculated to preserve class distinctions. It seems to be a perversion of Adam Smith's economic theories possible only in an absolutistic state: "As subsistence is, in the nature of things, prior to conveniency and luxury, so the industry which procures the former, must necessarily be prior to the increase of the town, which furnishes only the means of conveniency and luxury."[18] There is no room in Smith's sober and serious view of a nation's economic prosperity for the advocacy of luxurious living as a solemn national duty.

The eighteenth-century German bourgeois woman was, of course, intended to be the consumer of the articles described in the Journal des Luxus und der Moden.[19] Relegated to a space removed from the active male world of politics and economics--the single family house--her role was determined by pragmatics: her contribution to society was to consist of the bearing of children and the supervision of the household.[20] But she also had another value for the middle-class male: historically his property,[21] she attained an ornamental or exhibitional value, much like his house or other possessions. Woman also functioned as an erotic object, as an antidote to the supression of sexuality in the masculine world of commerce and politics. Masculine ideas of feminine beauty determined her desirability and were to be reflected not only in a woman's dress, in the accouterments of physical beauty displayed for her in such journals as the Journal des Luxus und der Moden, but also in her body. Thus the Frauenzimmerlexikon of 1715, in an earnest desire to promote contentment, lists some thirty requirements for perfection including: "nicht zu fett, nicht zu mager; ein holdseliges Lächeln; kleine röthliche Ohren, so nicht allzuweit von dem Haupt abstehen; eine zarte Haut, mit kleinen blauen Aederlein unterleget; ein langer elfenbeinener Hals" (Theweleit 1: 345). The eighteenth-century woman was not left in doubt about what was expected of her!

Presumably, the woman living up to masculine ideals of beauty possesses the erotic attraction necessary to interest a man. Through her eroticism, however, the male now perceives her to have gained a fatal power over him, an evaluation of womanhood not only stressed by the church, but also by the influential Rousseau (Elshtain 162). For Rousseau, in Silvia Bovenschen's words, it is one of the "Fatalitäten der weiblichen Natur, daß die Frauen diese Macht über Gebühr auszudehnen suchen" (178). Inherent in Rousseau's educational program, therefore, is an attempt to contain the erotic power women have over men (Bovenschen 178). This perception, the desire to "domesticate" women, seems to spill over into the women's journals. Theirs is a two-fold mission: 1) to instruct the female and 2) to control her. The journals accomplish this in three ways: they 1) mold, 2) frighten, and 3) silence women into submission. In their pages, the emphasis on physical beauty and on domesticity is unmistakable. Articles such as "Mittel, die weibliche Schönheit zu erhalten" (228), "Historische Bemerkungen über den Gebrauch der Schminke" (233), "Etwas von den rothen Haaren" (241), "Empfehlung eines Universal-Schönheitsmittels" (244), and the new year's message "Frieden der Welt, die Palme dem Helden, Lorbeer den Musen, und Hauben und Hüthe den Schönen zum Neuen Jahre,"[22] are abundant in the Journal des Luxus und der Moden. "Häuslichkeit ist die Zierde des Weibes"[23] is the reassuring conclusion of the Leipziger Taschenbuch short story "Luise Selneck, Oder: der Sieg über den Hagestolz," whose beautiful, reformed heroine had shown dangerous signs of independence. The sketch "Louise, ein

Gemählde unsrer Zeit" proclaims "schön ist die Rose; doch schöner noch das Veilchen" (Leipziger Taschenbuch 1784, 102). Women are taught to be patient and humble rather than independent and active; therefore, the rebellious "rose" is doomed to remain a "Blüthe ohne Frucht" (104), while the obedient and submissive violet is rewarded with a husband and children. Natural law is the authority in the poem "Die Bestimmung. Ein Trinklied für Frauenzimmer," which summarizes social and moral values appropriate for women and is to be sung in a "stillvergnügt" tone. The rhetoric would have appealed to ideologues of National Socialism, for it combines an emphasis on woman's "natural destiny for motherhood" with patriotism: women are urged to feel "der Bestimmung Würde, / . . . Pflänzerin der Welt zu werden / . . . Und dann--deutsches Weib zu seyn" (Leipziger Taschenbuch 1784, 234-36).

Did it occur to eighteenth-century society that woman might rebel against the confined and tedious life her solely domestic role prescribed? The women's journals are replete with fiction warning women of the pitfalls and danger lurking outside the house. Erring women in most dire and pitiful circumstances are depicted in the fiction which constitutes a large portion of the journals. A typical example is the short story "Amalie. Oder: die Unglücklichen [sic] durch Selbstschuld" whose heroine marries well, but feels lonely and dissatisfied after a brief interlude during which the couple had participated in court life. Yearning to partake of the greater world which is denied her on the samll estate she inhabits with her husband, Amalie squanders her husband's fortune and lavishes her attention on others. Although her husband-teacher, whose perspective the narrator adopts, is an angel of mercy who forgives all, "divine" justice is not so generous, for at the hour of death poor Amalie pays for her irresolute life by suffering the tortures of hell dying a death that predicts eternal damnation: "Und mit einemmahl ward ihr Auge starr, stammelnde Worte, die sie sprach, trugen die Marter der Hölle, und ihr Geist entfloh unter den schrecklichsten Verzückungen des Körpers (Leipziger Taschenbuch 1799, 146). Amalie's widower takes their son and the young girls of the town to his wife's grave to tell them her lamentable story "zur lehrreichen Warnung" (146). The warning, printed in spaced type for those who still did not get the point, is: "A r m e A m a l i e! w i e h a r t b ü s s t m a n f ü r d i e T h o r h e i t e n d e r g r o s s e n W e l t!" (146).

172

The journal Flora, whose predecessor Ameliens Erholungsstunden had shown such promise under the editorship of Marianne Ehrmann, deteriorated to such a degree that even Schiller was moved to criticize its triviality. In a letter to the editors dated November 14, 1794, he begins with a polite praise of the journal, but adds: " . . . Aber ich kann es Ihnen kaum verzeihen, daß Sie sich bisher blos auf eine angenehme Unterhaltung des schönen Geschlechts einschränken, das einer ernsthaftern Belehrung und Bildung so sehr empfänglich und würdig ist."[24] However, the man who penned the lines "Der Mann muss hinaus / Ins feindliche Leben, / . . . Und drinnen waltet / Die züchtige Hausfrau" did not necessarily advocate enlarging women's horizons, but merely favored more serious instruction in their role as wife and mother.[25] His poem "Die Kindsmörderin," whose text and music were printed in Flora in April 1793, seems to be his idea of a serious topic for "das schöne Geschlecht." The pathos and sentimentality of its narration of an unmarried mother's plight is calculated to create fear of the world outside the safety of the house. The real social problem of the unmarried maidservants, however, who did not have the protection of a patriarchal father and who committed most of the infanticides, is not addressed.

Amalie's point of view is not addressed in the above short story nor is the child murderess allowed to speak, for the eighteenth-century woman was discouraged from thinking and speaking independently. The most notable example is probably Luise Adelgunde Victoria Gottsched who, for the most part, subordinated her literary activity to that of her husband. On a less spectacular level, the editor of the Leipziger Taschenbuch leads the reader to believe that his wife Caroline, whose articles reveal her to be a competent and pragmatic person, is incapable of counting to three without his assistance. He describes the following scene: while sitting in his library contemplating his many children and potential grandchildren--"Bey Gott! ich weiss mich nicht vor Wonne zu lassen" (Leipziger Taschenbuch 1784, 200)--Caroline quietly slips into the room and he gives her the pen. "Und was damit machen? Väterchen?" she asks (a peculiar question for an adult). "Schreiben.--Und was?--Alle die goldnen Regeln, wodurch du deine Töchter zu solchen brauchbaren Hausmüttern erzogst" (200). And thus began the literary career of Caroline Ehrenberg!

In spite of the essays Caroline produced for Flora, masculine authority was preserved because she was writing under the editorship of her husband. All he had to do was take away his pen, and she would once again be silent. "Go back within the house and see to your daily duties, / your loom, your distaff, and the ordering of your servants; / for speech is man's matter, and mine above all others, / for it is I who am master here" Telemachus scolds his mother Penelope in this telling scene from the Odyssey.[26] The eighteenth century reiterated this ancient view of women at a time when the rights and duties of political participation were being extended to or demanded by more and more European males. A revealing example of the triumph of male authority over women who wish to speak on their own behalf is the "great corset debate" published in the Journal des Luxus und der Moden.

The corset appears to be a foolish and unhealthy absurdity of fashion. It was used as early as the sixteenth century to shape and mold the female figure so that it might more closely resemble prevailing ideals of beauty. By the eighteenth century, the manufacture of the increasingly intricate whalebone garment supported a coterie of highly skilled craftsmen. The corset had evolved to a detail of design which permitted a more shapely figure and narrow waist "by placing the bones diagonally at the front to narrow the waist. . . ."[27] The resulting considerable distortion of the body not only caused frequent discomfiture but also serious pain. For many, the German word Schnürbrust, which so graphically describes the garment's physical function, became an icon of oppression, constriction, and domination and was used as such by Schiller and Goethe. In Die Räuber, for example, Karl Moor cries out: "Ich soll meinen Leib pressen in eine Schnürbrust und meinen Willen schnüren in Gesetze,"[28] and in the essay "Zum Shakespeares-Tag" Goethe decries the narrowness of a century in which "wir von Jugend auf alles geschnürt und geziert an uns fühlen und an andern sehen."[29] The corset is not only a fitting symbol for women's condition but also represents actual physical confinement. Women were relieved of the corset during the latter part of the eighteenth century only to exchange it for the confinement of the house.

The corset was worn primarily by women belonging to the nobility and the upper middle class. Toward the end of the eighteenth century, the corset was found to be hazardous to its wearer's health. As a gesture of public service the editors of the Journal des Luxus und der Moden, in an article entitled "Die Schnürbrust vor einem weiblichen Tribunale" (107-17), introduced the topic by presenting the facts of the situation: in the manner of

174

the reformist eighteenth century's attempt to resolve problematic issues by posing public questions or contests (Preisfragen),[30] Herr Professor Salzmann of Schnepfenthal had asked: "ist die Schnürbrust dem weiblichen Körper schädlich oder unschädlich?" (107).[31] Both prize-winning essays responding to the challenge were written by men and found the corset to be physically harmful. The two essays, one by the anatomist Professor Sömmering and the other by an anonymous author, were published in 1788 under the title: "Über die Schädlichkeit der Schnürbrüste." The editors add: "ein kleines Buch von vorzüglichem Werthe, dessen Lectüre wir sorgfältigen Müttern die Töchter zu erziehen haben, nicht genug empfehlen können" (108). They then explain that they had hoped the scientific inquiry by experts (anatomists and physiologists) would resolve the matter once and for all, but to their astonishment, a female defender of the corset submitted a letter to the Journal inviting the editors to publish it, so that the matter could be judged by female readers rather than by male professors. The editors, who announce that they regard themselves not as the judges of customs but only as their historians, conceded to this request and agreed to publish the letter by the female proponent of the corset, along with a response by a female opponent.

The exchange presents itself as a serious debate between two intelligent women—the editors assure the reader that both women are "Damen von Geist"—but it soon becomes clear that the editors at all times retain their position of power along clearly established patriarchal lines, and that they have no intention of letting the two women decide the issue for themselves. As men of reason they cannot, of course, condone the health-impairing institution of the corset, and one can certainly not argue that they were mistaken in encouraging its elimination. One is, however, alerted by the tone they adopt toward the two women, a mode of speaking to and about them which smugly reiterates the traditional notion that decisions concerning women's lives are best made by men.[32]

The opponent of the corset, who happens to agree with the editors' point of view, is introduced as "eine Dame von Geist, die glückliche Mutter mehrerer gesunder und schon gewachsener Kinder ist, und die durch ihre Erfahrung und hellen Verstand sich vollkommen zu der, von unserer anonymen Correspondentin verlangten Richterin qualifizirte" (109). The proponent is said to defend "ihren Liebling, die Schnürbrust, im Namen ihres ganzen

175

Geschlechts, mit vielem Geiste, Sophisterey und Scheingründen"; further, she "protestirt geradezu gegen das
Urtheil der Männer, die nie eine Schnürbrust trugen, als
incompetente Richter in dieser Sache und appelirt . . .
an ein weibliches Tribunal" (109).

By the late eighteenth century, the corset had already fallen out of fashion in favor of the "natural"
neoclassical French model of the Directoire--the loosely
draped Empire style which focused on natural body shape.
The opponent of the corset can therefore not be regarded
as the plucky rebel she would have been at a time when
the Paris fashion dictum had not yet declared the garment's obsolescence. Nevertheless, the language she used
in her letter indicates a long-standing rebellion toward
an untenable societal demand: "Noch mit Schaudern er-
innere ich mich einer Schnürbrust, die ich in meiner
frühen Jugend getragen, welche freylich in ihrer Art
nicht von der besten Sorte war. Aber was half es? Es
ging damit wie mit hundern andern Dingen in der Welt;
alle Jahre bekam ich einen dergleichen neuen Panzer . . ." (115).[33] Ironically, however, because she
happens to agree with a male-determined new dictum, one
which apparently has already been accepted as the norm
by influential segments of society, the potential rebel
is cast in the role of exemplary sustainer of the mainstream culture: her credentials as a happy mother of
several healthy and attractive children establish her
credibility beyond all doubt. The proponent of the corset, however, who remains anonymous but could well also
be the happy mother of several healthy and attractive
children, is branded as untrustworthy because she has
committed the fatal error of disagreeing with a masculine decision about women, of protesting the judgment
of men on the grounds that female experience is ultimately a better judge than male theory.

In their introduction to the two letters, the editors, who portray themselves as enlightened reformers
determined to eliminate a dangerous threat to women's
health--the wearing of a corset is "eine schlimme
Sache" which they do not wish to defend (109)--never-
theless agree that they will let the two women of
"Geist" (109) decide the matter, humbly reserving for
themselves only the right to a few brief footnotes. However, there are no footnotes to the opponent's letter,
only to that of the proponent! The notes, interjected at
propitious times, quickly make it clear that the editors
intend to ridicule the position of the corset's proponent in case the reader is unable to decide for her-

or himself that her argument is replete with the "Sophisterey und Scheingründen" (109) to which they had already referred in the introduction, and that they have no intention of letting the women themselves resolve a question so intensely concerned with their own bodies.

In the time-honored manner of pedantry, the footnotes in the proponent's letter are plentiful, on one page longer than the text of the letter itself, a graphic response to her query: "Wer nie eine Schnürbrust trug, kann der wohl so richtig von ihren Folgen urtheilen, als der den tägliche Erfahrung davon belehrt? und ist eben darum das Zeugnis eines Frauenzimmers nicht gültiger in dieser Sache als das Urtheil der Männer?" (112). The sarcastic footnote provides the answer that a woman's experience is not sufficient evidence: "O gewiss, und wenigstens eben so richtig und gültig, als das Urtheil des Gelbsüchtigen von Farben. Wer wollte aus Mangel von Respecte daran zweifeln?" (112).

The editors' most successful attempt to trivialize the proponent's arguments is the following exchange: the author states: "Aber die Sache ist zum Glück, so gefährlich nicht, sonst müsste das weibliche Geschlecht der höheren Stände längst ausgestorben seyn" (111). To demonstrate her lack of reasoning powers, the editors interrupt: "Diess ist eine falsche Consequenz. Die physische und moralische Natur des Menschen kann sehr viel Mishandlungen an ihr ertragen ehe sie ganz unterliegt, und hat unglaubliche Kraft, sich demungeachtet zu erhalten und wieder herzustellen" (111); the proponent continues: "und wäre sie es, so würde doch schwerlich eine gelehrte Abhandlung die Abschaffung einer Mode bewürken, gegen welche Rousseaus einnehmende Beredsamkeit nichts vermogte" (111), to which the editors respond: "Wie aber, wenn diese Mode schon wirklich abgeschafft wäre? Denn in Frankreich und England trägt keine Dame, von gesundem Leibe, eine eigentliche Schnürbrust mehr" (111). The proponent seems to have a better understanding of the social dynamics which supported the wearing of the corset than the editors have, for she recognizes that common sense has no impact on fashion. In her next sentence, however, she adopts an expected and approved female stance when she refers to the difficulty of the experts' treatises and claims that she could not understand their scientific language. She seems to have absorbed the rules of eighteenth-century successful womanhood when she writes: "Wir Weiber wollen nun einmal zugleich unterhalten seyn, wenn wir etwas lesen, und werden lieber eine steife Schnürbrust anziehen, als eine

Schrift lesen, die uns lange Weile macht, weil wir sie nicht verstehen" (111). This, of course, gives the editors a good opportunity to respond with "Ey! Ey!!" (111) with two exclamation points after the second Ey.

The corset's opponent, the would-be rebel redeemed only because she concurs with the editors, agrees that the treatises are difficult to understand, but has an original interpretation of the motivation behind the professors' intentions: "Ich will alle die gelehrten und uns unverständlichen Abhandlungen der Herrn Aerzte und Anatomiker in ihren Ehren und Werthe lassen, die eigentlich mehr zu ihrem eignen Behufe, als zu unserer Ueberzeugung geschrieben zu seyn scheinen" (115). Like the corset's proponent, she relies on her own experience and observation in formulating her assessment of the controversy. The two women, both of whom had personal experience wearing a corset, arrive at completely contradictory conclusions, however, indicating that there is much more at stake here than the simple question whether or not the corset is detrimental to women's health. The dispute suggests that the corset is not simply a garment, but that the social practice of wearing it is a "sign" representative of a condition.[34]

The corset signifies both the condition of women as a sex, and their class status as ornamental luxuries. On the one hand, it signifies the female situation itself—imprisonment and enmeshment in the whale-bone structure of patriarchal society's restrictions and demands. The imagery applied by the corset's opponent in particular indicates this. She compares the experience of wearing the corset to that of "ein armer Gefangner in seinem Kerker und Fesseln" (115), describes the ill-fitting garment into which her body was forced as a young girl as a "Panzer" (115), a military reference suggesting protection from the outside world but at the same time seclusion, and calls it a "Plage" (116), implying the confinement of illness and disease. Both women use language borrowed from the political discourse of the times, a rhetoric that stresses the liberation of the individual. The opponent decries the "hölzernen Puppen" (116), manipulated women who are not even capable of bending down to pick up their own handkerchiefs (116), who have been denied personal freedom, while the proponent, albeit arguing the reverse, speaks of the "Tiranney der Schnürbrüste" (110) and the dilemma of women "die man wider ihren Willen 'in Freyheit setzen will'" (110). The desire to be rid of the corset voiced by the garment's opponent is a declaration of female autonomy and self-determination comparable to contemporary feminists' bra-burning, an act ridiculed by society because it is unconsciously perceived as a threat.

On the other hand, the corset's proponent gives politically charged class significance to the corset wearer. The wasp-waisted, extravagantly coiffed lady, erect and immobile, smiling and waiting for an admirer to retrieve the handkerchief she dropped and cannot reach herself, is significative of the decadent, late eighteenth-century aristocracy: the threat of the elimination of the garment is subconsciously perceived by the letter-writer as a threat to the privileged classes. Her letter is published under the heading "Vertheidigung der Schnürbrüste gegen die, denselben drohende Revolution" and she compares the situation of the embattled corset to that of the King of France. She begins her epistle with "Das achtzehnte Jahrhundert scheint mit grossen Begebenheiten endigen zu wollen. An den Ufern der Seine empört sich eine Nation wider den ältesten Monarchen Europens, und im Reiche der Mode, will man der Schnürbrust ihre verjahrte [sic] Rechte rauben" (110); she complains that unlike the "königliche Gewalt" (110), the corset is not finding enough defenders. Her passionate rhetoric is a reminder that the corset not only shaped the body according to a specific notion of beauty, but that it signified wealth and status, for it rendered its wearer inactive and immobile inducing an enforced state of leisure, a privilege only the aristocracy could afford. The interests of the emerging bourgeoisie, however, required active participation by all citizens, with the female members of society restricted to domestic activity, a fact reiterated again and again in the women's journals. While the corset is designed to shape the female body, its elimination implies the reshaping of society, a political implication, disguised as a health hazard, apparently recognized by the garment's defender.

As enlightened citizens, the editors state their opposition to "unnatural" exercises of power, to despotism and tyranny. "Sobald die königl. Gewalt in Despotismus ausartet," they write, "macht sie den Staats-Körper zum Krüppel, und muss in die Schranken ihrer rechten, natürlichen und nur wohlthätigen Form zurückgebracht werden, wenn die Nation nicht in den elendesten Marasmus verfallen soll" (110). A major principle of the right, natural, and beneficent mode, that is, of the patriarchal system they seek to guard, is that women be held in tutelage, that they become willing and silent

workers in the bourgeois household (Cocalis 52; Duden
126). The German word is bevormunden and means that
somebody speaks for you and you do not speak for your-
self. Like Telemachus silencing his mother Penelope, the
two editors successfully deny the two women the right to
speak for themselves. Even though the opponent seems to
be speaking independently, the editors make it mani-
festly clear that she espouses their opinion and thus is
really speaking for them. The proponent's arguments are
consistently ridiculed. By trivializing the proponent's
comments and transforming the opponent into their mouthpiece, the editors have silenced the women and safe-
guarded male authority.

To what extent did women attempt to protest the restrictions imposed upon them during the Age of Enlightenment? It is clear that efforts were made. Marianne
Ehrmann's and Sophie von La Roche's albeit short-lived
journals, which questioned the traditional self-
understanding of women as passive and completely dependent, have already been mentioned. On a more private
level, in their correspondence, women express their dissatisfaction quite freely. Thus even Luise Gottsched,
the model wife, complains of the hardships of her life
in her letters to Dorothea Runckel and Wilhelmine
Schulze[35]; Charlotte von Stein, who is only identified
with Goethe in literary histories, shows that she
thought independently when she wrote to Charlotte
Schiller:

> Ich glaube, daß wenn ebenso viel Frauen
> Schriftstellerinnen wären, als Männer es
> sind, und wir nicht durch so tausend
> Kleinigkeiten in unserer Haushaltung her-
> abgestimmt würden, man vielleicht auch
> einige gute darunter finden würde, denn
> wie wenige gute gibt es nicht unter den
> Autorn ohne Zahl.[36]

Yet women in Germany did not express their rebellion
on the larger political level, as happened in France and
England. Significantly, the only German equivalent to
Olympe de Gouges' Declaration of the Rights of Women
(1791) and Mary Wollstonecraft's A Vindication of the
Rights of Woman (1792) is by a man: Theodor Hippel's
didactic Über die bürgerliche Verbesserung der Weiber
(1792). In Germany, the Journal des Luxus und der Moden
did bring material of a political nature to the attention of its readers. A letter entitled "Klagen und
Bitten des schönen Geschlechts an den jetzigen

französichen Reichstag," written by a French woman
revealing the writer's political consciousness, was
printed in the Journal. She writes:

> Wohlan dann, versammelte Väter des Volkes,
> wenn die Nation, wenn die Menschheit und
> ihre heiligen Rechte eure ganze Kraft und
> Zeit fordern, so wisset daß auch unser
> Geschlecht die eine Hälfte der Menschheit
> und der Nation ausmacht. Warum sollt' es
> denn nicht eben so gut als euer Geschlecht
> bey der gesetzgebenden Versammlung Zutritt
> geniessen? (290).

The Journal did not fail to publish its opinion: "Wir
glauben, daß eine Frau nie aus ihrem Familienkreise her-
austreten dürfe, um sich in Geschäfte der Staatsver-
waltung zu mischen. . . . Sie sind überall Hörerinnen,
nie Sprecherinnen" (Schumann 160). Representative of the
destruction of any gains women may have made earlier in
the century (if indeed the emphasis on weibliche
Gelehrsamkeit is sufficient to regard it as progress for
women), is the French attorney general's response to
Olympe de Gouges' declaration: "Woman is born free and
lives equal to man in her rights."[37] When in 1793 all
women's organizations were dissolved in France and women
were forbidden to gather in groups larger than five,
Chamette, the attorney general, responded with:

> Die Natur sagte der Frau: Sei Weib! . . .
> die Erziehung der Kinder, die häuslichen
> Sorgen, die süssen Mühen der Mutterschaft
> - das ist das Recht deiner Arbeit. . . .
> Im Namen der Natur, bleibt was ihr seid,
> weit entfernt davon, uns um die Kämpfe un-
> seres Lebens zu beneiden, begnügt euch da-
> mit, sie uns vergessen zu machen" (Braun
> 88).

The evidence that the Enlightenment failed women is
unmistakable. As the tone of the three journals indicates, their male editors regarded themselves as per-
forming an important role in the instruction of women.
While they published articles and letters written by
women, these were always printed under the careful
editorship of men. The corset debate especially shows
how men manipulated women's opinions to suit their own
point of view. The Enlightenment claimed that it based
its understanding of the role of women on natural law,
which questioned long-existing authority structures and

181

claims of divine law. For women, however, equality and self-determination were not realized and "natural law" merely came to represent the substitution of one authority for another.[38]

Notes

[1] See Ernst Cassirer, The Philosophy of the Enlightenment, trans. Fritz C.A. Koelln and James P. Pettegrove (Princeton: Princeton University Press, 1979) 234-53. Thomas Hobbes Elements of Law Natural and Politic was written in 1639. Additional references are placed in the text.

[2] On women in social and political thought, see Jean Bethke Elshtain, Public Man, Private Woman (Princeton: Princeton University Press, 1981). Additional references are placed in the text.

[3] His essay in defense of women's rights to education is entitled "Von dem Vorzug des weiblichen vor dem männlichen Geschlecht."

[4] A well-known essay is Christian Lehms's support of female education entitled "Daß das weibliche Geschlecht so geschickt zum Studieren als das männliche" (1715). Lily Braun notes that between 1657 and 1727, at least eighteen treatises and dissertations supporting the point of view that women did have the potential to be educated were written. She calls the women scholars of the seventeenth and eighteenth centuries the "Triebfeder der deutschen Frauenbewegung." See Die Frauenfrage (1901; Berlin: Dietz, 1979) 66. Additional references are placed in the text.

[5] Londa Schiebinger, "Skeletons in the Closet: The First Illustrations of the Female Skeleton in Eighteenth-Century Anatomy," Representations 14 (1986): 43. Additional references are placed in the text.

[6] See Karin Hausen, "Die Polarisierung der 'Geschlechtscharaktere' - Eine Spiegelung der Dissoziation von Erwerbs- und Familienleben," in Sozialgeschichte der Familie in der Neuzeit Europas (Stuttgart: Klett, 1976) 363-93. Additional references are placed in the text. Also see Jürgen Habermas, Strukturwandel der Öffentlichkeit, 8th ed. (Neuwied/Berlin: Luchterhand, 1976) especially 74.

[7] For an analysis of "weibliche Gelehrsamkeit" see Silvia Bovenschen, Die imaginierte Weiblichkeit. Exemplarische Untersuchungen zu kulturgeschichtlichen und literarischen Präsentationsformen des Weibliche (Frankfurt: Suhrkamp, 1979) 65-149. Additional references are placed in the text.

[8] On women's education in the eighteenth century, see Ulrich Herrmann, "Erziehung und Schulunterricht für Mädchen im 18. Jahrhundert," in Wolfenbütteler Studien zur Aufklärung, Band III (Wolfenbüttel: 1976) 101-127.

[9] See Klaus Theweleit, "Die Sexualisierung der bürgerlichen Frau im 17/18 Jahrhundert," in Männerphantasien, Frauen, Fluten, Körper, Geschichte, 2 vols. (Reinbek bei Hamburg: Rowohlt, 1980) 1: 344-60 and Christine Touaillon, Der deutsche Frauenroman des 18. Jahrhunderts (Wien/Leipzig: Braumüller, 1919) 54. Additional references are placed in the text.

[10] See Barbara Duden, "Das schöne Eigentum," Kursbuch 47 (1977): 135. Additional references are placed in the text.

[11] See Sabine Schumann, "Das 'lesende Frauenzimmer': Frauenzeitschriften im 18. Jahrhundert," in Die Frau von der Reformation zur Romantik, ed. Barbara Becker-Cantarino, 2nd ed. (Bonn: Bouvier, 1985) 139. Additional references are placed in the text.

[12] An earlier fashion magazine was the Mode- und Galanteriezeitung published in Erfurt in 1758. It had a very short life. The Journal des Luxus und der Moden was published between 1786-1827.

[13] Joachim Kirchner, Die Zeitschriften des deutschen Sprachgebietes von den Anfängen bis 1850 (Stuttgart: Hiersemann, 1969). Also see Hugo Lachmanski, "Die deutschen Zeitschriften des 18. Jahrhunderts," Diss. Berlin, 1900 and Edith Krull, Das Wirken der Frau im frühen deutschen Zeitschriftenwesen, Beiträge zur Erforschung der deutschen Zeitschrift (Charlottenburg: Lorentz, 1939). Concerning moral weeklies, which contain many pages devoted to women, see Wolfgang Martens, Die Botschaft der Tugend: Die Aufklärung im Spiegel der deutschen moralischen Wochenschriften (Stuttgart: Metzler, 1968) and Ursula Menck, "Die Auffassung der Frau in den frühen moralischen Wochenschriften," Diss. Hamburg, 1940.

[14] On Marianne Ehrmann's journalistic activities, see Edith Krull, Das Wirken der Frau im frühen deutschen Zeitschriftenwesen (Charlottenburg: Lorentz, 1939) 236-76. Additional references are placed in the text.

[15] The author of this article has read a paper on Marianne Ehrmann, "Addressee Unknown: Marianne Ehrmann's Letters from Gottfried August Bürger," Div. on Eighteenth and Early Nineteenth Century German Literature, MLA Convention, New York, 28 Dec. 1986. She is in the process of collecting materials for a monograph on Ehrmann.

[16] Journal des Luxus und der Moden, ed. F.J. Bertuch and G.M. Kraus, 1786-1827, partial rpt., ed. Werner Schmidt, 4 vols. (Hanau/Main: Müller und Kiepenheuer, 1967-1970) 1: 24. Additional references are placed in the text. All references are to volume 1.

[17] Johann Georg Büsch, a Hamburg writer and publicist who opened a "Handlungsakademie" in Hamburg in 1767, is known for his writings about commerce; among others, Schriften über Staatswirtschaft und Handlung, 1784.

[18] Adam Smith, An Inquiry into the Nature and Causes of the Wealth of Nations, ed. Edwin Cannan (Chicago: University of Chicago Press, 1976) 402.

[19] Schumann identifies middle-class women and to some degree aristocratic women as readers of the women's journals (139).

[20] See Dagmar Grenz, Mädchenliteratur, Von den moralisch-belehrenden Schriften im 18. Jahrhundert bis zur Herausbildung der Backfischliteratur im 19. Jahrhundert (Stuttgart: Metzler, 1981) 18-19.

[21] Touaillon 34-37. Also see Dagmar Lorenz, "Vom Kloster zur Küche: Die Frau vor und nach der Reformation Dr. Martin Luthers," in Die Frau von der Reformation zur Romantik 7-35.

[22] Title page of Volume VI of the Journal des Luxus und der Moden.

[23] Leipziger Taschenbuch für Frauenzimmer zum Nutzen und Vergnügen, ed. Franz Ehrenberg (Leipzig: Bohme, 1797) 103. Subsequent references to this and other volumes are placed in the text.

[24] Flora, 3.1 (1795): 101-102.

[25] Flora, 102-103.

[26] Lawrence Lipking, "Aristotle's Sister: A Poetics of Abandonment," in Canon, ed. Robert von Hallberg (Chicago and London: University of Chicago Press, 1984) 90.

[27] Encyclopedia Americana, 30 vols. (Danbury, Connecticut: Grolier, 1984) 8: 23. Also see Norah Waugh, Corsets and Crinolines (1954; New York: Theatre Arts Books, 1970). In this thoroughly researched study, Waugh cites contemporary commentaries concerning the corset, including the following amusing observation by Horace Walpole: "There has been a young gentlewoman overturned and terribly bruised by her Vulcanian stays. They now wear a steel busk down their middle, and a rail of the same metal across their breasts. If a hero attempts to storm such strong lines, and comes to a close engagement, he must lie as ill as ease as St. Lawrence on his gridiron" (65).

[28] Friedrich Schiller, Werke, 3 vols. (München: Hanser, 1966) 1: 67.

[29] Johann Wolfgang von Goethe, Werke, 14 vols. (München: Beck, 1973) 3: 227.

[30] Another well-documented essay contest dealing with a contemporary social problem was one announced in 1781 in Mannheim by an anonymous friend of humanity. It sought to diminish the murder of newborn infants without increasing incontinence. See J.M. Rameckers, Der Kindesmord in der Literatur der Sturm und Drang Periode (Rotterdam: Nijgh and Van Ditmar, 1927) 83.

[31] That the corset could indeed be a health hazard is corroborated by this statement from the Autobiography and Correspondence of Mrs. Delany: "I hope Miss Sparrow will not fall into the absurd fashion of ye wasp-waisted ladies. Dr. Pringle declares he has had four of his patients martyrs to that folly (indeed wickedness), and when they were open'd it was evident that their deaths were occasioned by strait lacing." Cited by Waugh 60.

[32] See Susan Cocalis, "Der Vormund will Vormund sein: Zur Problematik der weiblichen Unmündigkeit im 18. Jahrhundert," Amsterdamer Beiträge zur neueren Germanistik, 10 (1980): 43, 48-49. Additional references are placed in the text.

33 The letter writer's complaint is reiterated by a fellow sufferer in the British Isles, Elizabeth Ham, who writes in 1792-93: "The first reformation made in my appearance was effected by a stay-maker. I was stood on the window-seat, whilst a man measured me for the machine, which, in consideration of my youth, was to be only what was called half-boned, that is, instead of having the bones placed as close as they could lie, an interval the breadth of one was left vacant beneath each. Notwithstanding, the first day of wearing them was very nearly purgatory, and I question if I was sufficiently aware of the advantage of a fine shape to reconcile me to the punishment." Cited by Waugh 71.

34 On the signifying nature of fashion see Roland Barthes, "The Vestimentary Sign," in The Fashion System, trans. Matthew Ward and Richard Howard (New York: Hill and Wang, 1983), 212-21. Julia Kristeva writes: "What semiotics has discovered . . . is that the law or, if one prefers, the major constraint affecting any social practice lies in the fact that it signifies, i.e. that it is articulated like a language." See Terence Hawkes, Structuralism and Semiotics (Berkeley and Los Angeles: University of California Press, 1983) 125.

35 See Ruth H. Sanders, "'Ein kleiner Umweg': Das literarische Schaffen der Luise Gottsched," in Die Frau von der Reformation zur Romantik 173 and 190.

36 Cited by Gisela Brinker-Gabler, Deutsche Dichterinnen vom 16. Jahrhundert bis zur Gegenwart (Frankfurt: Fischer, 1978), 45. Also see my paper "The German Woman--A Neglected Topic in German Studies," in German Studies in den USA--Soll und Haben, Proceedings of the International Symposium on German Studies, Taos Ski Valley, New Mexico, July 1985.

37 Article I of Olympe de Gouges's Declaration of the Rights of Woman (Les Droits de la Femme, 1791) in Women in Revolutionary Paris 1789-1795, trans. Darline Gay Levy, Harriet Branson Applewhite and Mary Durham Johnson (Urbana/Chicago/London: University of Illinois Press, 1979) 90.

38 I would like to thank Ingrid Stipa for her helpful suggestions while writing this article.

Hexenjagd in Gelehrtenköpfen*

Sigrid Brauner

Das Thema "Hexen" wird in unserer Disziplin weitgehend mit Schweigen übergangen. Es scheint peinlich. Von Hexenliteratur zu reden, gehört nicht zum "guten Ton" und schon gar nicht in den Literaturkanon. Diese "Peinlichkeit" verweist auf ein größeres Problem. Die Hexenverfolgungen der Neuzeit sind lange aus der traditionellen Geschichtsschreibung als Sonderfall ausgegrenzt worden.[1] In den letzten zehn Jahren aber haben sich feministische Forscherinnen, Sozialhistoriker und Anthropologen mit dem Phänomen neuzeitlicher Hexenverfolgungen auf neue Weise auseinandergesetzt.[2] Sie beschäftigen sich vor allem mit der sozialgeschichtlichen Relevanz der Prozesse. Obwohl weder die Quellenforschung abgeschlossen ist, noch die verschiedenen Thesen über Genese und Funktion der Verfolgungen ausdiskutiert sind,[3] zeichnen sich doch verschiedene Hypothesen ab. Eine der Thesen ist, daß die Hexenprozesse Praktiken der Volksmagie kriminalisierten und dadurch zur Sozialdisziplinierung der Unterschichten beitrugen.[4] Andere Erklärungsansätze zeigen, daß die den Prozessen zu Grunde liegende Vorstellung und Verteufelung von Hexerei und Magie eine wichtige Rolle für die Entwicklung verschiedener moderner Kulturmuster gespielt hat; so zum Beispiel für die Herausbildung des mechanistischen Weltbildes, der instrumentellen Vernunft oder für die Genese des bürgerlichen Begriffs von der Natur der Frau.[5] Die für unseren Zusammenhang zunächst wichtigste Hypothese ist jedoch, daß das den Prozessen zu Grunde liegende Hexenbild einer mit Satan paktierenden Sekte vor allem durch klerikale Literatur vom Mittelalter bis zur Neuzeit tradiert und systematisiert wurde.[6]

Vorchristliche Vorstellungen von nachtfahrenden Geistern, volkstümliche Vorstellungen von Schadenzauber, Elemente gelehrter ritueller Magie, sowie Imaginationen von kannibalistischen und orgiastischen Ketzersekten gingen in das klerikale Hexenbild ein, wurden verfremdet und ideologisiert. Vorstellungen von dämonischen, orgiastischen und kannibalistischen Sekten, die den

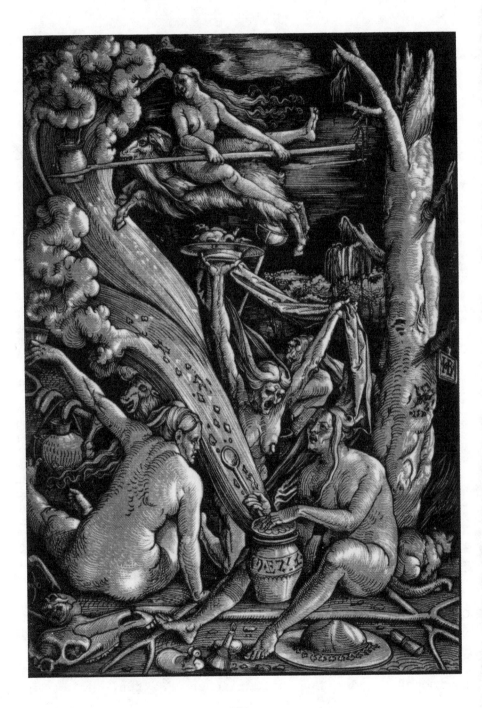

politischen Status Quo unterminieren, gehen bis in die Antike zurück, wurden von mittelalterlichen klerikalen Autoren übernommen und verändert auf die verschiedensten häretischen Gruppen angewandt. Zu Beginn der Neuzeit wurden diese Vorstellungen in das entstehende Hexenbild integriert.[7] Vom Mittelalter, als sich die ersten Elemente des späteren Hexenbildes ausbildeten, wie dämonische Sekten und Satansanbetung, bis in die Neuzeit hinein, ergaben sich immer wieder Überschneidungen zwischen theologischen und volkstümlichen Vorstellungen. In Predigten wurden paganistische Gestalten satanisiert, unter der Folter (gezwungen) gestanden Ketzer und später Hexen, an satanischen Ritualen teilgenommen zu haben, und gaben den ihnen unbekannten Teufeln in ihrer Angst Namen, die sie kannten, nämlich Namen lokaler Haus- und Waldgeister, die dann wieder in klerikaler Literatur als Satansnamen auftauchten. Zum Teil veränderten sich dadurch auch die volkstümlichen Vorstellungen von der dämonischen Welt und näherten sich in der Neuzeit allmählich den theologischen an.[8] Die klerikale Literatur spielte als Systematisiererin, autoritäre Interpretin und Umformuliererin der dämonischen Welt eine ebenso große Rolle bei der Vorbereitung der Hexenprozesse wie die Übernahme inquisitorischer Elemente in die Hexenprozeßführung.[9] Diese tragende Rolle der klerikalen Literatur ist auch schon immer in der Forschung zum Thema betont worden.[10] Dennoch findet man auch in einer neueren Literaturgeschichte die Erwähnung der Prozesse höchstens als ein quasi außerliterarisches Ereignis. Die immerhin umfangreiche literarische Tradition von Hexenbüchern, Zauberei- und Teufelsliteratur wird in derselben Literaturgeschichte als "volkstümlich" und als "Nachtseite" der Geschichte abgetan.[11] "Peinliche" Texte. Sie passen nicht in ein lineares Geschichtsbild, sie sind nicht "kanonfähig". Kann eine solche Ausgrenzung weiterhin gerechtfertigt werden? Was erzählen uns zum Beispiel Hexenelemente in der Literatur des frühen sechzehnten Jahrhunderts, kurz vor dem Einsatz der großen Hexenverfolgungen um 1680 über diese "Nachtseite" der Geschichte?

Der vorliegende Beitrag geht einigen Hexenvorstellungen in der Literatur nach. Er lädt zu einer kurzen Spritztour duch ein paar Gelehrten- und Literatenköpfe aus der ersten Hälfte des sechzehnten Jahrhunderts ein und sieht, was es in ihnen mit Hexen so auf sich hat.

Die Vorstellung von Hexenwesen ist zu Beginn des sechzehnten Jahrhunderts innerhalb der orthodoxen Theologie in den Grundzügen ausgeprägt und bestimmt die gelehrte Definition der Hexe bis in das achtzehnte Jahrhundert hinein.[12] Am ausführlichsten beschrieben ist dies im Malleus Maleficarum, einem theologisch-juristischem Handbuch für Hexenprozesse, verfaßt von zwei Dominikanern und päpstlichen Inquisitoren für das deutsche Gebiet, Henricus Institoris und Jakob Sprenger im Jahre 1487. Dieses Werk wurde zu einem der meistverlegten Bücher aus der Frühphase des Buchdrucks; es wurde bis Mitte des sechzehnten Jahrhunderts allein 13 mal aufgelegt und das ausschließlich in Latein;[13] das heißt, es gab eine relativ große Leserschaft dafür in den Gelehrtenkreisen. Das Buch summiert die theologische Tradition zum Problem Hexenwesen, wie Teufelspakt, Hexenflug, Kannibalismus, Häresie, und Beischlaf mit dem Teufel. Unter das Verbrechen der Hexerei fällt vor allem volkstümlicher Schaden- und Heilzauber, aber Formen der gelehrten Magie, der Magia Naturalis sind auch einbegriffen.[14] Der Malleus zeichnet sich aber durch verschiedene ganz neue Elemente aus. Erstmals werden hier Frauen systematisch als Hexen defamiert. Die Autoren benutzen zur Begründung das gesamte Repertoire klerikaler Misogynie des Mittelalters und verbinden es mit der Vorstellung von Hexerei, die bisher eigentlich nicht geschlechtsspezifisch war.[15] So lautet ihre Argumentation im ersten Teil des Malleus: Frauen sind das schwächere Geschlecht, das heißt sie haben keine Intelligenz, keine Selbstdisziplin, eine animalische, unersättliche Sexualität und sind aus all diesen Gründen leichter vom Teufel verführbar als Männer. Dieser zwingt sie durch sexuelle und andere Versprechungen in den Teufelspakt, macht sie sich hörig, um dann durch sie als Medium seinen Schadenzauber auszuführen wie Unwetter, Vergiftung der Nahrung, Impotenz und Unfruchtbarkeit, Krankheiten und Mißgeburten. Die Hexen mögen glauben, daß sie solches zaubern könnten, das ist aber nur eine weitere Sinnestäuschung des Teufels; er selbst führt diese Akte aus und auch das nur dann, wenn Gott es zuläßt. Obwohl die Frauen also nicht eigenständig handeln, was sie ja auch qua ihrer inferioren Natur gar nicht könnten, sind sie doch verantwortlich für solche hexerischen Taten. Ihr Vergehen ist es, dem Teufel zu verfallen und damit die höchste Form der Häresie, ein Crimen Exceptum[16] zu begehen, das mit dem Tode bestraft werden muß. Das häretische Moment wird dabei auch als Umkehrung christlicher Praktiken verstanden. In ihrer sexuellen Verbindung mit dem Teufel werden die Hexen zu Satansbräuten, schreckliches Gegenbild zu den Christusbräuten, den Nonnen, die der Malleus wegen ihres Keuschheitsgelübdes von den Vorwürfen der Hexerei ausschließt.

Die beiden Dominikaner befürchten eine wahre Hexen-
epidemie; sie glauben, daß jede Frau dem Teufel zufallen
könne und dieser nun die weltliche und göttliche Ordnung
mit einem riesigen Hexenheer bedrohe.[17] Als Prävention
sollen daher Prozesse schnell und effektiv geführt
werden. Hexen - so wird in Teil II argumentiert - sind
nicht nur Ketzerinnen, sondern sie schaden vor allem
auch dem weltlichen Staat durch Schadenzauber an Personen, Hab und Gut.[18] Daher müssen - so Teil III -
weltliche Gerichte ebenso wie die Kirche an der Aus-
rottung der Hexen interessiert sein. Um die Prozeß-
führung voranzutreiben, sollen Elemente des Inquisi-
tionsprozesses verstärkt angewandt werden. Die Autoren
erklären Folter und Denunziation zu expliziten Verfah-
rensweisen und lassen weder Verteidigung noch mildernde
Umstände zu. Damit zeigte der Malleus die Richtung an,
die sich verheerend für die Prozesse der Neuzeit
auswirken sollte, nämlich die Übernahme inquisitorischer
Verfahren in die weltliche Rechtsgebung zum Hexenprozeß.

Das lateinisch verfaßte Werk fand ungeteilte Zu-
stimmung bei Teilen der intellektuellen Elite. Argumente
des Malleus finden sich in den Schriften des dem
Humanismus nahestehenden Abtes Johann Trithemius, des
populären Predigers Geiler von Kaysersberg sowie in der
zweiten Ausgabe des Laienspiegels von Ulrich Tengler.[19]
Martin Luther, Phillip Melanchthon sowie der Hofjurist
Ulrich Molitor beziehen sich in ihren Schriften zum
Thema nicht nachweisbar auf den Malleus, argumentieren
aber auch, daß Hexen vor allem weiblich seien und daß
Hexerei mit Tod zu bestrafen sei.[20] Das Hexenwesen war
für die Gelehrten des sechzehnten Jahrhunderts Tages-
thema. Meinungsunterschiede bezogen sich vor allem auf
den Problemkreis der gelehrten Magie; Autoren wie Johann
Trithemius, Agrippa von Nettesheim und Theophrastus
Paracelsus bezeichneten Formen der Magia Naturalis wie
Astrologie, Traumdeutung, Alchemie im Gegensatz zu dem
Malleus nicht als Hexerei, sondern sie sahen die Magia
Naturalis - wie viele Humanisten - als eine positive
Wissenschaft. Es herrschte noch keine Übereinstimmung
über die Realität des Hexensabbats und des Hexenfluges;
oft noch wurde argumentiert, daß dies nur eine vom
Teufel produzierte Einbildung sei. Manche Autoren
wollten volkstümlichen Heilzauber nicht mit Todesstrafe
belegt wissen; er sollte nur als Aberglauben bestraft
werden. Erst gegen Ende des Jahrhunderts wurde die harte
Position des Malleus gegen alle Formen der Hexerei
aufgenommen, weiter ausgebaut und wurde zur dogmatischen
Lehrmeinung. Die Forschungsliteratur spricht daher von
einer "offenen" Diskussion über Hexerei im frühen 16.

Jahrhundert.[21] Dabei wird aber übergangen, daß die im Malleus systematisierte Verbindung von Frau und Hexerei in dieser "offenen" Diskussion nie zur Debatte stand. Sie wurde akzeptiert, oder die Autoren kamen unabhängig vom Malleus zu ähnlichen Schlüssen. Ein Grund dafür mag sein, daß zu dieser Zeit in denselben Gelehrtenkreisen eine lebhafte Diskussion über Ehe und Familie, über die Natur und Bestimmung von Geschlechtsrollen geführt wurde. Protestanten und Humanisten, die dabei die Ehe aufwerteten, beriefen sich aber für die weiterhin untergeordnete Rolle der Frau immer wieder auf deren physische und geistige Inferiorität und übernahmen die lange Tradition klerikaler Misogynie. Gleichgültig also, ob diese Autoren im Verlauf der Reformation Katholiken blieben oder Protestanten wurden, ob sie dem Humanismus nahestanden oder nicht, sie stimmten in einem überein: Hexerei gibt es, sie wird vom Teufel beeinflußt oder ausgeführt, Hexerei ist vor allem Schadenzauber, und Hexen sind vorwiegend Frauen. Todesstrafe für Hexerei muß sein, weil sie Häresie ist.[22]

Der humanistisch-alchemistische Wissenschaftler Agrippa von Nettesheim wird oft als einzige Gegenstimme zu dieser Position zitiert. 1519 hatte er erfolgreich eine als Hexe angeklagte Bäuerin in Metz verteidigt. In seiner Schrift De incertitudine et vanitate scientiarum[23] bezieht er sich auf diesen Fall und greift die Praxis der Hexenprozesse und vor allem die Rolle päpstlicher Inquisitoren an. Aber auch er behauptet an anderer Stelle in der gleichen Schrift, daß Frauen der Hexerei zugeneigter seien als Männer und daß Bestrafung der Hexerei göttliches Gesetz sei.[24] 1529 widerlegte er in seiner Schrift De nobilitate et praecellentia foemenei sexus ejusdemque supra virilum eminentia die kirchliche Lehre von der Inferiorität der Frau durch Material aus dem Alten und Neuen Testament, aus der Kabbala, aus antiker Mythologie und Geschichte. Aber diese Schrift hatte keine große Verbreitung und war wohl auch eher als Dedikation an eine ehemalige Mäzenin gedacht denn als öffentliche Streitschrift.[25] So erscheint auch Agrippa nur als sehr eingeschränkter Verteidiger der Frauen. Aber wegen seiner kritischen Haltung den Hexenprozessen gegenüber und wegen seines eigenen Interesses an gelehrter Magie geriet er selbst in den Ruf der Hexerei und wurde von kirchlichen Autoritäten angegriffen.

Dem Hofarzt Johann Weyer, einem Schüler Agrippas, der in den sechziger Jahren mit seiner Streitschrift De Praestigiis Daemonum et Incantatibus ac Veneficiis dafür plädierte, die Hexenprozesse abzuschaffen und

stattdessen Hexen ärztlich zu behandeln und so "umzuer-
ziehen", erging es wenig besser; er wurde erbittert be-
kämpft. So zum Beispiel von dem Protestanten Johann
Fischart, der, um Weyer zu widerlegen, gelehrte Hexen-
bücher, darunter den Malleus, neu herausgab.[26] Auch der
Arzt Theophrastus Paracelsus hatte schon vor Weyer in
seiner Schrift De sagis et earum operibus (1537) an die
Umerziehung der Hexen gedacht aber diese Schrift wurde
erst nach seinem Tode veröffentlicht, und wir wissen
nicht, wie bekannt sie war; es ist aber anzunehmen, daß
Paracelsus' Argumente in Gelehrtenkreisen diskutiert
wurden. Wichtig ist, daß die Schriften dieser beiden
Ärzte, auch wenn sie den Hexenprozeß ablehnen,[27] in zwei
Punkten völlig mit den Argumenten des Malleus über-
einstimmen; Hexen sind nämlich auch für sie vorwiegend
Frauen. Wiederum begründen sie es damit, daß Frauen
schwach sind und ein leicht beeinflußbares Gemüt haben.
Für Weyer sind Hexen kranke Melancholikerinnen, die der
Gesellschaft schaden können, aber durch Behandlung kon-
trollierbar sind; ein Argument, das sich mit der Aufklärung durchsetzen sollte und das moderne Hexenbild
vorwegnimmt: die Hexe als zu hospitalisierende Geistes-
kranke, die Hysterikerin Charcot'scher Prägung. Auch
Paracelsus glaubt, daß die Frauen für Gemütskrankheiten
anfälliger seien, aber Hexen haben für ihn noch ganz
bestimmte asoziale Qualitäten, nämlich: Sie fliehen Männer; sie verbergen sich, wollen alleine sein; sie suchen
Künstler auf; sie schließen sich an Zauberinnen an und
lernen, wozu sie der Geist treibt; sie sehen Männer
nicht an; sie kochen nicht, sie waschen sich nicht; sie
liegen gern faul herum and sperren sich alleine ein.[28]
Für Paracelsus sind Hexen also Frauen, die ihre soziale
und sexuelle Rolle verweigern, die den Männern Körper
und Geist entziehen und damit die patriarchalische
Weltordnung bedrohen.

Paracelsus und Weyer argumentieren nicht nur wie die
Autoren des Malleus, daß Hexerei mit der weiblichen Natur zusammenhänge, sondern sie bauen das Argument auch
weiter aus. Das Bild der Hexe nimmt zunehmend asoziale
Züge an, die über die Vorwürfe der Häresie, des Schadenzaubers und Teufelspaktes hinausgehen und sich auf Ab-
weichungen von sozialnormativen Geschlechtsrollen konzentrieren. Aus dem bisher Gesagten kann man dieses neue
Element des Hexenbildes der gelehrten Elite des sechzehnten Jahrhunderts wohl in den folgenden Punkten zu-
sammenfassen: 1) Hexerei wird geschlechtsspezifisch,
Hexen sind überwiegend Frauen; 2) Frauen können ihren
Sexualtrieb nicht beherrschen, sind insgesamt disziplin-
los und daher asozial; 3) die Phantasie von Frauen ist

leicht vom Teufel beeinflußbar, denn ihnen fehlt die Intelligenz, um zwischen Gut und Böse zu unterscheiden; 4) Frauen haben keine eigene Macht, d.h. sie können nicht kreativ sein oder selbständig handeln, sondern etwas anderes, nämlich das Böse (=der Teufel) handelt durch sie.[29]

Soweit die Gelehrten. In der Frühphase des 16. Jahrhunderts gingen die Hexenprozesse nach ersten größeren Pogromen um die Jahrhundertwende zurück. Im Gegensatz zu den päpstlichen Inquisitoren Institoris und Sprenger waren die anderen hier erwähnten Autoren nicht so brennend daran interessiert, ihre Haltung zur Hexerei in Taten umzusetzen.[30] In den Wirren der frühen Reformationszeit blieb die Hexerei nur ein intellektuell interessierendes Thema; der Alltag wurde von anderen, vor allem religiös-politischen Konflikten bestimmt. Aber die Juristen und Theologen, die die Prozesse gegen Frauen ein halbes Jahrhundert später unter veränderten sozialpolitischen Bedingungen durchführten, lernten von dieser literarischen Tradition.

Wie aber wurde dieses neue und veränderte Hexenbild unter die Leute gebracht? Wie konnte es für den größten Teil der Bevölkerung so attraktiv und/oder einfach nur normal werden, daß sie den Verfolgungen zu Ende des 16. Jahrhunderts keinerlei Widerstand entgegensetzten? Wie konnte es dazu kommen, daß Schauverurteilungen mit Massen von Frauen stattfinden konnten, von denen eine jede auch von den Zuschauern als Hexe akzeptiert wurde? Natürlich gab es auch populäre Vorstellungen von Hexerei, unabhängig von dem theologischen Hexenbild. Diese konzentrierten sich aber nicht auf Frauen sondern auf Heil- oder Schadenzauber, der von "weisen" Personen beiden Geschlechts ausgeübt werden konnte. Letzterer war gefürchtet und diese Furcht trug bestimmt zu einer Bereitschaft der Bevölkerung bei, Schadenzauber zu bestrafen. Aber eine solche Latenz kann die Massenprozesse nicht erklären.[31]

Merkwürdig ist ja auch, daß das den Prozessen zu Grunde liegende Hexenbild schon zu Beginn des sechzehnten Jahrhunderts innerhalb der intellektuellen Elite vorformuliert war, die Massenprozesse aber erst fünfzig Jahre später einsetzten. Es liegt also nahe anzunehmen, daß es vor den Massenprozessen Medien gegeben haben muß, die zumindest Teile der Bevölkerung auf das neue Hexenbild vorbereiteten. Eines dieser Medien war natürlich die Predigt, wie das Beispiel des populären Straßburger Predigers Geiler von Kaisersberg zeigt, der sich vorwiegend mit dem Thema Hexe beschäftigte. Auch protestantische Autoren verfaßten Hexenpredigten.[32] Predigten wurden schon früh gedruckt und zirkulierten oft unter Predigern als Vorlagen. Die Autoren des Malleus wiesen auch auf die Predigt als wichtiges Medium der Volkserziehung zum Hexenwesen hin und gaben genaue Predigtanweisungen in ihrem Buch.

Kann man aber für das frühe 16. Jahrhundert nur eine solche traditionelle Vermittlung der Theorie über das Hexenwesen von theologischen Experten über Prediger zur Bevölkerung annehmen? Wie steht es mit der Verbreitung des Hexenbilds durch weltliche populäre Literatur? Die Literatur des sechzehnten Jahrhunderts war ja nicht mehr nur klerikal. Sie richtete sich auch nicht mehr nur an eine kleine gelehrte Elite, sondern gerade auch an den "gemeinen Mann", was sich durch die Ereignisse der Reformation und der Bauernkriege noch verstärkte. Zum ersten Mal war Literatur auch vor allem Gebrauchs-literatur, sie nahm zu den religiösen und politischen Tagesthemen Stellung und verstand sich als moralische Hilfestellung für Lebensfragen.[33] Gedrucktes konnte durch die Fortschritte im Buchdruck nun massenweise her-gestellt werden.[34] Zudem war der Anteil der Bevölkerung, der lesen konnte, größer als je zuvor und sogar höher als im darauffolgenden Jahrhundert, und besonders in den Städten war Lesefähigkeit nicht nur in den Oberschichten verbreitet.[35] Vorstellungen von Hexen, die durch popu-läre Literatur verbreitet wurden, dürften von daher dort wohl eine relative große Leserschaft beeinflußt haben.

Die meistern Verfasser dieser neuen Literatur waren gebildet, waren als Gelehrte, als Theologen, oder - wie im Falle des Schuhmachers Hans Sachs - als Autodidakten mit dem aktuellen Diskussionsstand der Gelehrten auch zum Thema Hexe vertraut. Sehen wir uns also ein paar repräsentative Werke des wohl erfolgreichsten Autors zu Mitte des Jahrhunderts, Hans Sachs aus Nürnberg, an. Eines der Hauptthemen seiner Dramen und Schwänke ist das problematische Verhältnis der Geschlechter in der Ehe[36]; in zahllosen Negativbeispielen zeigt der überzeugte Protestant, was passiert, wenn Mann oder Frau sich nicht ihrem Ehestand entsprechend verhalten.Es ist kein Zu-fall, daß die Ehe ein so zentrales Thema für ihn ist; schließlich wurde sie von Luther zur Basis der weltlichen Ordnung erklärt. Aber für Sachs ist die Ehe auch vor allem eine soziale Institution; sie sichert das materielle Überleben der Stadtbürger. In Nürnberg, wie wohl auch in anderen Städten der Zeit, gab es neue Probleme mit den Eheschließungen. Die Situation der

Handwerker, für die Sachs wohl am meisten spricht, hatte sich in Nürnberg schon während des vorhergehenden Jahrhunderts verschlechtert. Zünfte waren aufgelöst und der größte Teil der Handwerker arbeitete nicht mehr in selbständiger Produktion, sondern zunehmend für Stücklohn. Gesellen hatten kaum Aussicht, Meister zu werden. Das beeinflußte auch die Familienstruktur. Kleinfamilienstrukturen lösten die Haushaltsfamilie des Handwerksmeisters ab. Die Ehefrau war nicht mehr Mitarbeitende im Familienbetrieb, sondern es scheint, daß es ihre neue Rolle war, die knappen Einkünfte dieser Haushalte sparsam zu verwerten, und wenn möglich außerhalb dazu zu verdienen. Das Überleben in einer solchen Familie erforderte daher nun einen größeren Triebverzicht und eine stärkere Arbeitsethik, versprach aber keineswegs Belohnung durch einen verbesserten sozialen Status.[37]

Diese Situation erzeugte wohl Spannungen in ehelichen Beziehungen und Sachs spricht manches davon an. So werden Männer wie Frauen, die faul sind oder Geld verschwenden, angeprangert.[38] Meistens aber ist für Sachs das Problem in der Ehe die Frau: sie ist faul, widerspenstig, geht egoistisch ihren eigenen Interessen nach, sie sucht sich zum Beispiel Liebhaber oder ißt dem Mann die letzten Speckeierpfannkuchen weg oder will in der Ehe die Hosen anhaben; kurz sie ist ein böses Weib. Diese Bosheit liegt nach Sachs in der Natur des Weibes, wie er in seinem Schwank und poeterey, Die vier natur einer frawen darlegt.[39] Danach sind Frauen zu drei Teilen schlecht, denn sie haben eine unbändige Pferdenatur, eine wollüstige Schweinenatur, eine bissige Hundenatur und nur einen Teil guter Honigwabennatur, nämlich die Fähigkeit zu guter Haushaltsführung. Trotz dieser schlechten Disposition ist nicht alle Hoffnung verloren. In Die neunerley heud einer bösen frawen sambt ihren neun eygenschafften[40] und in anderen Sprüchen und Schwänken demonstriert Sachs, daß ein rechtschaffener Mann seine Frau umerziehen kann. Im Idealfalle mit guten Worten; falls das nicht hilft mit Gewalt: Aderlaß,[41] Schläge und andere Brutalitäten sind hier das Repertoire. Die Frau dagegen kann ihren faulen oder trunksüchtigen Ehemann nur durch Geduld und liebe Worte umerziehen. Wenn er sie schlägt, muß sie es ertragen; schlägt sie zurück, wird sie sofort zum bösen Weib und bedroht die Eheordnung. Diese Ungleichheit in dem Mann und Frau zur Verfügung stehenden ehelichen Korrektionsmittel kommt natürlich daher, daß Sachs sehr ungleiche Vorstellungen vom männlichen und weiblichen sozialen Rollenideal hat. Der Mann ist Haushaltsvorstand und

Erzieher der Frau, weil Frauen nicht eigenständig mora-
lisch handeln können.

Hier zeigen sich Einflüsse protestantischer Ge-
schlechtsrollenvorstellungen, die ihrerseits von der
langen Tradition klerikaler Misogynie zehren. Die Frau
im Naturzustand ist, ohne die vermittelnde moralische
Erziehung des Mannes, unmoralisch. Die erfolgreich erzo-
gene Frau nimmt quasi eine zweite moralische Natur an;
sie wird passiv, gehorsam, zügelt ihre sexuelle Trieb-
haftigkeit, und akzeptiert ihre untergeordnete Stellung.
Jegliche Form eigenständiger Handlung, die über ihre
festgeschriebene Funktion innerhalb familiärer Haushaltsführung hinausgeht, kann nur Ausdruck ihrer unmo-
ralischen, ursprünglichen Natur sein und gilt von daher
als sozialgefährlich. Die Frau, die Gleichberechtigung
fordert, die sich gegen Schläge verteidigt, faul ist,
die Haushaltsführung verweigert, egoistisch handelt,
sich sexuell entzieht oder gar nicht heiratswillig ist,
ist Sachs zufolge asozial, d.h. "böse".

Das böse Weib oder "böse wîp" ist kein neuer Charakter der Schwankliteratur, sondern geht bis ins frühe
Mittelalter zurück. Zum Teil hatten die früheren
Schwänke auch sozial affirmativen Charakter. Jedoch kon-
zentrierte sich die Kritik meist auf den Ehemann, der
unfähig ist, seine Frau zu beherrschen und dadurch zum
Narren wird. Auch fehlt das Repertoire von Umerziehungs-
anweisungen, denn meistens enden diese älteren Schwänke
damit, daß die böse Frau mit ihrem verkehrten Handeln
gewinnt. Die böse Folge umgekehrter Geschlechterrollen
ist auch nicht, wie bei Sachs, die Gefährdung des
materiellen Überlebens sondern, wenn überhaupt kom-
mentiert, der Verlust ewigen Seelenheils.[42]

Neu bei Hans Sachs ist aber nicht nur diese Kon-
zentration auf die materielle Sphäre, sondern auch, daß
er die Figur des bösen Weibes mit dem gängigen Hexenbild
der Elite verbindet. Der Schwank Der Teufel mit dem
alten Weib, den Sachs seit 1524 in verschiedenen Fas-
sungen vorgelegt hat,[43] kann das verdeutlichen. In
diesem Schwank versucht der Teufel schon seit Jahren die
dreißigjährige Ehe eines gottesfürchtigen Ehepaares zu
zerstören. Allerdings ohne Erfolg, denn das Ehepaar ist
vernünftig und läßt sich auch nicht durch Alpträume über
Ehestreitigkeiten, die ihnen der Teufel eingibt, be-
einflussen. In seiner Not wendet sich der Teufel an ein
altes Weib, das vespricht ihm zu helfen, wenn er ihr ein
Paar neue Schuhe besorgt. Die Alte macht sich sofort an
die Arbeit und belügt zunächst die Ehefrau nach Strich

197

und Faden über heimliche Liebesaffären ihres Mannes,
dann redet sie dem Ehemann ein, seine Frau wolle ihn
vergiften. Beide Ehepartner sind sofort aufgebracht wie
die Taranteln und stürzen aufeinander los, um sich ordentlich zu verprügeln. Der Teufel freut sich, die Alte
nicht, denn der Belzebub will ihr ohne Bezahlung ent-
wischen. Sie schlägt daher einen Kreis und beschwört den
Teufel, der kleinlaut angefahren kommt und sich in ihre
Macht begibt, denn die Alte ist stärker als er, wie er
nun zugibt:

> "Ja, ich foercht mich so hart vor dir.
> Ich bin ein einziger Satan,
> Du hast eine ganze Legion
> Teufel, so dir all wohnen bei
> mit argen Listen allerlei.[44]

Die Alte ist hier ganz deutlich als Hexengestalt ge-
zeichnet: sie schließt einen Pakt mit dem Teufel, kann
zaubern und wird von Sachs "Die alt Wettermacherin",
"die alt Unhold", oder "alt Hex" genannt.[45] Sie ist
nicht allein, sondern befiehlt über ein Heer von
Dämonen. Es wird impliziert, daß sie, wie alle Hexen
auch, eine Satansbraut ist, also des Teufels Weib. Hier
hat sie alle Eigenschaften des bösen Weibs, denn in
dieser Ehe hat die Alte die Hosen an, sie bestimmt über
den Teufel, sie schlägt ihn, usw.

Sachs hat dieses Thema noch öfter behandelt, so zum
Beispiel in dem Schwank Der Teufel nahm ein alt Weib zu
der Eh, die ihn vertrieb (13. Mai 1557).[46] Hier be-
schließt der Teufel, die Freuden des Ehestandes zu
kosten und zu heiraten. Er sucht sich eine alte Frau,
weil er sich der Sexualität einer Jungen nicht gewachsen
fühlt. Er muß seine Wahl aber bald bereuen, denn die
Alte richtet ihn so zu, daß er sich in die Hölle retten
muß. In beiden Fällen ist das Verhältnis Teufel-Hexe
satirisch umgedreht: der Teufel ist machtlos gegenüber
der Frau: er wird dadurch besonders lächerlich gemacht
und seine Machtlosigkeit wird demonstriert. Die Alte
dagegen, Versinnbildlichung des bösen Eheweibs, wird für
alle Mißverhältnisse verantwortlich gemacht. Im ersten
Schwank ist daher auch nicht der Teufel, sondern das
Geschwätz der Alten schuld an dem Ehekrach. Sie hetzt
dadurch die Ehefrau so auf, daß diese zum bösen Weib
wird, ihre anerzogene Rolle vergißt, in ihren "natürlichen" Zustand von Unmoral fällt und ihren Mann
schlägt. Nach Sachs besteht die Lehre dieser Geschichte
im folgenden: dem Geschwätz von alten Weibern soll man
keinen Glauben schenken.[47] Wenn die Alte auch gegenüber

dem Teufel machtvoll erscheint, so hat doch ihr Trug keine Macht über das Ehepaar, denn das kann sich seiner Vernunft besinnen und verträgt sich wieder.

In einem anderen Schwank, dem Kampf mit dem bösen Weib (9. November 1541)[48] ist die Verschmelzung von bösem Weib und Hexenbild noch direkter. Sachs beruft sich dabei auf eine Geschichte, die sich ein paar Jahre zuvor in Siebenbürgen tatsächlich zugetragen habe; er präsentiert sie also als Beispiel aus dem Leben. Ein Bauer erwischt eine Frau und einen Pfaffen in Flagranti und schimpft die Frau eine Pfaffenhure. Die Frau ist wütend und verlangt Genugtuung durch einen Zweikampf. Dieser wird arrangiert; der Bauer erhält ein kurzes Schwert, die Frau, die keine Waffen tragen darf, nur eine lange Stange; sie verliert nach langem Kampf. Im Sterben entdeckt sie ihre wahre Identität: sie wird eine Wetterhexe und macht noch schnell ein Hagelwetter. Der siegreiche Bauer aber kann sich nicht lange freuen, er wird auf dem Nachhauseweg von Freunden des bösen Weibes umgebracht. Hier sind alle Elemente des bösen Weibes und der Hexe enthalten: die Frau will die Hosen tragen, sie ist widerspenstig, wollüstig und eine Hexe, die Wetter macht. Sie agiert nicht alleine, sondern ist von Freunden umgeben, die ihre üblen Taten weiterführen. Sachs hält diese Geschichte, so der moralische Schluß, für einen guten und lehrreichen Beweis über das Ausmaß des Übels das von bösen Weibern komme: "Des ist ains der neun poesen wuerm: / Ein poes weib in der welde".[49] Er setzt somit das "böse Weib" mit der "Hexe" gleich.

Sachs hat aber auch direkt zum Hexenwesen Stellung genommen. In Ein wunderlich gesprech von fünff Unhulden (9. April 1531)[50] erscheinen ihm fünf Hexen im Traum und diskutieren ihre Künste. Als er erwacht, erkennt er, daß all das nur Traum und "fantasey" sei, das gesamte Hexenwesen eine Einbildung und ihre Künste nur Täuschungen. Dem gottesfürchtig Gläubigen kann dieser Spuk Sachs' Meinung nach nichts anhaben - soweit die Gläubigen Männer sind. Hier teilt Sachs auch die Spekulation des Malleus, daß Frauen potentielle Hexen seien, denn er sagt im gleichen Spruch nur von Frauen: "Der teuffel lest ein weib sich zwingen, / So ferr ers im unglaub mug bringen".[51] Das scheint in Anbetracht der Masse von bösen Weibern in seinen Werken kein Problem für den Teufel zu sein.

Nicht nur Hans Sachs hat mit dem Hexenbild sein dramatisches Repertoire erweitert; es ist auch fester Bestandteil bei anderen Autoren. Der Protestant Rebhuhn

präsentiert in seiner Hochzeit zu Cana einen Teufel mit
kooperierender Hexe in ganz ähnlicher Weise wie Hans
Sachs und auch hier siegt Vernunft über den Teufel und
die Hexe.[52] Beide Protestanten nutzen so die Teufel-
Hexen Gestalt als dramatisches Mittel, um eine Krise im
Alltag gottesfürchtiger Menschen herzustellen und demon-
strieren dann, wie diese Krise durch vernünftiges Handeln überwunden werden kann. Auch ein weiterer Protestant, Fischart, benutzt Hexengestalten, zum Beispiel in
Flöhhatz, Weibertratz,[53] wo er alte Marktfrauen mit un-
flätigen Hexen gleichsetzt und sie der tugendhaften
jungen Bürgerstochter entgegensetzt.

Diese Beispiele legen nahe, daß sich protestantische
Autoren des Hexenbildes aus zwei Gründen bedienen. Zum
einen benutzen sie es als wirksames dramatisches Ab-
schreckmittel, als negatives weibliches Rollenmodell,
und zum anderen, weil sie selbst auch an das Potential
des Bösen in der Frau glauben. Die Protestanten glauben
nicht so ausschließlich daran wie die Autoren des
Malleus; sie schaffen auch positive Frauengestalten. Sie
wissen, wie Hans Sachs im Hundschwanz[54] sagt, daß die
Männer ohne die Arbeit der Frauen nicht auskämen, und
auch Luther gibt in den Tischreden[55] zu, daß ohne den
Beitrag der Frauen keine soziale Ordnung möglich sei.
Gute Frauen aber sind, wie gute Männer, nur die, die
ihren sozialen Stand völlig akzeptieren und sich in Ehe,
Kirche und Staat unterordnen. Die soziale Gefährlichkeit
der Bosheit des Mannes und der Frau ist in ihrem Modell
aber asymmetrisch verteilt. Der "böse Mann" verweigert
seine eigentliche überlegene Natur, wenn er faulenzt,
trinkt und seine Frau nicht durch ein gutes Vorbild
erzieht. Die "böse" Frau dagegen verfällt in ihren amoralischen Naturzustand, wenn sie dasselbe tut und bedroht dadurch weitaus mehr die immer noch göttlich
gedachte soziale Ordnung. Daher hat die Gestalt der Hexe
bei diesen protestantischen Autoren einen ganz konkreten
sozialen Charakter: es ist die widerspenstige Ehefrau.
Das ist ihr Beitrag zum Hexenbild.

Als letztes Beispiel für die Durchsetzung des neuen
Hexenbildes werde ich zwei Flugschriften zitieren. Die
Flugschrift ist das machtvollste neue Massenmedium. Zu-
meist von Gebildeten verfaßt, ist sie populär gehalten,
billig, schnell herzustellen, und wird meist mit Holz-
schnitten geschmückt, die auch für den Analphabeten den
Inhalt in Form einer Bildergeschichte wiedergeben. Diese
Flugschriften kann man als Vorläufer der Lokalpresse
bezeichnen.[56] Sie vermitteln Lokalnachrichten, meist mit

Sensationsinhalten wie das Erscheinen von Kometen, Gewaltverbrechen, Feuerbrünste und Hexenprozesse.

Die erste Flugschrift stammt von 1549 und ist betitelt: Ein unerhört übernatürliche gestalt einer großgeschwollenen Jungkfrauen zu Esslingen.[57] Der Verfasser ist der Maler Hans Schiesser aus Worms, vermutlich ein fahrender Maler und Journalist, der im Auftrag der Stadt Esslingen diese Geschichte aufschrieb und die kranke Jungfrau im Bild festhielt. Laut Flugschrift ist die Tochter von Hans Ulmer seit vier Jahren krank. Ihr Bauch ist unnatürlich geschwollen, wächst ständig und hat schon eine unerhörte Größe erreicht. Sie kann nur kalte Kost zu sich nehmen, hat keinen Stuhlgang und gibt alles wieder von sich. Chirurgen, Hofärzte, Edelleute und Durchreisende besuchen sie und bestaunen ihren Wunderbauch. Auf der Abbildung der Flugschrift lächelt die Jungfrau recht holdselig unter der riesigen Kugel ihres Bauches hervor, als gehe sie mit aller Gutheit der Welt schwanger.

Die zweite Flugschrift stammt von 1551 und behandelt den Fortgang der Geschichte. Ihr Titel ist Newe Zeitung: Wie wunderlich Gott den unmenschlichen un vom teuffel zugerichten großen bauch an der Jungfrauen zu Esslingen offenbaret hat.[58] Aus der Wundergeschichte ist eine Hexengeschichte geworden, denn die Jungfrau ging nicht mit Göttlichem schwanger. Vier Jahre lang - so der Inhalt der Flugschrift - haben Arm und Reich diese Jungfrau "mit andacht heimgesucht",[59] und viel Geld und Geschenke da gelassen. Im Jahre 1550 entschloß sich der Rat der Stadt Esslingen, der schon lange um die Gesundheit der jungen Frau besorgt war, die Jungfrau aufzuschneiden um sie von ihrem Leiden zu befreien. Ein Barbier, ein Doktor, ein Apotheker und eine Hebamme waren anwesend, als man den Bauch aufschnitt und feststellte, daß er teuflischer Betrug sei. Der Mutter der Jungfrau wurde daraufhin Zauberei vorgeworfen und beide Frauen wurden wegen Hexerei angeklagt. Die Mutter wurde verbrannt, der Tochter wurden die Backen gebrannt, sie wurde eingemauert und starb bald darauf. Im Gegensatz zu Sachs' Geschichten über Hexen läßt sich für diese Flugschrift ein reales Vorkommnis dokumentieren: 1551 wurden Frau Ulmer und Tochter nach einem Hexenprozeß in Esslingen wirklich hingerichtet.[60] Das Ver-rückte aber ist, daß die Flugschrift ganz genau beschreibt, wie Mutter und Tochter zusammen den Betrug ausführten. Der Bauch war mit Nähkunsten und viel Raffinesse so hergestellt, daß er echt aussah. Er konnte durch das Ziehen an einer Schnur vergrößert und verkleinert werden und

Ein vnerhörte vbernatürliche gestalt einer

groß geschwollenen Junckfrawen zu Eßlingen/
als hie fürgemalet/vnd hernach gemelt wäre.

Der sich sechzehen zeigen frey/   Wie groß der Bauch geschwollen sey.

Die Junckfraw ist von frommen ehrlichen eltern geporn/so wonhafftig sind zu Eßlingen/in der vorstatt Bläsin/in der

war abnehmbar. All das war offensichtlich kein Teufelswerk, sondern ein kreatives Machwerk der Frauen. Den gemacht, sondern der Stadtrat hielt einen Hexenprozeß ab. Die Mutter wurde gefoltert und bekannte, eine Hexe zu sein und die Tochter verführt zu haben.

Für den Verfasser der Flugschrift lag zwischen dem nachweisbaren Betrug und der Anklage wegen Hexerei kein logischer Bruch vor, er hielt sich auch nicht einmal damit auf, noch weitere Greueltaten der Frauen auszumalen und sie dadurch zu dämonisieren. Er berichtet ganz de facto and selbstverständlich, daß zwei Frauen wegen einfachen Betrugs als Hexen gerichtet wurden. Warum? Die für die modernen Leser und Leserinnen fehlende Logik kann man leicht mit Elementen des gelehrten Hexenbilds ergänzen. Mutter und Tochter Ulmer sind Hexen, denn Frauen sind schwach, sie können nicht eigenständig handeln. Wenn sie es aber dennoch tun, dann nur deswegen, weil sie eben dieser ihrer Schwäche, ihrer Sexualität und Phantasie und somit dem Teufel nachgegeben haben. Sozial abweichendes und im Extremfall kriminelles Handeln der Frau kann demnach nicht von ihr selbst kommen, da sie qua ihrer Inferiorität nicht handeln kann. Erscheint sie dennoch als Handelnde, so versteckt sich hinter diesem unnatürlichen Trugbild der Teufel selbst. Der Verfasser der Flugschrift gibt der Neuigkeit wie üblich eine moralische Lehre bei. Aber diese lautet keineswegs, sich von Hexerei fernzuhalten, wie das wohl naheläge, sondern es geht ihm um Völlerei, Lustprinzip des Magens und der Sinne. Den Frauen wird nämlich der Vorwurf gemacht, sie hätten das eingenommene Geld nachts versoffen und verpraßt und all das ohne Wissen des Ehemanns. Hier taucht dasselbe Motiv vom weiblichen Eigennutz und weiblicher Gefräßigkeit auf, das wir auch bei Hans Sachs' bösen Weibern finden, die den Ehemännern den Speck wegfressen. Die beiden Ulmer Frauen sind also nicht nur Hexen, sondern auch böse Eheweiber, Eigenschaften die scheinbar nicht mehr trennbar sind.61 Damit enthält diese Flugschrift in der expliziten (Völlerei) und impliziten (Schwäche des Weibes) Begründung für das hexerische Vergehen von Mutter und Tochter genau die gleichen Elemente des Hexenbilds, wie sie bei den Gelehrten und dann schon verändert in der populären Literatur erscheinen: Hexen sind ungehorsame (Haus)Frauen; wenn Frauen handeln, kreativ sind, kann nur der Teufel die Hand im Spiel haben.

Wie diese Beispiele meiner Ansicht nach zeigen, ist die Literatur des sechzehnten Jahrhunderts stark vom vorhandenen gelehrten Hexenbild beeinflußt und baut es noch weiter aus, indem es das Hexenbild vor allem in die häusliche Sphäre lenkt. Obwohl das hier skizzierte Bild dieser Entwicklung durch weitere Forschung ausgebaut werden müßte, lassen sich doch die folgenden Hypothesen für eine weitere Diskussion aufstellen.

Die Gleichsetzung weiblicher moralischer Inferiorität mit größerer Anfälligkeit der Frau für das Verbrechen der Hexerei wird erstmals von katholischen orthodoxen Autoren, im Malleus, formuliert. Ihre Argumentation baut auf der mittelalterlichen und patristischen Tradition klerikaler Misogynie auf. Darin symbolisiert die Frau auf Grund ihrer Physis eine elende, sündenvolle und daher abzulehnende Welt. Die "gute Frau", vom Vorwurf der Hexerei ausgenommene Frau, ist daher im Malleus nur die Nonne, die durch ihr Keuschheitsgelübde ihre weibliche Physis negiert. Humanistische und protestantische Autoren, die im frühen 16. Jahrhundert das Hexenwesen diskutieren, übernehmen ohne Widerspruch die Formel, daß Frauen eher der Hexerei zugeneigt seien. Diese Behauptung wird in den erwähnten Werken nicht weiter diskutiert. Es ist anzunehmen, daß diese Behauptung in Verbindung steht mit dem neuen Diskurs über Geschlechtsrollen in Ehe und Familie, in dem die Frauen noch analog der klerikalen Tradition als inferiore Wesen dargestellt werden. Im Gegensatz zur Ansicht des Malleus gilt nun das monastische Leben nicht mehr als einzig mögliche Korrektur der weiblichen amoralischen Natur, sondern die Frauen sollen von ihren Ehemännern zu guten Weibern erzogen werden.

Vor diesem Hintergrund ließe sich auch erklären, warum bei Theophrastus Paracelsus nun eine Hexenbeschreibung auftaucht, in der das Kennzeichen der Hexe besonders auch die Verweigerung traditioneller Frauenrollen ist. Sie erscheint schon als das "Böse Weib", wird aber nicht so genannt. Obwohl die Popularisierung der Vorstellung vom vorwiegend weiblichen Hexenwesen wahrscheinlich vor allem durch die Hexenpredigten erfolgte, taucht die Hexe auch als neue Gestalt in populärer Literatur auf. Kennzeichnend für die erwähnten populären Texte von Sachs, Rebhuhn und den Flugschriften ist, daß die Hexe zwar mit den theologischen Vorstellungen ausgestattet sein kann wie mit dem Teufelspakt, Fähigkeit zum Schadenzauber wie Wettermachen, daß aber ihr Vergehen vor allem als Durchbrechen der sozialen Frauenrolle beschrieben wird. Die Hexe wird daher mit der literarischen Tradition des rebellischen, bösen Weibes in Verbindung gebracht, und das Hexenbild wird in die häusliche Sphäre gelenkt. Die Motivation für die

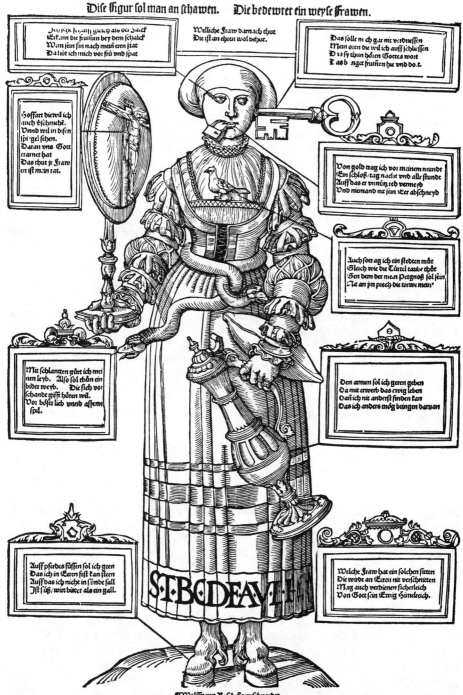

Dise figur sol man an schawen.   Die bedewtet ein weyse Frawen.

Ich sich gemug gleich als der Luck
Erkenn die sünen bey dem schalck
Wem sein sin nach mein eren stat
Da hüt ich mich vor frü vnd spat

Welliche Fraw darnach thut
Die ist an ehren wol behut.

Das solle ich gar nit verdriessen
Mein oren die wil ich auff schliessen
Do ich sy thun hören Gottes wort
Las hinger frumen hie vnd do.t.

Hoffart dieweil ich
auch vfchnuhe.
Vnnd wil in disen
spigel sehen.
Daran vns Gott
erarnet hat
Das thut jr Fraw
en ist mein rat.

Von gold trag ich vor meinem munde
Ein schloß trag nacht vnd alle stunde
Auff das er vnnütz red vermeyd
Vnd niemand nit sein eer abschneyd

Auch sol trag ich ein stedten mut
Gleich wie die Türtel taube thut
Sen der der mein Petgnoß sol sein
Hat an jn piech die trewe mein

Mit schlangen gürt ich mei
nen leyb.   Also sol thun ein
bider weyb.   Die sich vor
schande gifft hüten wil.
Vor böser lieb vnnd affem
spil.

Den armen sol ich geren geben
Da mit erwerb das ewig leben
Dann ich nit anderst finden kan
Das ich anders mög bringen daruan

Auff pferdes füssen sol ich geen
Das ich in Eeren fest kan steen
Auff das ich nicht in sünde fall
Ist süß, wirt bitter als ein gall.

Welche Fraw hat ein solchen sitten
Die wirdt an Eeren nit verschnitten
Mag auch verdienen sicherleich
Von Gott sein Ewig hümelreich

S·T·B·C·D·E·A·V·H·

Wolffgang Resch Formschneyder.

205

Benutzung der Hexengestalt als negatives Rollenvorbild
kommt wohl einmal von dem Wunsch protestantischer
Autoren, ein neues Ehefrauideal zu propagieren. Aber es
scheint auch, daß dieses Ideal der sparsamen und tüch-
tigen Hausfrau zumindest bei Sachs als wichtiger Bestandteil einer neuen ökonomischen Überlebensstrategie
für untere städtische Schichten gesehen wird. Es wäre
daher für eine weitere Untersuchung notwendig, die
sozialen und ökonomischen Veränderungen in Familien- und
Erwerbstrukturen des frühen 16. Jahrhunderts mit einzu-
beziehen. Erst dann könnte die Frage untersucht werden,
ob für Gruppen der Bevölkerung das Böse Frau-Hexenbild
eine willkommene Erklärung für soziale Probleme war und
ob es von daher mithalf, eine passive Bereitschaft zu
den Hexenverfolgungen vorzubreiten.

Klerikale, gelehrte und populäre Literatur des früh-
en 16. Jahrhunderts beschäftigte sich recht ausführlich
mit dem Begriff der Hexerei und der Hexe. Magie,
Zauberei, Hexerei waren nicht a priori "volkstümliche"
Themen, sondern Literatur spielte eine Rolle bei ihrer
Popularisierung. Sie repräsentieren auch nicht eine ir-
rationale "Nachseite" unserer Geschichte. In der Auseinandersetzung mit den Inhalten solcher Werke können
Elemente von Sozialgeschichte sichtbar werden, zum
Beispiel die veränderte Einstellung zu sozialen Geschlechterrollen. Unsere Literaturgeschichten aber haben
die Hexenverfolgungen als absurdes Exotikum ausgeschlossen, sie tabuisiert und trivialisiert. Es ist an
der Zeit, daß wir sie zum Teil des Curriculums machen.

Anmerkungen

* Dieser Artikel baut auf einem gleichnamigen Vor-
trag auf, den ich im Oktober 1984 bei der Annual Con-
ference of Women in German hielt. Ich möchte Jeannine
Blackwell, Ritta Jo Horsley, Marianne Burkhard und
Jeanette Clausen für ihre hilfreichen Kommentare bei der
Umarbeitung dieses Artikels danken.

1 Zum Teil lag das daran, daß die Pioniere der
Hexenforschung des 19. und frühren 20. Jahrhunderts wie
Joseph Hansen, Zauberwahn, Inquisition und Hexenprozeß
(1900; Repr. Aalen: Scientia Verlag, 1964); Henry C.
Lea, Materials Toward a History of Witchcraft (1939;
Repr. New York: Thomas Yoseloff, 1957, III Bde.); und
Wilhelm G. Soldan, Heinrich Heppe, Geschichte der Hexen-
prozesse (Stuttgart: Cotta, 1880, II Bde.) den Komplex
Hexenverfolgung als ein vorwiegend mittelalterliches

Problem sahen und vor allem die Frauenfeindlichkeit der
mittelalterlichen katholischen Kirche dafür verantwortlich machten. Der Hexenwahn war für sie ein Überrest
irrationalen, mittelalterlichen Denkens, das in die
Neuzeit überschwappte und endlich von dem neuen rati-
onalen Denken der Aufklärung aufgehoben wurde. Diese
These wird heute von den meisten Forschungen zum Thema
in Frage gestellt. Aber auch moderne Hexenforscher haben
zur Mystifizierung beigetragen, indem sie die Hexenverfolgungen oftmals als Extremfall oder Ausrutscher der
Geschichte gewertet haben. Mary Daly beschreibt diese
patriarchalische Ausgrenzung der Hexe und der Hexenverfolgungen aus der Geschichte sehr gut im sechsten
Kapitel ihres Buches Gyn/Ecology (Boston: Beacon, 1978).

2 Vgl. für feministische Ansätze: Gabriele Becker,
Sylvia Bovenschen, Helmut Brackert u.a., Aus der Zeit
der Verzweiflung: Zur Genese und Aktualität des Hexenbildes (Frankfurt: Suhrkamp, 1977); Helen Berger,
"Witchcraft and the Domination of Women: The English
Witchtrials Reconsidered", Diss. New York University,
1983; Jeannine Blackwell, "'Die Zunge, der Geistliche
und das Weib': Überlegungen zur strukturellen Bedeutung
der Hexenbekenntnisse von 1500 bis 1700", Innsbrucker
Beiträge zur Kulturwissenschaft 31: 1-20, 1985; Anne-
marie Droß, Die Erste Walpurgisnacht: Hexenverfolgung in
Deutschland (Frankfurt: Roter Stern, 1978); Claudia
Honegger (Hrsg.), Die Hexen der Neuzeit: Studien zur So-
zialgeschichte eines kulturellen Deutungsmusters (Frank-
furt: Suhrkamp, 1978); Ritta J. Horsley, Richard A.
Horsley, "On the Trail of the 'Witches': Wise Women,
Midwives and the European Witchhunts, Women in German
Yearbook 3 (Lanham, MD: University Press of America,
1986), S. 1-28; Sigrid Schade, Schadenzauber und die
Magie des Körpers: Hexenbilder der frühen Neuzeit
(Worms: Wernersche Verlagsanstalt, 1983); für sozial-
historische Ansätze: Carlo Ginzburg, The Night Battles:
Witchcraft and Agrarian Cults in the Sixteenth and
Seventeenth Centuries (London: Routledge & Kegan Paul,
1983), Gunnar Heinsohn, Otto Steiger, Die Vernichtung
der weisen Frauen: Beiträge zur Theorie und Geschichte
von Bevölkerung und Kindheit (Herbstein: März, 1985);
Michael Kunze, Die Straße ins Feuer: Vom Leben und
Sterben in der Zeit des Hexenwahns (Kindler: München,
1982); für anthropologische Ansätze: Hans P. Duerr,
Traumzeit: Über die Grenze zwischen Wildnis und Zivili-
sation (Frankfurt: Syndikat, 1978); Richard A. Horsley,
"Who Were the 'Witches'? The Social Role of the Accused
in the European Witch Trials", Journal of Interdisciplinary History, 9: 689-715, 1979.

[3] Einen guten Überblick über den neuesten Stand der Forschung zu den deutschen Hexenprozessen, der auch die neueren Ansätze mit einbezieht, gibt Gerhard Schormann, Hexenprozesse in Deutschland (Göttingen: Vandenhoeck & Ruprecht, 1981).

[4] So Duerr und Droß (Anm. 2). Die wichtigste ältere Studie dazu ist Keith Thomas, Religion and the Decline of Magic (London: Weidenfeld & Nicolson, 1970).

[5] So Becker, Bovenschen, Brackert u.a. (Anm. 2), Berger (Anm. 2) und Honegger (Anm. 2). Die Rolle der Hexenverfolgungen für die Herausbildung des mechanistischen Weltbildes wird ausführlicher von Brian Easlea, Witchhunting, Magic and the New Philosophy (Sussex: Harvester Press, 1980) and von Carolyn Merchant, The Death of Nature: Women, Ecology and the Scientific Revolution (San Francisco: Harper & Row, 1980) behandelt.

[6] Die beste neuere Studie dazu ist Norman Cohn, Europe's Inner Demons (London: Heinemann, 1975). Der folgende historische Abriß stützt sich auf sein Buch.

[7] Cohn (Anm. 6), S. 225 ff. Er gibt hierfür das Datum 1430.

[8] Diese Annäherung erfolgt eigentlich erst in der Zeit der großen Hexenverfolgungen, d.h. während des 17. Jahrhunderts, wo volkstümliche Vorstellungen von Schadenzauber mit den gelehrten Vorstellungen von Hexerei in den Prozessen konfrontiert werden und sich dann vermischen. Am besten beschrieben ist das von Christina Larner, Witchcraft and Religion (New York: Blackwell, 1984), S. 42-56. Larner sieht, wie Cohn (Anm. 6), den Anfang dafür in den ersten Pogromen um 1430. Sie mißt aber der Hexenliteratur des 16. Jahrhunderts größere Eigenständigkeit bei. Sie betont auch mehr als Cohn die sozialen Konflikte des 17. Jahrhunderts als Motivation für Hexenprozesse.

[9] Für die Übernahme inquisitorischer Elemente auch in die weltliche Hexenprozeß-Rechtsprechung vgl. Larner (Anm. 8) und Schormann (Anm. 3).

[10] Das war auch schon die grundlegende These der Hexenforscher des 19. Jahrhunderts, so Hansen, Lea, und Soldan, Heppe (Anm. 1).

[11] "Im Hintergrund erfolgt eine gewisse Kulmination des reichstädtischen Lebens, die Entwicklung eines auf Bergbau und Fernhandel gestützten frühen Kapitalismus . . . , die immer stärker zu Bewußtsein kommende Verweltlichung der Kirche . . . , Judenaustreibungen und Hexenverfolgungen (der Malleus maleficarum erscheint 1487) vervollständigen das Bild." Max Wehrli, Geschichte der Deutschen Literatur vom Frühen Mittelalter bis zum Ende des 16. Jahrhunderts. Geschichte der Deutschen Literatur von den Anfängen bis zur Gegenwart, Bd. I (Stuttgart: Reclam, 1980), S. 904. Wir erfahren also, daß es Hexenprozesse gab, daß irgendein Buch dazu erschien, aber ansonsten wird das Thema in den 250 Seiten über die Literatur des 16. Jahrhundert nur noch einmal erwähnt, im Kontext des Faustbuches: "Die Wissenschaft der Renaissance überschritt noch leicht die Grenzen zur Nachtseite von Natur oder Geschichte"; ebda. S. 1145. Das Thema wird disqualifiziert.

[12] Vgl. dazu: Honegger (Anm. 2), Kapitel III; Becker, Bovenschen, Brackert u.a. (Anm. 2), Abteilung II.1, III.

[13] Vgl. Russel Hope Robbins, The Encyclopedia of Witchcraft and Demonology (New York: Crown, 1959), S. 337.

[14] Das einzige wichtige Element der Hexenvorstellung, das im Malleus noch nicht ausführlich beschrieben ist, ist der Hexensabbath. Vgl. Russel Hope Robbins (Anm. 13), S. 415 ff.

[15] Das gilt für die gelehrte Tradition ebenso wie für die volkstümliche. Thomas von Aquinas zum Beispiel hielt eine sexuelle Beziehung zwischen Dämonen, Männern und Frauen für möglich. In der volkstümlichen Vorstellung konnte Heil- und Schadenzauber von "weisen Personen" männlichen oder weiblichen Geschlechts ausgeführt werden.

[16] Der Malleus benutzt noch nicht diesen juristischen Begriff, beschreibt ihn aber schon. Crimen Exceptum beschreibt ein außergewöhnliches Vergehen wie Majestätsbeleidigung. Die Definition von Hexerei als Crimen Exceptum spielte eine entscheidende Rolle bei der späteren juristischen Auffassung der Hexenprozesse. Dadurch wurde der Hexenprozeß als juristischer Ausnahmefall gesehen, bei dem Folterung und Denunziation erlaubt waren, und zwar in einer Zeitperiode, in der sich das moderne Zivilrechtssystem mit seinem Schutz des

Angeklagten entwickelte. Dieses Problem wird ausführlich diskutiert von Larner (Anm. 8), S. 43 ff.

[17] Die Theorie über die Staat und Kirche gefährdende Hexensekte wird im Malleus vor allem als sexuelle Verschwörung der Hexen gesehen. Vgl. Malleus Maleficarum, Übers. Montague Summers (London: Rodker, 1928), Pt. I, Qu. VI., S. 48 ff.

[18] Die Bestrafung des Schadenzaubers gab es im weltlichen Recht während des Mittelalters. Er wurde aber nie mit dem Tode bestraft.

[19] Johann Trithemius, Liber Octo Questiorum (Oppenheim 1515) und ders. Antipalus Maleficorum (Ingolstadt, 1555). Lea (Anm. 1) Bd. I, S. 369 ff., sieht den Einfluß des Malleus auf Trithemius' Hexenschriften. Geilers Hexenpredigten zeigen nach Schade (Anm. 2), S. 35 ff. einen starken Einfluß des Malleus. Sie wurden nach dem Gedächtnis von dem Franziskaner Johann Pauli niedergeschrieben: Johann Geiler von Kaysersberg, Die Emeis (Straßburg, 1516); Ulrich Tengler, Der neu Layenspiegel, Hrsg. Christoph Tengler (Augsburg, 1511). Kunze (Anm. 2), S. 273, verfolgt den Einfluß des Malleus auf diese zweite Ausgabe des Layenspiegels. Seiner Ansicht nach ist der Sohn Christoph dafür verantwortlich, der Theologieprofessor in Ingolstadt war.

[20] Luther beschäftigte sich zwar nicht ausführlich mit dem Hexenproblem, aber in seinen Erklärungen zu 3.1 des Galaterbriefes von Paulus und zu 6.1-4 des ersten Buch Moses nimmt er dazu Stellung. Ebenso am 25. August 1538 in den Tischreden. Vgl. Georg Längin, Religion und Hexenprozeß (Leipzig: Wiegand, 1888), S. 169 ff. Melanchthon nimmt ähnlich wie die Malleus Autoren an, daß der Teufel die Frauen durch Träume zur Hexerei verführt. Vgl. "Erinnerung Phillippi Melanchthonus von mancherley Geschlächten der Träume samt ihrer bedeutung", in Bretschneider und Bindseil, Corpus Reformatorum (Leipzig: Heinsius, 1834-), Bd. 13, S. 5-178. Ähnlich wie Luther trat er für die Bestrafung der Hexerei ein. Vgl. dazu Nikolaus Paulus, Hexenwahn und Hexenprozeß (Freiburg: Herder, 1910), S. 121. Ulrich Molitor, De Lamiis et Pythonicis Mulieribus (Konstanz, 1489). Zum Verhältnis von Molitors Schrift zum Malleus vgl. Helmut Brackert, "Unglückliche, was hast du gehofft? Zu den Hexenbüchern des 15. bis 17. Jahrhunderts" in Becker, Bovenschen, Brackert (Anm. 2), S. 143 ff.

[21] Vgl. dazu Erik H.C. Midelfort, Witchhunting in South-Western Germany, 1582-1684 (Stanford: Stanford University Press, 1972), S. 10-29.

[22] Als Begründung wird dabei vor allem das Alte Testament (Exodus XXII.18) herangezogen, d.h. es wird mit der Tradition "göttlichen Gesetzes", nicht mit strafrechtlicher Tradition für die Todesstrafe plädiert.

[23] Vgl. dazu Kapitel 96, "De Arte Inquisitorum", in Agrippa von Nettesheim, De incertitudine et vanitate scientiarum (Köln: 1527). Zur Darstellung des Prozesses siehe Wolfgang Ziegeler, Möglichkeiten der Kritik am Hexen- und Zauberwesen im ausgehenden Mittelalter (Köln und Wien: Böhlau, 1973), S. 137 ff.

[24] Vgl. Kapitel 45, "De Goetia et Necromantia", in Agrippa von Nettesheim, De incertitudine.

[25] Agrippa widmete sie der literarisch gebildeten Margarete von Österreich, an deren Hof in Dôle er sich aufhielt.

[26] Fischart übersetzte das sich stark auf den Malleus stützende Hexenbuch des modernen französischen Staatstheoretikers und Anwalts Bodin als Kampfmittel gegen J. Weyer: De Magorum Daemonomania. Vom außgelaßnen Wütigen Teufelsheer...Gegen Doctor J. Wier Buch von der Geister verführungen, durch..Johann Bodin..auß gegangen. Nun erstmals durch H. Johann Fischart .. Auß Frantzösischer Sprach trewlich ins Teutsche gebracht.. (Straßburg: Jobin, 1581). Doch damit nicht genug: 1582 besorgte er eine kommentierte Neuausgabe des Malleus, der sechzig Jahre lange nicht mehr gedruckt worden war.

[27] Paracelsus unterstützt trotz seiner Forderung nach Umerziehung der Hexen auch die Todesstrafe bei "hoffnungslosen" Fällen. Vgl. dazu Walter Pagel, Paracelsus (Basel: Karger Libri, 1958), S. 152.

[28] Paracelsus erstellt im fünften Traktat seines De sagis et earum operibus eine Liste mit zwölf Hexenzeichen. Neben den von mir erwähnten finden sich dort auch körperliche Male. Seine Hexentheorie wird ausführlich diskutiert von Klaus Schneller, "Paracelsus: Von den Hexen und ihren Werken" in Becker, Bovenschen, Brackert u.a. (Anm. 2), S. 240-59.

[29] Diese Definition der Frau ist in ihren Grundzügen nicht neu, sondern lehnt sich stark an die theologische

211

Diskussion der Frau an, besonders an diejenige von Thomas von Aquin und anderen scholastischen Autoren. Neu ist, daß die schon vorhandenen Elemente mit dem Hexenbegriff verbunden werden.

[30] Die beiden Inquisitoren initiierten ab 1484 eine ganze Reihe von Prozessen, bei denen die Mehrzahl der angeklagten Frauen waren. Vgl. Droß (Anm. 2), S. 221 ff.

[31] Es gibt verschiedene Erklärungen der Verfolgungen im sechzehnten Jahrhundert, unter anderem die Popularisierung des gelehrten Hexenbildes, die zunehmende Betonung des geheimen Hexensabbaths in dieser Theorie zu Ende des 16. Jahrhunderts, Veränderungen im Strafrecht, Zunahme von sozialen Konflikten, daher Interesse an sozialer Befriedigung mittels der Prozesse seitens der Herrschenden, seitens der Bevölkerung größere Bereitschaft zu Hexereianklagen als Ventil sozialer Frustration. Vgl. dazu Larner (Anm. 8), S. 58 ff.

[32] Vgl. dazu Midelfort (Anm. 21), S. 30 ff.

[33] Vgl. dazu Barbara Könneker, Die Deutsche Literatur der Reformationszeit: Kommentar zu einer Epoche (München: Winkler, 1975), S. 7-9.

[34] Verschiedene Hexenforscher halten die Verbreitung des elitären Hexenbildes durch den Buchdruck für einen entscheidenden Faktor. Vgl. dazu: Bruno Gloger, Walter Zöllner, Teufelsglaube und Hexenwahn (Leipzig: Köhler & Amelang, 1983), S. 175 ff; Droß (Anm. 2), S. 222; Jeffrey Burton Russell, Witchcraft in the Middle Ages (Ithaca, NY: Cornell University Press, 1972), S. 234; Hansen (Anm. 1), S. 526.

[35] Vgl. dazu Rolf Engelsing, Analphabetentum und Lektüre (Stuttgart: Metzler, 1973), S. 20-41. Er gibt folgende Daten für das 16. Jahrhundert: zwischen 1/3 und 2/3 der männlichen Bevölkerung kann lesen; über 5% der Gesamtbevölkerung hat Lesekenntnisse; in den Städten können auch viele Frauen und Leute der Unterschichten lesen; der Bildungsstand von Handwerkern, Bürgern und Adeligen unterscheidet sich kaum; das gelehrte Publikum umfaßt im 16. Jahrhundert 50.000 Personen, 1773 dagegen nur 20.000. Zudem nimmt er an, daß Analphabeten nicht von der Kultur der Lesenden ausgeschlossen waren, sondern daß Lesen oft noch eine kollektive Tätigkeit war. Es bestand aus Vorlesen, Zuhören, Bilder ansehen.

212

36 Vgl. auch Barbara Könneker, "Die Ehemoral in den Fastnachtspielen von Hans Sachs. Zum Funktionswandel des Nürnberger Fastnachtspiels im sechzehnten Jahrhundert" in H. Brunner, G. Hirschmann, F. Schnellbögel, Hans Sachs und Nürnberg: Bedingungen und Probleme reichstädtischer Literatur (Nürnberg: Selbstverlag des Vereins für Geschichte der Stadt Nürnberg, 1975), S. 219-45.

37 Den Einfluß sozialer Eheprobleme auf Sachs' Werk analysieren Erika Kartschoke, Christiane Reins, "Nächstenliebe-Gattenliebe-Eigenliebe: Bürgerlicher Alltag in den Fastnachtspielen des Hans Sachs" in Thomas Cramer, Erika Kartschoke, Hans Sachs-Studien zur frühbürgerlichen Literatur im 16. Jahrhundert, Beiträge zur Älteren Deutschen Literaturgeschichte, Bd. 3 (Frankfurt: Lang, 1978), S. 105-39.

38 So zum Beispiel in den beiden Spruchgedichten Wie siben weiber über ihre ungeratne Mender klagen (3. März 1531) und Ein gesprech zwischen 7 mendern, darinn sie ihre weiber beklagen (6. März 1531) in Max Geisberg, The German Single-Leaf Woodcut: 1500-1550, Übers. Walter L. Strauss (New York: Hacker Art Books, 1974), Bd. III, S. 1124 und 1125. Im Folgenden zitiert als Max Geisberg.

39 Vom 7. Juli 1562 in Hans Sachs, Hrsg. Adelbert von Keller und Edmund Goetze (1870; rpt. Hildesheim: Georg Olms Verlagsbuchhandlung, 1964), Bd. XXI, S. 144-47 (im Folgenden zitiert als KG). Vgl. dazu auch Richard M. Allen "Rebellion within the Household: Hans Sachs's Conception of Women and Marriage," Essays in History (Charlottesville: University of Virginia), Bd. 19, 1975, S. 43-74.

40 Vom 17. Mai 1539, KG Bd. V, S. 232-36.

41 Eine widerspenstige Ehefrau wird durch Aderlaß gezähmt in Ein Faßnachtspiel mit drey Personen: Die Bürgerin mit dem Thumbherrn (24. Oktober 1563) in Neudrucke Deutscher Literaturwerke des 16. Jahrhunderts (Halle/Saale: Max Niemeyer, 1876-1958), Bd. 51-52, S. 110-17. Im Folgenden zitiert als Neudrucke.

42 Vgl. für die älteren Schwanke: Franz Brietzmann, Die böse Frau in der deutschen Literatur des Mittelalters (Berlin: Mayer & Müller, 1912). Aber das "böse wip" gehört auch zum mittelalterlichen und neuzeitlichen Topos der verkehrten Welt und kann, je nach dem Kontext

in dem es gebraucht wird, neben affirmativen auch sozialkritischen oder gar gesellschaftstransformierenden Charakter haben. Vgl. dazu Natalie Zemon Davis, "Women on Top" in diess., Society und Culture in Early Modern France: Eight Essays (Stanford: Stanford University Press, 1975), S. 124-51.

[43] Als Fastnacht=spiel mit 4 personen (19. November 1545), in Paul Merker und Reinhard Buchwald, Hans Sachs, ausgewählte Werke (Leipzig: Insel, 1961), Bd. II, S. 54-67; als Schwank Der Teufel mit dem alten weib (30. März 1546) in Joseph Kürschner, Deutsche Nationalliteratur (Berlin und Stuttgart: W. Spemann), Bd. 20, Hrsg. Arnold, S. 84-87. Im Folgenden zitiert als DNL.

[44] Merker und Buchwald (Anm. 43), Bd. II, S. 65.

[45] Merker und Buchwald (Anm. 43), S. 61, S. 54, S. 64. "Unhold" ist eine althochdeutsche Bezeichnung für Geister und Götter, die im 16. Jahrhundert nun auf weibliche Hexen angewandt wird.

[46] Merker und Buchwald (Anm. 43), Bd. I, S. 185-89, und als Ein Fastnachtsspiel mit fünff Personen. Der Teufel nahm ein alt Weib zu der Ehe (24. September 1567).

[47] Vgl. Merker und Buchwald (Anm. 43), Bd. II, S. 66-67.

[48] Neudrucke, Bd. 164-73, S. 284-85.

[49] Neudrucke, Bd. 164-73, S. 285.

[50] In "Materialien zur Geschichte der Hexenverfolgungen", in Becker, Bovenschen, Brackert u.a. (Anm. 2), S. 365-68.

[51] Becker, Bovenschen, Brackert, u.a. (Anm. 2), S 367. Hervorhebung d. Verf.

[52] Von 1546. In: Paul Rebhuhns Dramen, Hrsg. Hermann Palm (Darmstadt: Wissenschaftliche Buchgesellschaft, 1969), S. 95 ff. Rebhuhn nennt den Teufel dort "Eheteufel".

[53] Von 1594. In: DNL, Bd. 18.1, S. 1-131.

[54] Vom 4. Dezember 1557. In KG, Bd. IX, S. 303-07.

55 Vgl. Kurt Aland, Luther Deutsch. Die Werke Martin Luthers in neuer Auswahl für die Gegenwart (Stuttgart: Klotz, 1960), Bd. 9, S. 279.

56 Vgl. dazu Paul Roth, Die neuen Zeitungen in Deutschland im 15. und 16. Jahrhundert (1914; rpt. Leipzig: Zentral-Antiquariat der Deutschen Demokratischen Republik, 1963).

57 Abgedruckt in Max Geisberg, Bd. III, S. 1066.

58 Flugschrift 1550/4 (Staatsbibliothek Preussischer Kulturbesitz, Berlin).

59 Flugschrift 1550/4, Blatt 2.

60 Vgl. Droß (Anm. 2), S. 230.

61 Offenkundig legt aber diese Geschichte von dem geschwollenen Bauch einer Jungfrau noch etwas anderes nahe: Die Macht der Frau, ihre Reproduktionsfähigkeit, ist nicht ihre Sache. Der Bauch gehört nicht ihr, er ist entweder in Gottes oder in des Teufels Besitz. Den Bauch abnehmen, über ihn verfügen, ihn zu finanziellen Quelle zu machen, das alles ist höchste Form der Häresie und somit Hexerei.

Verzeichnis der Abbildungen

S. 188: Hans Baldung Grien, "Hexensabbath", Holzschnitt, 1510. Max Geisberg, The German Single-Leaf Woodcut: 1500-1550, Übers .Walter L. Strauss (New York: Hacker Art Books, 1974), Bd. I, G 121. Im folgenden zitiert als Max Geisberg. Hans Baldung Grien war der bekannteste Hexenmaler des 16. Jahrhunderts.

S. 202: Hans Schiesser, "Ein unerhörte übernatürliche gestalt einer großgeschwollenen Junckfrauen zu Eßlingen", Flugblatt, 1549. Max Geisberg, Bd. III, G 1118.

S. 205: Wolffgang Resch Founschneyder, "Dise Figur sol man an schawn. Die bedwtet ein weyse frawen", Holzschnitt, 1525. Max Geisberg, Bd. IV, G 1558. Allegorische Darstellung des neuen Hausfrauenideals.

Gespräch mit Herrad Schenk

Susan Wendt-Hildebrandt

Die Romane der Bonner Schriftstellerin Herrad Schenk sind in Nordamerika - unberechtigterweise - relativ unbekannt. Selbst in der Bundesrepublik ist Schenk eher - um sie selbst zu zitieren - als "feministisch engagierte Sozialwissenschaftlerin" bekannt. Dennoch gilt ihr Roman Unmöglich, ein Haus in der Gegenwart zu bauen in weiblichen akademischen Kreisen der Bundesrepublik als Geheimtip; dieser Roman befaßt sich zum großen Teil mit den Problemen, Ängsten und Wahlmöglichkeiten von Akademikerinnen in den 70er und 80er Jahren.

1948 in Detmold geboren, studierte Schenk Sozialwissenschaften in Köln und York, England; von 1972 bis 1980 war sie wissenschaftliche Assistentin an der Universität Köln. Danach verließ sie die Universität, wie im ersten Interviewauszug geschildert wird. 1979 bekam sie den Förderpreis des Georg-Mackensen-Literatur-Preises. Seit den späten 70er Jahren veröffentlicht sie mehr oder weniger abwechselnd Sachbücher und Erzählungen bzw. Romane.

Zu den Sachbüchern gehören feministische Standardwerke wie Die feministische Herausforderung und Frauen kommen ohne Waffen. In Die feministische Herausforderung untersucht Schenk die "alte" (d.h. die Mitte des 19. Jahrhunderts entstandene) und die "neue" Frauenbewegung (d.h. die Bewegung, die Ende der 60er/Anfang der 70er Jahre in der Bundesrepublik entstanden ist), wobei sowohl Gemeinsamkeiten als auch Unterschiede hervorgehoben werden. Behandelt werden außerdem der Komplex Feminismus/Marxismus, der neue Weiblichkeitsmythos, die Struktur des Patriarchats und Strategien zur Auflösung der patriarchalischen Grundstruktur der Gesellschaft.

Die Einleitung zu Frauen kommen ohne Waffen enthält Schenks Bekenntnis:

Ich sehe in der Friedensbewegung eine große Hoffnung und fühle mich ihr

217

zugehörig; trotzdem geht es mir in dieser Arbeit mehr um die Frauen- als um die Friedensbewegung, weniger um eine Analyse des Beitrags, den die Frauen zur Friedensbewegung leisten oder leisten könnten, als um die Frage, was die Berührung mit dem Pazifismus für den Feminismus bedeutet (S. 9).

Neben einer Untersuchung zur Rolle der Frau in der Geschichte des Krieges enthält dieses Werk eine eingehende Analyse der kulturellen Definition von Mann und Frau. Schließlich entwickelt Schenk ihre Strategien für einen gewaltfreien Kampf sowohl innerhalb der Friedensbewegung als auch gegen das Patriarchat. Schenks Sachbücher sind übrigens wohltuend sachlich, verständlich - und auch überzeugend - geschrieben.

Drei der bisher erschienenen längeren Prosawerke - Abrechnung, Unmöglich, ein Haus in der Gegenwart zu bauen und Die Unkündbarkeit der Verheißung - stellen die Welt einer jeweils anderen Ich-Erzählerin dar. Jedesmal geht es um die Situation einer begabten Frau in der akademischen Welt, um problematische Vater-Tochter-Beziehungen und um (noch) zu treffende Entscheidungen in bezug auf Karriere, Heirat, Kinder. Im Vordergrund steht bei Schenk die Darstellung der inneren Konflikte ihrer Ich-Erzählerinnen, die an der Kluft zwischen "männlichen" und "weiblichen" Zielen leiden, wie z.B. die Erzählerin in Die Unkündbarkeit: "Ach ja: Familienstand ledig, Kinder keine. . . . Leider, leider: beim Promovieren versackt. Weder in der männlichen noch in der weiblichen Disziplin das Klassenziel erreicht" (S. 25). Eine weitere wichtige Rolle in diesen drei Werken, besonders in Unmöglich, spielt die projizierte Zukunft, wobei eine utopische Vorstellung der fernen Zukunft (nach der Pensionierung) mit einer Angst vor den Problemen der Gegenwart gekoppelt ist.

Schenks 1986 erschienener Roman Die Rache der alten Mamsell ist in manchem eine Synthese ihrer Sachbücher und Prosawerke. Hier wird das Leben der Schriftstellerin und Ahnfrau des Trivialromans Eugenie Marlitt (1825-1887) aus wechselnden Perspektiven erzählt: es ist eine Mischung aus Recherchiertem und Erfundenem, aus Biographischem und Vorgestelltem. Wieder treten die Themen der begabten Frau, der engen Vater-Tochter-Beziehung auf; dazu kommen u.a. fingierte Streitgespräche zwischen Vertretern des Literaturverständnisses des 19. Jahrhunderts, der modernen Literaturwissenschaft und der

Psychoanalyse, in denen über die Bedeutung E. Marlitts in der Literaturgeschichte diskutiert wird. Schenk entlarvt ein Literaturverständnis, das Werke von Frauen systematisch vom literarischen Kanon fernhält. Wie in den anderen Romanen sind auch hier Humor und Satire feste Bestandteile der Erzählstruktur.

Während eines Sabbaticals in der Bundesrepublik hatte ich die Gelegenheit, ein längeres Gespräch mit Herrad Schenk zu führen. Wir sprachen über Autobiographisches, über das Schreiben im allgemeinen und über erschienene und geplante Werke. Durch das Gespräch zog sich als Leitfaden die Unmöglichkeit des Nicht-Schreibens: ". . . ich kann mir nie vorstellen zu leben, ohne zu schreiben".

Folgende Auszüge entstammen der Tonbandabschrift des Gesprächs, das im späten Herbst 1983 stattfand. (Der Auszug "Zum neuen Roman" bezieht sich übrigens auf den 1984 erschienenen Roman Die Unkündbarkeit der Verheißung.)

I. "Wissenschaftlich arbeiten . . ."

Frage: Sie haben ja Wissenschaften studiert; es gibt in Unmöglich eine Stelle, wo die Erzählerin meint: "Wissenschaftlich arbeiten heißt - in meiner Umgebung jedenfalls - das eigene Produkt bis zur totalen Austauschbarkeit von jeder Individualität zu reinigen" (S. 106). Haben Sie es auch so empfunden?

Schenk: Doch, ja, das ist auch einer der Gründe, warum ich keine Lust mehr hatte, an der Uni zu bleiben. Die Wissenschaftstradition, in der ich groß geworden bin, hält das Objektive ganz groß, das Objektive, das Wertneutrale, das Nicht-Engagierte, und es wird als nicht wissenschaftlich angesehen, die eigene Person in das Werk, in die Arbeit hineinzubringen. Und ich glaube nicht, daß es so sein muß. Ich kann mir vorstellen, daß es auch Wissenschaft geben könnte und ein Wissenschaftsverständnis, wo die eigene Person mit der Arbeit eine Beziehung eingeht und es trotzdem Wissenschaft bleibt. Aber da, wo ich gearbeitete habe, war das nicht anders möglich und eine Arbeit war wirklich umso besser, je mehr sie bei anderen Leuten zusammengeschrieben war. Wissenschaftliche Arbeit bestand darin, möglichst viel zu lesen, und das zu kompilieren aus verschiedenen Arbeiten, und eigentlich nichts Eigenes da hineinzubringen.

219

Frage: Sind Sie deshalb von der Universität weggegangen?

Schenk: Ja, es gab äußere und es gab innere Gründe. Der äußere Grund war, daß ich auf einer zeitlich befristeten Stelle war, die nach 8 Jahren auslief. Ich hätte rechtzeitig entweder ein neues Forschungsprojekt suchen müssen, oder ich hätte mich habilitieren müssen. Das wäre auf der Stelle möglich gewesen, auf der ich war, hätte aber geheißen, daß ich mindestens 3 Jahre, bevor die Zeit abgelaufen war, mir ein Thema hätte suchen müssen, und daß ich, je nachdem, wahrscheinlich 3 bis 5 Jahre nur an einem ganz kleinen, ganz eng umgrenzten Thema hätte arbeiten müssen. Und ich habe die Situation schon bei meiner Dissertation als unbefriedigend empfunden. Ich habe gerne an meiner Doktorarbeit über Gerontologie geschrieben, aber ich hatte das Gefühl, daß alles, was mir an dem Thema wichtig war, über Altern – das war ein teils theoretische, teils empirische Arbeit – daß alles, was mir wichtig war, hinterher den Kompromissen des Wissenschaftsbetriebes zum Opfer gefallen ist. Und da habe ich zum ersten Mal gewußt, ich will anders schreiben, ich will nicht so schreiben, wie das der Universitätsbetrieb von mir fordert. Ich glaube aber, daß die speziellen Bedingungen da, wo ich war, besonders hart in diese Richtung waren. Ich kann mir andere Universitätsstädte oder Stellen bei anderen Professoren denken, wo es besser gewesen wäre, wo ich das hätte machen können, was ich gewollt hätte. Und dann gab es noch andere äußere Gründe. Ich habe Schwierigkeiten mit dem Chef meines Institutes gehabt, weil ich mich für Frauenforschung interessiert habe, und er hat mir sehr deutlich klargemacht, daß er nicht möchte, daß ich mich mit Frauenthemen befasse; er wollte, daß ich weiter an der Gerontologie arbeite, und ich wußte, daß für mich keine weitere Entwicklung möglich war, wenn ich da bliebe. Deswegen bin ich dann weggegangen. Aber mein Wissenschaftsverständnis hat sich sehr verändert und gewandelt. Ich würde im Rahmen der Universität keine Wissenschaft mehr machen wollen bei uns.

Frage: Werden Sie jetzt mit den Sachbüchern die Möglichkeit haben, das Kreative mit der Wissenschaft zu verbinden?

Schenk: Genau, ich glaube, daß für viele Leute meine Sachbücher jetzt nicht im engen Sinne ernstzunehmende Wissenschaft sind, sondern populärwissenschaftlich genannt werden würden. Ja, teils, teils. Ich weiß, daß sie häufig an der Universität gelesen werden, aber das hängt sehr vom Lehrstuhl, sehr von den Professoren ab, die das machen. Mein ehemaliges Institut würde das, was ich jetzt mache, nicht wissenschaftlich nennen, obwohl ich weiß, daß meine Bücher in den wissenschaftlichen Bibliotheken stehen und auch benutzt werden. Nur, ich habe jetzt das Gefühl, ich kann etwas Eigenes machen; mir ist gar nicht wichtig, wer das wissenschaftlich oder nicht wissenschaftlich nennt, sondern ich will das machen, was ich machen möchte und das kann ich jetzt.

Frage: Es fiel Ihnen also nicht so schwer, von der Universität wegzugehen?

Schenk: Überhaupt nicht. Ich habe das nie bereut und nie bedauert. Das einzige, was ich an der Universität wirklich schön fand und gern gemacht habe, waren Seminare, der Kontakt mit den Studenten. Das habe ich jetzt auf eine andere Art auch wieder, weil ich oft von Universitäten eingeladen werde, zu Vorträgen, und weil ich auch noch viele Seminare und Vorträge halte. Der Kontakt mit Menschen ist also noch da.

Frage: Wenn Sie zum Beispiel einen Vortrag an der Universität halten: ist das über Literatur oder hat das etwas mit Ihren Sachbüchern zu tun?

Schenk: Meistens werde ich jetzt eingeladen zu den Themen meiner Bücher, also schon zu Bereichen, über die ich gearbeitet habe. Meistens dann soziale Bewegungen, Frauenbewegung, Zusammenhänge Frauenbewegung - Friedensbewegung, Geschlechtsrollen und ihre Veränderungen. Manchmal lese ich auch Erzählungen oder Geschichten vor, das aber eher außerhalb der Uni. Meistens sind das Vorträge oder Lesungen aus den Büchern, und damit wieder kann ich selbst bestimmen, was ich machen möchte.

Frage: Betrachten Sie sich jetzt in erster Linie als Schriftstellerin oder als Journalistin?

Schenk: Es ist schwierig. Meine Wunschidentität ist Schriftstellerin. Es gibt eine Stelle bei Sylvia Plath, wo sie sagt: Ich wollte immer Schriftstellerin werden, aber das war das einzige, was ich nicht konnte. Manchmal habe ich auch das Gefühl, daß ich das am liebsten wäre, aber ich glaube, in der Öffentlichkeit bin ich am ehesten durch meine Sachbücher bekannt, bin ich am ehesten als - wie heißt es immer so schön? - feministisch engagierte Sozialwissenschaftlerin bekannt, werde oft so genannt, wenn ich eingeladen werde. Ich bin weniger als Romanautorin bis jetzt bekannt, sondern als Sozialwissenschaftlerin, die in gut lesbarer Form, aber doch halbwegs differenziert, Sachbücher schreibt. Ich wäre aber lieber Schriftstellerin. Ich möchte beides sein, aber das ist für mich höherwertig.

II. Die Entstehung eines Romans

Frage: Können wir jetzt über die Entstehung eines Romans sprechen? Wie beginnen Sie die Arbeit an einem Roman?

Schenk: Ich habe einen Arbeitsrhythmus, der sich in den letzten Jahren herauskristallisiert hat; ich glaube, das ist nicht ganz zufällig, daß bei mir immer Sachbuch und Roman abgewechselt haben. Bei Sachbüchern ist es ja so, das Thema ist genau gestellt, da habe ich immer ein genaues Exposé, da weiß ich, ich muß das und das und das dafür lesen, halte auch immer ziemlich genaue Zeitpläne ein, bin also ziemlich rigide in meiner Arbeit und auch sehr diszipliniert und gehe sehr handwerklich vor bei Sachbüchern. Und ich habe immer das Gefühl gehabt, daß während ich ein Sachbuch schreibe, gerade durch diese Disziplin des Handwerklichen, also wie ich es an der Uni gelernt habe, in meinem Unterbewußten sich alle möglichen Gedanken dann ansammeln, die dann hinterher die neue Idee für den Roman ergeben. Es war fast immer so, daß, wenn ich mit dem Sachbuch fertig war, erst mal eine furchtbare Leere entstand und ich dachte, was soll ich jetzt tun, um Gottes willen, ich habe nichts zu tun; das hielt dann vielleicht drei, vier Wochen an, und plötzlich war mir klar: Ich will über den und den Bereich einen Roman schreiben, und das wird das Thema. Und dann ist das Thema oft nur etwas wie ein Problem, oder eine Frage oder manchmal auch oft nur eine Atmosphäre, eine bestimmte Stimmung, die ich im Kopf habe und mit der das zu tun haben soll.

Ich habe ja vorhin schon erwähnt, daß ich Tagebücher schreibe und auch jetzt noch sehr, sehr exzessiv, wobei der Teil "Festhalten von Gelebtem" zur Zeit kaum darin vorkommt; es kommt sehr, sehr selten vor, daß ich z.B. eine Reise skizziere. Meistens sind es Gespräche oder Skizzen von Ideen, oder was Leute erzählt haben, oder auch ganz absurde Sachen, also wenn ich über die Straße gehe und mir irgend etwas Besonderes auffällt, eine besondere Beleuchtung, oder wie die Leute miteinander reden oder auch nur Satzfetzen. Ich kann das sehr schwer beschreiben; mir kommt manchmal in sonderbaren Stimmungen alles Mögliche bedeutsam vor. Dann schreibe ich das irgendwie hin. Wenn ich jetzt nach einem Sachbuch anfange, zu wissen, das oder das ist eigentlich das

Thema von dem nächsten Roman - also zum Beispiel, es hat mit meinem Vater zu tun, könnte ich jetzt sagen, bei dem neuen Roman - dann gucke ich mir meine Notizbücher der letzten drei Jahre quer an und habe auch einmal das Gefühl, daß alle möglichen Dinge, die ich vorher scheinbar ziellos gesammelt habe, wie ein Altwaren-, Lumpensammler, irgendwo aufgepickt habe, daß die sich kristallisieren, um ein bestimmtes Thema, ohne daß ich das vorher wußte. Ich merke plötzlich, eigentlich hat mich die letzten drei Jahre schon immer das Problem, z.B. des Vergehens der Zeit beschäftigt - ich drücke das jetzt mal pathetisch aus - und dann picke ich aus meinem Tagebuch die ganzen Stellen heraus, von denen ich denke - das sind dann nicht alle, aber ziemlich viele - daß sie mit dem neuen Problem zu tun haben. Dann tippe ich sie ab, und sehr oft ist es so, daß beim Abschreiben von einer Szene, einem Gespräch, einer Stimmung, daraus ein Umfeld entsteht. Das ist die erste Phase.

Die nächste Phase ist dann, daß ich ziemlich genau eine Idee habe, wie das Ganze verlaufen oder aussehen soll und daß ich dann um diese Idee herum anfange zu schreiben, wobei ich die Abrechnung und den jetzigen Roman einigermaßen in der richtigen Reihenfolge auch geschrieben habe und beim Haus die Komplexe schon hintereinander, aber nicht genau in der Reihenfolge, wie sie hinterher standen. Das Haus-Buch ist übrigens auch eine sehr konstruierte Sache, was die meisten Leute gar nicht denken. Es sieht wie eine lockere Abfolge von Situationen und Szenen aus, aber es ist im Grunde ganz genau, symmetrisch zueinander aufgebaut gemeint gewesen. Vielleicht habe ich es überkonstruiert, so daß es deswegen manche nicht gemerkt haben. Ich habe dann in der zweiten oder dritten Phase sehr stark einen Strukturplan, auch bei Romanen.

Frage: Einige Schriftsteller arbeiten ohne festen Plan und wissen nicht, wie es am Ende ausgehen wird.

Schenk: Bei einzelnen Stücken, also in der Frühphase, wo ich die Stücke sammele, ist es auch oft ziellos, da weiß ich auch noch nicht, wohin es mich trägt. Ich habe ja zuletzt meistens in Ich-Form geschrieben, bin aber relativ sicher, daß mein nächster Roman nicht in Ich-Form sein wird. Und es ist so, daß bei diesem ziellosen Suchen am Anfang ein Bild von diesem Ich entsteht, was da redet; ich habe vorhin schon gesagt, das ist ein Stück, ein Teil von mir, aber das bin ich nie ganz. Es ist auch etwas, worüber sich Leute sehr oft gewundert haben, auch in Rezensionen, die kriegten immer das Ich

in diesem Buch nicht zusammen mit dem gelebten Ich; sie
verstanden nie, warum man so depressiv ist und dem Leben
so schlecht klarkommt. Das hängt natürlich damit zusammen, daß das nur ein Teil von mir ist.

Frage: Viele Leute verwechseln Autor und Erzähler?

Schenk: Ja, vielleicht weil bei dieser sogenannten
"Frauenliteratur" immer angenommen wird, daß es da nur
um Erfahrungen geht, und auch nur um Erfahrungen, die
ganz unmittelbar dargestellt werden, ohne irgendwelche
Verfremdungs- oder Formungsprozesse. Vielleicht gehen
davon auch die Rezensenten oder Rezensentinnen aus.

Meine Romane sind viel, viel konstruierter, als die
meisten Leute denken. Ich glaube, ich konstruiere anders, ich konstruiere sicher nicht formal, vielleicht
nicht wie eine Germanistin konstruieren würde, sondern
mir geht es dann, glaube ich, schon mehr um die Vermittlung von bestimmten Gedanken, also Gedanken oder
Ideen dahinter; in Unmöglich, ein Haus ist es eigentlich
die Sache mit der Zeit: daß der Augenblick, immer wenn
man ihn festhalten will, tatsächlich leer wird, daß man
eigentlich immer nur in der Vergangenheit oder Zukunft
lebt und eben heute besonders.

III. Das Ziel der Prosa

Frage: Was sehen Sie als Ziel Ihrer Prosa an? Wollen Sie
etwas Bestimmtes mit Ihren Werken erreichen? Das ist
vielleicht jeweils anders bei den Sachbüchern und bei
den Romanen.

Schenk: Ja, bei den Sachbüchern ist es klar. Bei den
Sachbüchern ist es so, daß ich schon eine engagierte
Perspektive für irgendein Sozialproblem vermitteln will:
das ganze Umfeld, die Fürs und Widers klarmachen, alles,
was mit einer bestimmten Frage zusammenhängt, einen
Überblick geben und gleichzeitig meine eigene Einstellung, meine eigene Wertung des Problems auch vermitteln. Und vielleicht auch ein bißchen gesellschafts-
verändernd wirken - das ist ein sehr pathetischer und
sehr hochgestochener Anspruch, aber in Sachbüchern
möchte ich das bestimmt. In Anführungszeichen, mit aller
Vorsicht, würde ich sagen: Bei den Sachbüchern geht es
mir irgendwie um "Richtung auf eine besseres Leben",
also "wie lebt man besser" oder "das richtige Leben",
aber eben nur ganz mit Vorsicht.

224

Bei den erzählenden Sachen, bei der Prosa, ist das sehr schwierig. Da würde ich eine ganze Menge von Zielen, nicht nur eins im Vordergrund sehen. Ich würde schon sagen, daß Prosa, Literatur überhaupt, ein ganzheitlicherer Zugang zu Leben ist als ein Sachbuch oder eine Wissenschaft, daß das synthetischer ist, daß es umfassender ist, als ein Sachbuch. Ein Sachbuch ist eigentlich nur die intellektuelle Ebene, abgelöst. Ich weiß nicht, ob ich so etwas wie Lebenshilfe mit den Büchern geben möchte. Das bestimmt nicht mit der Prosa. Aber wenn das auch dazu genommen wird, finde ich das nicht notwendig etwas Schlechtes - "Lebensbewältigungshilfe".

Romane können unterhaltende Funktion haben, dabei finde ich auch nichts Negatives. Bei uns in Deutschland wird ja immer die Trennung gemacht zwischen der sogenannten "hohen" Literatur, die muß mühsam und kompliziert und langweilig zu lesen sein, die darf nur ja keinen Spaß machen. Das ist ähnlich wie bei Kant mit der Pflicht und der Neigung; all das, was Spaß macht, das ist auch nicht ethisch und nicht hochwertig. Das finde ich eigentlich ziemlichen Quatsch, weil ich glaube, daß viele gute Literatur, und darunter auch viele, die ich gern lese, sowohl Spaß macht beim Lesen, also Lesegenuß vermittelt, als auch gleichzeitig noch andere Ziele verfolgt.

Dann kann es eskapistische Funktion haben, also auch die Funktion, daß der Leser oder die Leserin vorübergehend aus dem eigenen Leben heraus in ein anderes versetzt wird. Das kann auch etwas Befreiendes haben, besonders, wenn man das eigene Leben als bedrängend oder eng empfindet. Wenn ich es mir überlege, will ich auch immer eine Mischung zwischen Identifikation und Distanz erzielen, also immer beides, ein Stück Identifikation und ein Stück liebevoll-humorvolle Distanz zu der Person, die da redet, möglicherweise mit einem bestimmten Ergebnis auch für Verhalten. Das ist jetzt sehr abstrakt, ich erzähle das nochmal an dem Haus. Da möchte ich eigentlich nicht nur, daß Leute sich mit dem Ich identifizieren und sagen, "ja, so ist es, so langweilig ist der Alltag" und so leer ist der Alltag, daß sie sich mit dieser Haltung der Person identifizieren, die immer ein bißchen am Rand steht und sich nicht einlassen kann. Aber ich möchte auch, daß die, die das lesen, für sich zu dem Schluß kommen, daß sie anders sind und anders sein wollen, also daß sie den Teufelskreis der Stagnation schon durchbrechen, nicht, indem das in dem Buch angeboten wird, als Lösung, sondern das sollen die Leser außerhalb des Buches für sich tun. Aber es wäre zu weit gegriffen, wenn ich sagen würde, daß ich beim Schreiben die Absicht habe, diesen Effekt bei den Lesern zu erzeugen. Ich glaube vielmehr, daß ich den beim Schreiben in mir selbst erzeugen will und daß das eine zweite Wirkung ist, daß sie dann möglicherweise auch für den Leser erzeugt wird.

Frage: Also als Nebenprodukt?

Schenk: Ja, ich glaube, daß ich mir mit meinen Büchern schon auch immer einen Tritt in den Hintern in irgendeine Richtung geben will und ich glaube, daß ich das gar nicht schlecht fände, wenn das bei den Lesern auch wäre. Aber, wenn Leute sagen würden, daß das nicht bei ihnen der Fall ist, daß sie das nur lesen, weil sie das amüsiert oder weil sie das unterhält, oder weil sie das hübsch finden, oder weil es ihnen eine Hilfe zur Lebensbewältigung gibt, dann würde mich das überhaupt nicht kränken. Ich würde es nicht als Negativurteil ansehen, weil ich überhaupt die Vorstellung habe, daß Prosa dazu da ist, daß sich viele Leute viel Verschiedenes herausholen für sich. Und es ist mir eigentlich auch ziemlich egal, was dann.

IV. "Frauenliteratur"

Frage: Können wir jetzt ein bißchen über das Thema "Frauenliteratur" reden? Gibt es das überhaupt? In allen Verlagsprospekten gibt es verschiedene Kategorien: Romane, Lyrik usw.; meistens gibt es dann die weitere Kategorie "Frauenliteratur" und darunter sind aber auch Romane.

Schenk: Ja, die Verlage machen das natürlich so, weil das offensichtlich noch immer ein expansionsträchtiger Bereich ist. Gibt es Frauenliteratur? Ich würde sagen, es gibt schon Eigenarten der Prosa von vielen Frauen, die in der Mehrzahl der Literatur von Männern nicht auftaucht. Solange die grundsätzlichen Erfahrungsbereiche von Frauen im allgemeinen sich noch sehr von der der Männer unterscheiden, wird es auch unterschiedliche Verarbeitungsformen geben. Aber das läßt sich nicht global sagen, es ist schon ein fließender Unterschied. Der besteht einmal in den Gegenständen, die beschrieben werden, glaube ich, also in der Themenwahl. Ich denke schon, daß im allgemeinen Frauen mehr diese berühmten "Beziehungsthemen" bearbeiten, mehr als Männer im Schnitt, und daß weniger solche Erfahrungen der äußeren Welt da zu Wort kommen als Erfahrungen der inneren Welt. Es ist ja auch häufiger, daß sie solche Gegenstände thematisieren wie Krankheit, negatives Selbstbild usw. Aber da könnte man viele Beispiele auch aus der Männerliteratur nehmen, das ist ja auch nicht so, als wären die literarischen Gegenstände von Männern immer der Beruf oder die Karriere, zumal Schriftsteller meistens ja auch keine anständigen Berufe haben, auch männliche Schriftsteller, sondern auch im Grunde genommen immer das eigene Ich und seine Beziehungen oder Beziehungslosigkeit thematisieren.

Es gibt auch einen Unterschied in der Selbstsichtweise, nicht bei allen Frauen gegenüber allen Männern, aber bei vielen Frauen gegenüber vielen schreibenden Männern. Es ist mir an Romanen, in der Zeit, als ich noch alle Neuerscheinungen verfolgte, sehr aufgefallen, welche Romane von männlichen Jungautoren hochgejubelt werden und wie diese angelegt sind. Ich habe dann versucht, in solchen Romanen, wenn ich "Ich" gelesen habe, mir vorzustellen, daß eine Frau so über sich redet, sich so darstellt, und ich würde sagen, daß eine Tendenz, sich selbst ernster zu nehmen, deutlich spürbar ist. Wenn man sich vorstellt, an manchen Stellen sei das Ich eine Frau, dann kommt einem das lächerlich vor, wirklich lächerlich, so wichtigtuerisch über sich selbst daherzureden. Ich fand das damals furchtbar komisch, ich habe darüber gelacht, als mir aufgegangen ist, daß das wohl ein Unterschied it. Ich glaube schon, daß Frauen sich nicht ganz so furchtbar ernst nehmen; das Pathos des Leidens ist irgendwie aufdringlicher bei Männern. Und dann glaube ich, daß bei den Männern eine Tendenz zu mehr Techniken des Verfremdens und zu mehr Manierismus ist. Aber auch nur über den Daumen gepeilt. Es gibt einige Frauen, bei denen das auch ist, und es gibt einige Männer, bei denen das nicht ist. Zum Beispiel finde ich, bei Frisch ist das überhaupt nicht, und bei Handke ist es sehr; und Karin Reschke zum Beispiel ist für mich manieriert. Ja, aber das ist nur ein ganz allgemeiner Eindruck. Ich weiß nicht, ob ich die Kategorie "Frauenliteratur" noch angemessen finde. Ich weiß auch nicht, ob sie nicht den Autorinnen eher schadet, dem Umsatz sicher nicht, aber bei der Rezeption wahrscheinlich ja.

Frage: Würden Sie Ihre Werke zur "Frauenliteratur" rechnen?

Schenk: Ich weiß, daß sie dazu gerechnet werden, wobei witzigerweise die <u>Abrechnung</u> meistens dazugerechnet wird und das <u>Haus</u> nicht. Das hängt nun mit der Reihe "neue frau" zusammen. Ich glaube, daß <u>Unmöglich, ein Haus</u>

227

sicherlich sehr viele Dinge behandelt, die auch für Männer wichtig und spannend sind, die <u>Abrechnung</u> möglicherweise auch. Sie sind Frauenliteratur, weil sie von einer Frau geschrieben werden und sie sind Frauenliteratur, weil sie überweigend von Frauen gelesen werden.

Frage: Heinz Puknus meint, Frauenliteratur wäre "von Frauen verfaßt" und "Frauen betreffend".[1] Gibt es nun auch eine Männerliteratur?

Schenk: Kaum. Wenn ich nur bedenke, daß auch Männerliteratur, also die von männlichen Autoren, zeitgenössischen Romanschriftstellern verfaßte Literatur mehr von Frauen als von Männern gelesen wird. Ich glaube, daß Frauen überhaupt als Leserinnen anteilmäßig stärker vertreten sind, weil sie wohl insgesamt mehr zum Roman neigen; bei Männern sind das ausgesuchte kleinere Gruppen, die Romane lesen. Sofern Männer überhaupt noch lesen, dann überwiegend Sachbücher. Ich kann da keine Prozentzahlen sagen, aber ich habe auch literatursoziologische Untersuchungen gelesen, die in diese Richtung gehen. "Frauen betreffend": so wäre vielleicht noch der Begriff "Frauenliteratur" gerechtfertigt, wenn man damit meint, daß die Sichtweise von Frauen darin deutlicher ist als in den üblichen Männersachen. Es ist natürlich so, daß ich mich mit den weiblichen Figuren männlicher Autoren nur selten identifizieren kann, sehr selten darin wiederfinde, auch bei zeitgenössischen Autoren. Und umgekehrt weiß ich, daß manche Leute sich beschweren, daß die Männer in meinen Büchern so entsetzlich blaß und unwichtig sind, und warum nicht deutlicher und ein bißchen wichtiger.

Frage: Beschweren sich die Männer darüber oder die Frauen, oder ist das teils, teils?

Schenk: Die männlichen Rezensenten taten das zum Teil, die Frauen tun das eigentlich weniger. Das würde ich als Kritik auch nicht akzeptieren, weil das bei dem Buch nicht so wichtig ist. Ich würde auch manchen männlichen und sonstigen Autoren, egal wem, zubilligen, daß man ein sehr helles Licht auf eine bestimmte Stelle scheinen läßt und eine andere Stelle unwichtiger findet. Ich glaube, ich wäre sehr glücklich, wenn der Begriff "Frauenliteratur" irgendwann verschwände. Aber ich sehe ihn in einer Übergangszeit schon als unvermeidlich an, weil ich glaube, daß Frauen, wie gesagt, bestimmte Erfahrungsbereiche häufiger thematisieren, sie vielleicht in einer etwas anderen Art thematisieren und auch deutlicher ihre Selbstwahrnehmung thematisieren, in dieser Sorte von Literatur, als das vorher üblich war, also auch, als es von weiblichen Autoren vor dieser Frauenliteraturzeit gemacht worden ist.

Frage: Gehört das vielleicht schon zur "Kommerzialisierung des Feminismus . . . auf dem Literaturmarkt"? So haben Sie das in Die feministische Herausforderung (S. 222) formuliert.

Schenk: Ja, das würde ich sagen. Was Sie erwähnt haben – die Ankündigung in den Verlagsprospekten, daß es jetzt diese Kategorie "Frauenliteratur" überall gibt, und daß es eine verkaufswirksame Kategorie ist – gehört sicher schon zur Kommerzialisierung. Und darin sehe ich auch eine Gefahr; im Augenblick, wo das nicht mehr einkommensträchtig ist für die Verlage, wird das sofort wieder abserviert. Mit diesem Begriff verschwinden dann wahrscheinlich zig Autorinnen, die sich heute noch äußern. Das ist ein Teil Kommerzialisierung. Aber nur in seinen Randphänomenen. Ich glaube, der Gedanke kommt in der Feministischen Herausforderung nicht vor, wohl aber in Frauen kommen ohne Waffen: daß ein Teil der bisherigen Frauenunterdrückung darin bestand, daß sie dieses Monopol auf Welterklärung hatten und daß die Frauenliteratur es auf einer Dimension durchbricht, das Monopol auf Welterklärung. Das ist ein Begriff von der Marie-Luise Janssen-Jurreit. Das ist ja ein Kulturmonopol gewesen, daß in der Literatur das Bild, das Männer von sich, von Frauen und von der Welt haben, eigentlich festgehalten ist, und daß Frauen, wenn sie gelesen haben, dieses Bild verinnerlicht und sich auch daran orientiert haben. Und ich denke, daß es ein Verdienst der Frauenliteratur ist, daß dieses Monopol aufgeweicht wird, und daß jetzt auch Frauen andere Möglichkeiten haben, sich, Männer und die Welt wahrzunehmen. Insofern ist es schon etwas Neues, aber die rasche Kommerzialisierung macht das Ganze auch dafür anfällig, schnell wieder abserviert zu werden.

Frage: Meinen Sie, daß das jetzt kommt?

Schenk: Ich fürchte, daß es bevorsteht, weil ich viele Parallelen im Verlauf der jetzigen Frauenbewegung zu der Entwicklung um die Jahrhundertwende sehe. Um die Jahrhundertwende war auch die letzte Welle der Frauenbewegung eine Kulturwelle und eine allgemeine Verbreitung feministischer Ideen, und dann wird langsam das Desinteresse wieder über alle diese Dinge hereinbrechen. Auch in der Weimarer Republik war es so, daß die Literatur am längsten überlebt hat von der Frauenbewegung. Als die politischen Ansprüche schon längst verstummt waren, gab es immer noch Romane, die die "neue Frau" - die damalige neue Frau - dargestellt haben. Und immer noch eine Zeitlang Autorinnen und Wissenschaftlerinnen.

V. Zum neuen Roman

Frage: Können Sir mir sagen, was für einen Roman Sie jetzt geschrieben haben, oder ist das noch ein Geheimnis?

Schenk: Das ist ein bißchen schwierig, weil er ja noch nicht erschienen ist. Es ist ein Roman, der auf verschiedenen Ebenen handelt, falls man überhaupt von Handlung sprechen kann. Es ist wieder ein erzählendes Ich, eine Frau in einer Arbeitskrise, die an einer Dissertation schreibt, nicht voran kommt, in einer sozial ungesicherten Position lebt, mit einem Mann zusammenlebt, ohne verheiratet zu sein, und ein Stipendium hatte, das sich dem Ende zuneigt. Also befindet sie sich in einer Situation vorm Beginn der Arbeitslosigkeit. Sie kommt mit ihrer Arbeit nicht weiter, weil die Arbeit zu einer Auseinandersetzung mit dem Vater geführt hat. Dann wird auf einer Ebene das Leben des Vaters erzählt, auf der anderen Ebene das Alltagsleben der erzählenden Person; gleichzeitig hat sie sich in dieser Situation in einen Mann verliebt, sodaß es zu einer Dreiecksbeziehung kommt zwischen dem Mann, mit dem sie zusammenlebt, und dem Geliebten, der gleichzeitig sie an den Vater erinnert oder die Auseinandersetzung mit dem Vater auslöst. Eigentlich ist es aber ein Roman, der so etwas wie eine Reise nach innen darstellt, denn alle drei Männer - also der Vater, der Geliebte und der Mann, mit dem sie zusammenlebt - sind eigentlich Aspekte einer Vaterfigur, also verschiedene Seiten der Auseinandersetzung mit dem Vater. Und in dem Buch gibt es eine etwas surrealistische Ebene und eine einfache Tatsachenebene, wie das ein bißchen schon in dem Haus anfängt. Ich glaube, die meisten Leute haben das da nicht richtig wahrgenommen, wie das gemeint war.

Frage: Hat der neue Roman auch einen satirischen Aspekt?

Schenk: Ja, es kommen ganze satirische Passagen darin vor; im Augenblick heißt der Titel - aber ich weiß nicht, ob es dabei bleiben wird - Die Unkündbarkeit der Verheißung; ein Kernstück darin ist das Kündigungsschreiben an den Liebhaber, dem wird gekündigt mit einem formellen Geschäftsbrief, in dem genau die Form des Geschäftsbriefs eingehalten wird. Es gibt verschiedene

Passagen in dem Buch, wo emotionale Dinge in einer
merkantilen, kommerziellen Sprache abgehandelt werden,
das ist ein Strang des Buches. Zum Beispiel gibt es da
auch ein Kapitel über eine Gesellschaft, die sich
"Freundinnen und Förderinnen der Neben- und Außen-
beziehungen e.V." nennt. Da werden auch Geschäftsreden
gehalten, wie man ökonomisch eine Außenbeziehung ge-
staltet, so daß Aufwand und Ertrag sich gut rentieren.
Das ist eine Dimension. Ich möchte immer die etwas
düsteren und depressiven Stränge, die es bei mir eigentlich in allen Geschichten gibt, auch mit einem witzigen,
komischen - ich weiß nicht, wie ich das genau bezeichnen
soll - Gegengewicht wieder ausbalancieren. Das ist mir
ganz wichtig, vielleicht auch für mein eigenes Gleich-
gewicht wichtig. Wenn das Element nicht darin wäre,
würde ich ein falsches Pathos befürchten.

Anmerkung

[1] Heinz Puknus, ed., Neue Literatur der Frauen (München: Beck, 1980), S. 255.

Bibliographie

Erzählungen

Schenk, Herrad. "Wie dem auch sei". Merkur 318 (November
    1974).

----------. "Die Sache mit Conny". Pardon 11 (November
    1976).

----------. "Die Bellfahrt". Merkur 344 (Januar 1977).

----------. "Kaputte Blütenträume". Pardon 2 (Februar
    1977).

----------. "Es könnte daran liegen, daß ich häßlich
bin", "Das Interview", "Obst und Gemüse". In Frauen,
die pfeifen. Verständigungstexte. Hrsg. von Ruth
Geiger, Hilke Holinka, Claudia Rosenkranz, Sigrid
Weigel. Frankfurt: Suhrkamp, 1978 (= edition suhrkamp 968).

----------. "Nur eine Frage der Disziplin". Westermanns
Monatshefte (Dezember 1979).

----------. "Drei Biographien oder Das Traktat von der falschen und der richtigen Braut". Litfass 23 (April 1983).

----------. "Alle meine Kinder". In Kaum bin ich allein. Geschichten von der Nähe zu sich und den anderen. Hrsg. von Jutta Lieck und Frank Göhre. Reinbek: Rowohlt, 1985 (= rororo panther 5611).

Sachbücher

Schenk, Herrad. Geschlechtsrollenwandel und Sexismus. Zur Sozialpsychologie geschlechtsspezifischen Verhaltens. Weinheim: Beltz, 1979.

----------. Die feministische Herausforderung. 150 Jahre Frauenbewegung in Deutschland. München: Beck, 1980 (= BSR 213).

----------. Frauen kommen ohne Waffen. Feminismus und Pazifismus. München: Beck, 1983 (= BSR 274).

----------. Wir leben zusammen, nicht allein. Wohngemeinschaften heute. Köln: Kiepenheuer & Witsch, 1984.

Romane

Schenk, Herrad. Abrechnung. Reinbek: Rowohlt, 1979 (= neue frau, rororo 4424).

----------. Unmöglich, ein Haus in der Gegenwart zu bauen. Darmstadt: Luchterhand, 1980 (auch Ullstein Taschenbuch 26087).

----------. Die Unkündbarkeit der Verheißung. Düsseldorf: claassen, 1984.

----------. Die Rache der alten Mamsell. Eugenie Marlitts Lebensroman. Düsseldorf: claassen, 1986.

Anthologie

Schenk, Herrad, Hrsg. So nah und doch so fern. Die Geschichten mit den Eltern. Reinbek: Rowohlt, 1985 (= rororo panther 5670).

GDR Women Writers: The Post-War Generations
Bibliography of Narrative Prose, June 1987

Dorothy Rosenberg

In the 1970s, GDR women began writing about them-selves. Christa Wolf's Nachdenken über Christa T. was followed by Gerti Tetzner's Karen W., Brigitte Reimann's Franziska Linkerhand, and Irmtraud Morgner's Leben und Abenteuer der Trobadora Beatriz. These works were the first to challenge the idealized and convenient female stereotypes which had populated much of GDR literature in the 1950s and 1960s, in which women characters had been smoothly integrated into the flow of work life without significantly ruffling the surface of domestic tranquility.

In the small flood of novels and, in particular, the collections of short stories that followed, women began to write about the price of admission to the public sphere and the personal costs of leading a double life. Wolf, Tetzner, Reimann, and Morgner were joined by Maxie Wander (Guten Morgen, Du Schöne), Charlotte Worgitzky (Vieräugig oder Blind), and Renate Apitz (Evastöchter), from their own generation and a growing number of younger writers: Helga Königsdorf, Helga Schubert, Maria Seidemann, Monika Helmecke, Angela Stachowa, Christine Wolter, and Rosemarie Zeplin, among others.

The past ten years have seen the development of a body of GDR literature written by and about women which explores and discusses in depth the contradictions and problems of a society in which the economic organization and political ideology promote equality between the sexes, but in which cultural norms and individual atti-tudes toward sex roles and appropriate gender behavior lag far behind. With the major changes in social and economic structure largely accomplished, women writers in the 1980s have turned to address the much deeper challenge of sexual stereotyping and the social division of labor.

233

The writers listed below constitute the post-war generations in the sense that their concept of society has been either predominantly or exclusively determined by the experience of GDR socialism. Those who experienced the war did so as children. I have included several well-known writers born in the early 1930s (Wolf, Morgner, Reimann, and Wander) for the sake of completeness, but have tried to emphasize less well-known, younger writers. This is not a complete list of GDR women writers. It is a sample of prose works by women who fall into the above loose definitions and who write about questions of gender and society, broadly defined. My selection has been further limited by the practical question of accessibility: I have listed only works which I have been able to get copies of, read, and find interesting. I have listed GDR first editions wherever possible. West German editions are given for Wolf and Morgner (for convenience) and for works which did not appear separately in the GDR. As of June 1987, all of the authors except Katja Lange-Müller, Monika Nothing, and Doris Paschiller were GDR citizens.

Renate Apitz (1939)
    Evastöchter. (Erzählungen), Rostock: Hinstorff, 1981.
    Hexenzeit. (Roman), Rostock: Hinstorff, 1984.
Christiane Barckhausen (1942)
    Schwestern. Berlin: Verlag der Nation, 1985.
Daniela Dahn (1949)
    Spitzenzeit. (Feuilletons), Halle-Leipzig: Mitteldeutscher Verlag, 1978.
    Prenzlauer Berg-Tour, Halle-Leipzig: Mitteldeutscher Verlag, 1987.
Gabriele Eckart (1954)
    Per Anhalter: Geschichten und Erlebnisse aus der DDR. Berlin: Verlag Neues Leben, 1982.
    So sehe ick die Sache. (Protokolle), Köln: Kiepenheuer und Witsch, 1984.
    Der Seidelstein. (Novelle), Berlin: Buchverlag der Morgen, 1986.
Renate Feyl (1944)
    Rauhbein. (Roman), Rudolstadt: Greifenverlag, 1968.
    Bau mir eine Brücke. (Roman), Berlin: Verlag Neues Leben, 1972.
    Der lautlose Aufbruch. (Portraits), Berlin: Verlag Neues Leben, 1981.

Rosemarie Fret (1935)
Nachsaison. (Erzählungen), Rostock: Hinstorff, 1973.
Hoffnung auf Schneewittchen. (Erzählungen), Halle:
Mitteldeutscher Verlag, 1981.
Roswitha Geppert (1943)
Die Last die du nicht trägst. Halle: Mitteldeutscher
Verlag, 1978.
Christiane Grosz (1944)
"Der Trick" in: Das Kostüm.
"Der verlorene Ausdruck" in: Das Kostüm.
"Das würde dir guttun" in: Brautfahrt.
Monika Helmecke (1943)
Klopfzeichen. (Erzählungen), Berlin: Verlag Neues
Leben, 1979.
Ursula Höntsch-Harendt (1934)
Wir Flüchtlingskinder. Halle: Mitteldeutscher, 1985.
Rosita Ionescu (1941)
Lila, Kolorit auf Breitwand. Berlin: Aufbau, 1976.
Dorothea Iser (1946)
Wolkenberge tragen nicht. Berlin: Militärverlag,
1979.
Lea. Berlin: Militärverlag, 1983.
Neuzugang. Berlin: Verlag Neues Leben, 1985.
Sylvia Kabus (1952)
"Karls Reise" Temperamente 4/1981 pp. 63-83.
"Altes Weibchen" Temperamente 1/1979 pp. 84-89.
Helga Königsdorf (1938)
Meine ungehörigen Träume. (Geschichten), Berlin:
Aufbau, 1978.
Der Lauf der Dinge. (Geschichten), Berlin: Aufbau,
1982.
Hochzeit in Pizunda. (Erzählungen), Berlin: Aufbau,
1986.
Respektloser Umgang. Berlin: Aufbau, 1986.
Angela Kraus (1950)
Das Vergnügen. (Roman), Berlin: Aufbau, 1984.
Christine Lambrecht (1949)
Dezemberbriefe. (Geschichten), Halle: Mitteldeutsch-
er Verlag, 1982.
Männerbekanntschaften. Halle: Mitteldeutscher Ver-
lag, 1986.
Katja Lange-Müller (1951)
Wehleid - wie im Leben. Frankfurt/Main: S. Fischer,
1986.
Irina Liebmann (1943)
Berliner Mietshaus. (Begegnungen und Gespräche),
Halle: Mitteldeutscher Verlag, 1982.

Monika Maron (1941)
  Flugasche. (Roman), Frankfurt/Main: Fischer, 1981.
  Das Mißverständnis. Frankfurt/Main: Fischer, 1981.
  Die Überläuferin. (Roman), Frankfurt/Main: Fischer,
  1986.
Brigitte Martin (1939)
  Der Rote Ballon. (Geschichten), Berlin: Buchverlag
  der Morgen, 1978.
  Nach Freude anstehen. (Roman), Berlin: Buchverlag
  der Morgen, 1981.
Beata Morgenstern (1946)
  Jenseits der Allee. (Geschichten), Berlin: Aufbau,
  1979.
Irmtraud Morgner (1933)
  Hochzeit in Konstantinopel. Berlin: Aufbau, 1968.
  Die wundersamen Reisen Gustavs des Weltfahrers.
  Berlin: Aufbau, 1972.
  Leben und Abenteuer der Trobadora Beatriz nach
  Zeugnissen ihrer Spielfrau Laura. Berlin: Aufbau,
  1974. Darmstadt: Luchterhand, 1976.
  Amanda. Ein Hexenroman. Berlin: Aufbau, 1983. Darm-
  stadt: Luchterhand, 1983.
Christa Müller (1936)
  Vertreibung aus dem Paradies. (Erzählungen), Berlin:
  Aufbau, 1979.
Christine Müller (1949)
  Männerprotokolle. Berlin: Buchverlag der Morgen,
  1986.
Sibylle Muthesius (196?)
  Flucht in die Wolken. Berlin: Buchverlag der Morgen,
  1981.
Monika Nothing (1942)
  Ein Mantel aus Hoffnung. (Erzählungen), Rostock:
  Hinstorff, 1985.
Irene Oberthür (1941)
  Mein fremdes Gesicht. (Erzählbericht), Berlin: Buch-
  verlag der Morgen, 1985.
Doris Paschiller (1953)
  Die Würde. (Roman), Berlin: Buchverlag der Morgen,
  1980.
Lia Pirskawetz (1938)
  Der Stille Grund. Berlin: Verlag Neues Leben, 1985.
Brigitte Reimann (1933-1973)
  Der Tod der schönen Helena. (Erzählung), Berlin:
  Verlag des Ministeriums des Innerns, 1955.
  Die Frau am Pranger. Berlin: Verlag Neues Leben,
  1956.
  Die Kinder von Hellas. (Erzählung), Berlin: Verlag
  des Ministeriums für Nationale Verteidigung, 1956.
  Das Geständnis. (Erzählung), Berlin: Aufbau, 1960.

Ankunft im Alltag. Berlin: Verlag Neues Leben, 1961.
Die Geschwister. (Erzählung), Berlin: Aufbau, 1963.
Das grüne Licht der Steppen. Tagebuch einer Sibirienreise. Berlin: Verlag Neues Leben, 1965.
Franziska Linkerhand. Berlin: Verlag Neues Leben, 1974.
Brigitte Reimann in ihren Briefen und Tagebüchern. Berlin: Verlag Neues Leben, 1983.
Regine Röhner (1952)
Holunderzeit. (Erzählungen), Halle: Mitteldeutscher Verlag, 1981.
Jutta Schlott (1944)
Das liebliche Fest. Berlin: Verlag Neues Leben, 1984.
Helga Schubert (1940)
Lauter Leben. (Geschichten), Berlin: Aufbau, 1975.
Blickwinkel. (Geschichten), Berlin: Aufbau, 1984.
(Das verbotene Zimmer. Darmstadt/Neuwied: Luchterhand, 1982, largely overlaps Blickwinkel with some differences).
Helga Schütz (1937)
Vorgeschichten oder die schöne Gegend Probstein. Berlin: Aufbau, 1970.
Das Erdbeben bei Sangerhausen. (Geschichten), Berlin: Aufbau, 1972.
Festbeleuchtung. (Roman), Berlin: Aufbau, 1973.
Jetta in Dresden. (Roman), Berlin: Aufbau, 1977.
Julia oder die Erziehung zum Chorgesang. (Roman), Berlin: Aufbau, 1980.
Martin Luther. Eine Erzählung für den Film. Berlin: Aufbau, 1983.
In Annas Namen. Berlin: Aufbau, 1986.
Maria Seidemann (1944)
Der Tag an dem Sir Henry starb. (Geschichten), Berlin: Eulenspiegel Verlag, 1980).
Nasenflöte, Geschichten aus der Provinz. Berlin: Eulenspiegel Verlag, 1983.
Das geschminkte Chamäleon. Ein ironischer Roman, Berlin: Eulenspiegel, 1986.
Karin Simon (1940)
Drei Häute aus Eis. (Erzählungen), Rostock: Hinstorff, 1983.
Angela Stachowa (1948)
Stunde zwischen Hund und Katz. (Erzählungen), Halle: Mitteldeutscher Verlag, 1976.
Geschichten für Majka. Halle: Mitteldeutscher Verlag, 1978.
Kleine Verführungen. (Erzählungen), Halle: Mitteldeutscher Verlag, 1983.

Beata Stanislau (1942)
   Das Mädchen und der Alte. (Erzählungen), Halle: Mitteldeutscher Verlag, 1983.
   Die Erbschaft. (Erzählung), Halle: Mitteldeutscher Verlag, 1986.
Tanja Stern (1952)
   Fern von Cannes. (Erzählungen), Berlin: Buchverlag der Morgen, 1984.
Gerti Tetzner (1936)
   Karen W. Halle: Mitteldeutscher Verlag, 1974.
Maxie Wander (1933-1977)
   Guten Morgen, Du Schöne. Frauen in der DDR. (Protokolle), Berlin: Buchverlag der Morgen, 1977.
   Maxie Wander. Tagebücher und Briefe. Berlin: Buchverlag der Morgen, 1979.
Petra Werner (1951)
   Sich einen Mann backen. (Geschichten), Berlin: Verlag Neues Leben, 1982.
   Die Lüge hat bunte Flügel. (Erzählungen), Berlin: Verlag Neues Leben, 1986.
Maya Wiens (1950)
   Traumgrenzen. (Roman), Berlin: Verlag Neues Leben, 1983.
Christa Wolf (1929)
   Fiction:
   Moskauer Novelle. Halle: Mitteldeutscher Verlag, 1961.
   Der geteilte Himmel. Halle: Mitteldeutscher Verlag, 1963. Reinbek: Rowohlt, 1968.
   Juninachmittag. (Erzählung), Berlin: Aufbau, 1967.
   Nachdenken über Christa T. Halle: Mitteldeutscher Verlag, 1968. Darmstadt: Luchterhand, 1972.
   Till Eulenspiegel. (Erzählung für den Film) mit Gerhard Wolf, Berlin: Aufbau, 1972. Darmstadt: Luchterhand, 1973.
   Unter den Linden. Drei unwahrscheinliche Geschichten. Berlin: Aufbau, 1974. Darmstadt: Luchterhand, 1974.
   Dienstag der 27. September 1960. (Erzählung) Berlin: Aufbau, 1974.
   Gesammelte Erzählungen. Darmstadt: Luchterhand, 1974.
   Kindheitsmuster. Berlin: Aufbau, 1976. Darmstadt: Luchterhand, 1977.
   Kein Ort. Nirgends. Berlin: Aufbau, 1979. Darmstadt: Luchterhand, 1979.   Luchterhand, 1979.
   Kassandra. Vier Vorlesungen. Eine Erzählung. Berlin: Aufbau, 1983. Darmstadt: Luchterhand, 1983.
   Ausgewählte Erzählungen. Darmstadt: Luchterhand, 1984.

238

Erzählungen. Berlin: Aufbau, 1985.
Störfall. Nachrichten eines Tages. Berlin: Aufbau,
1987. Darmstadt: Luchterhand, 1987.
Essays:
Lesen und Schreiben. Aufsätze und Betrachtungen.
Leipzig: Reclam, 1971, erweitert 1973. Berlin: Auf-
bau, 1972.
Fortgesetzter Versuch. Leipzig: Reclam, 1979.
Karoline von Günderrode: Der Schatten eines Traums.
ed. with an essay by Christa Wolf. Berlin: Buch-
verlag der Morgen, 1979.
Voraussetzungen einer Erzählung. Kassandra. Darm-
stadt: Luchterhand, 1983.
Die Dimension des Autors. Aufsätze, Essays, Ge-
spräche, Reden 1959-1985. 2 vol. Berlin: Aufbau,
1987.
Christine Wolter (1939)
Meine italienische Reise. (Erzählung), Berlin: Auf-
bau, 1973.
Wie ich meine Unschuld verlor. (Erzählungen), Ber-
lin: Aufbau, 1976.
Die Hintergrundsperson, oder Versuche zu lieben.
(Roman), Berlin: Aufbau, 1979.
Die Alleinseglerin. (Roman), Berlin: Aufbau, 1982.
Areopolis. (Erzählungen), Berlin: Aufbau, 1985.
Charlotte Worgitzky (1934)
Die Unschuldigen. Berlin: Buchverlag der Morgen,
1975.
Vieräugig oder Blind. (Erzählungen), Berlin: Buch-
verlag der Morgen, 1978.
Meine ungeborenen Kinder. (Roman), Berlin: Buchver-
lag der Morgen, 1982.
Heute sterben immer nur die anderen. (Erzählung),
Berlin: Buchverlag der Morgen, 1986.
Rosemarie Zeplin (1939)
Schattenriß eines Liebhabers. (Erzählung), Berlin:
Aufbau, 1980.
Alpträume aus der Provinz. (Roman), Berlin: Aufbau,
1984.

Anthologies:

Edith Anderson, ed. Blitz aus heiterm Himmel. Rostock:
Hinstorff, 1975.
Meta Borst, ed. Angst vor der Liebe. Halle: Mittel-
deutscher Verlag, 1984.
Konrad Franke, ed. Gespräche hinterm Haus. Wien: Ull-
stein, 1981.

Almut Giesecke, ed. Brautfahrt. Geschichten über Begegnungen. Berlin: Aufbau, 1984.
Horst Heidtmann, ed. Im Kreislauf der Windeln. Basel: Beltz und Gelberg, 1982.
Bitterfisch. Baden-Baden: Signal, 1982.
Stefan Heym, ed. Auskunft 1. Reinbek bei Hamburg: Rowohlt, 1977.
Auskunft 2. Reinbek bei Hamburg: Rowohlt, 1981.
Ingrid Krüger, ed. Die Heiratsschwindlerin. Darmstadt und Neuwied: Luchterhand, 1983.
Helga Thron, ed. Das Kostüm: Geschichten von Frauen. Berlin: Aufbau, 1982.
Lutz W. Wolff, ed. Frauen in der DDR, 20 Erzählungen. München: DTV, 1976.

Comments and suggestions for additions are very welcome.

Dorothy Rosenberg
220 College St.
Lewiston, ME 04240

About the Authors

Charlotte Armster is an associate professor of German at Gettysburg College. In addition to teaching 19th- and 20th-century German literature, she has been active in several interdisciplinary programs, and has served as Women's Studies Coordinator representing Gettysburg College for the Central Pennsylvania Consortium. Her current research focuses on narrative and women in the Holocaust, and she is editing an anthology of critical essays on the writings of women of the Holocaust.

Sigrid Brauner studied German literature, political science, and pedagogy at the Goethe Universität in Frankfurt/Main and is currently completing her doctoral thesis on 16th-century literature at the University of California, Berkeley. She has taught and lectured on medieval and early modern women's writings and lives; her publications in this field include contributions to G. Becker et al., Aus der Zeit der Verzweiflung and to German and Women's Studies: New Directions in Literary and Interdisciplinary Course Approaches.

Renate Fischetti teaches German language and literature, the history of European film, and film theory at the University of Maryland/Baltimore County, where she is an associate professor. Her research interests have included Brecht studies, the Baroque period, and the New German Cinema; she has also made two films of her own. In 1983 she founded the Baltimore Women's Film and Video Festival, which includes an annual competition. Following the developments of German feminist film over the years, she has interviewed filmmakers Helke Sander, Claudia von Alemann, Valie Export, Ulrike Ottinger, Erika Runge, Ula Stöckl, Jutta Brückner, Heidi Genee, and Maria Knilli. Projects currently underway are a monograph on Helke Sander and a history of women in German film.

Renny Keelin Harrigan hopes to be writing more on Weimar popular literature, but constraints of a 12-month job make work very slow. She is working on an article about Zora Neale Hurston and a short translation of Mathilde

241

Franziska Anneke. Both these projects have come about directly or indirectly through her current job working in administration and faculty development at the Center for Women's Studies, University of Wisconsin-Milwaukee.

Lynda J. King, an assistant professor of German at Oregon State University since 1986, has also taught at the Universities of Minnesota and Texas and at a <u>Gymnasium</u> in Vienna. Besides language courses, she teaches and conducts research on literature and culture in Germany and Austria from 1890-1935. Her publications include reviews and articles on Robert Musil, on women in the 1920s, and on Vicki Baum, the subject of her book, <u>The Business of Best-Selling Books. Vicki Baum, Grand Hotel, and the House of Ullstein in Weimar Republic Germany</u> (Wayne State University Press, to appear 1988). King has received numerous research grants, most recently from Oregon State University, which funded her 1987 trip to the Literary Archive in Marbach to study urban themes and proletarian-revolutionary fairy tales in the twenties.

Helga Madland, an associate professor of German at the University of Oklahoma, received her Ph.D. from the University of Washington in 1981. Her research interests center on drama and dramatic theory, with a focus on Sturm und Drang. She is working on a book on J.M.R. Lenz. A new interest is 18th-century women, particularly the novels, plays, and editorial efforts of Marianne Ehrmann. Her teaching consists primarily of graduate level courses on the 18th and 19th century, and upper level literature and conversation courses. Presently, she is the Interim Chair of her department.

Jan Mouton is an associate professor in the Modern Language Department at Loyola University of Chicago where she teaches courses in German language and literature as well as in film, folklore, and women's studies. She has published articles on Bertolt Brecht, Günter Grass, Werner Herzog, Rainer Werner Fassbinder, and Margarethe von Trotta.

Luise F. Pusch, geb. 1944. Professorin für Sprachwissenschaft, berüchtigte "Radikalfeministin", daher für die deutsche Universität untragbar und stellungslos. Zwei Bücher und ca. 60 Aufsätze zur Grammatik des Deutschen, Englischen, Italienischen und Lateinischen. Seit 1979 Forschungsschwerpunkt Feministische Linguistik. Autorin von <u>Das Deutsche als Männersprache: Aufsätze und Glossen zur feministischen Linguistik</u> (1984); Herausgeberin von

Feminismus: Inspektion der Herrenkultur (1983) und _Schwestern berühmter Männer: Zwölf biographische Portraits_ (1985). Im Herbst 1987 soll _Töchter... und 1988 Mütter berühmter Männer_ erscheinen, außerdem ein zweites Buch über feministische Linguistik, mit neuen Glossen: _Alle Menschen werden Schwestern_ und ein Kalendar mit Frauen-Gedenktagen (1988ff).

Dorothy Rosenberg has taught courses in German and Women's Studies as an assistant professor at Colby College in Maine. She has written on leftist writers and literary theory in the Weimar Republic, women and popular culture, and women in GDR literature. She is currently living in Maine and co-translating and editing an anthology of contemporary GDR women writers with Nancy Lukens and writing a monograph on Women Writers in the GDR: Social Change and the Role of Literature.

Ricarda Schmidt, 33, lives in Manchester (GB) without permanent employment. She has taught German as a foreign language at Salford University (GB) and UMIST (GB), German literature at Hanover University (FRG) and Osnabrück University (FRG), and English literature at Hanover University. Her research interests include German and English women's literature of the 19th and 20th centuries, feminist theory, and E.T.A. Hoffmann.

Susan Wendt-Hildebrandt, an associate professor of German at the University of Windsor (Ontario, Canada), received her Ph.D. in German historical linguistics from the University of Michigan. Since then, however, her teaching and research interests have concentrated primarily on post-World War II German literature, with a further specialization in women writers of the Federal Republic of Germany.

Linda Kraus Worley received her doctorate from the University of Cincinnati in 1985. Her dissertation dealt with Louise von François. She has published and given papers on women travelers in the 19th century, the ugly woman as heroine, and Louise von François. Her current research interests revolve around women as readers and the ugly woman as heroine. She taught for the University of Maryland's European Division for eight years and is now an assistant professor at the University of Kentucky.